THE

HISTORY OF DAWLEY

(MIDDLESEX)

B . T . WHITE

Hayes & Harlington Local History Society

Published in 2001 by Hayes & Harlington Local History Society
14 North Way, Uxbridge, Middlesex. UB10 9NG

A catalogue record for this book is available from the British Library

ISBN 0-9540011-0-9

Printed and bound in Great Britain by The Short Run Book Company.
St Stephen's House, Arthur Road, Windsor. Berkshire. SL4 1RY

INTRODUCTION

This work had its origin in a discussion with Philip Sherwood, a fellow member of the Hayes and Harlington Local History Society.   The history of Dawley, we decided, would make an interesting but fairly straightforward subject for research. That was in 1974.

Preliminary investigation soon began to reveal some of the problems - how, for instance, was the late 17th century mansion depicted in a Kip engraving to be reconciled with a later view of an entirely different 18th century building (both long since demolished) on, apparently, a completely different site ?

Our combined efforts, with Philip concentrating on the (then) Middlesex Record Office archives and I following up other sources, mainly relating to the architecture of Dawley, resulted in a lot of information becoming amassed (and a great deal more was to come).   This included some surprising facts, such as that Queen Elizabeth had, indeed, 'slept here', and that three members of our own Local History Society were actually brought up in one of the buildings shown in the Kip engraving of c.1700. Much was discovered about successive owners of the Dawley estate, such as the mercurial Lord Bolingbroke and his literary circle, including Pope, Swift and Voltaire, and a Governor (for 35 hours) of Bengal.

Although our original intention was principally to chronicle the history of the houses on the site and the estate, the prehistory of Dawley, on the one hand, and the 200 years or so following the demolition of the last remaining mansion, on the other, proved to be of considerable interest.   Important discoveries from the Lower Palaeolithic era to the Iron Age have been made at Dawley.   In the late 18th to the early 19th century the Grand Junction Canal and the Great Western Railway both traversed the estate, the latter driving out Tattersall's distinguished equine residents. Agriculture was followed by brickearth and gravel extraction, to be succeeded in turn by 20th century industry - ranging from Glaxo's first pharmaceuticals to radar equipment by EMI and, today, by the highly acclaimed Stockley Park science and commercial estate.

An invaluable aid to understanding and interpreting much of our material has been the maps of Dawley, from the estate plan of c1721 onwards, reproduced to the same scale by Philip Sherwood.

Some of the results of our early investigations were written up by Philip Sherwood in our Society's Journal, but he eventually decided (wisely !) that he could no longer spare the time to continue detailed research into just one area of our local history, although he continued (and has continued up to the present time) to provide any further relevant information that came his way.

The present writer carried on the work on Dawley, although at a reduced rate more consistent with business and family commitments.   Our research had, by 1983, enabled me to contribute to The London Encyclopaedia (Macmillan: Editors Ben Weinreb and Christopher Hibbert) what is believed to be the first accurate, if brief, account of the evolution of the 17th-18th century houses at Dawley.   Retirement from full-time employment has finally enabled me to complete the task - as far as a wide-ranging subject like this can ever be finished.   As an amateur historian, I am well aware that there must be many faults in this work, for which I accept full responsibility.   However, all sources have been detailed as fully as possible so that my conclusions can be tested and accepted or rejected by future historians.

B T WHITE
Uxbridge, 1997

iii

ACKNOWLEDGMENTS

The long list that follows is of those individuals and organisations who have helped with information or advice or assistance in the writing and production of this book. Any omissions are greatly regretted - I am grateful to all. I would like to give thanks individually to Philip Sherwood, without whose cooperation in the early days, in particular, this book would probably never have seen the light of day. Brenda Povey, whose immaculate typing (and subtle corrections) of my messy drafts made publication begin to look like a possibility, and Chris Berridge who has seen the book through to publication - to which the A P Taylor Trust has given generous financial assistance - are also deserving of special mention. Of primary sources, the Paget papers, held in the Greater London Record Office, have proved invaluable for detail for a significant part of the book (17th-19th centuries) and like many historians, I am indebted to the Marquess of Anglesey for making these available.

G Allen
The Marquess of Anglesey
R L Anslow
Ashmolean Museum (J de Wit)
M Bawtree
C Berridge
British Library/British Museum
Christie's International plc (J Rex-Parkes)
Rev M Colclough
H M Colvin
T P Connor
Durham Record Office
EMI (Miss R Edge and others)
C Gadbury
Mrs M E Gibbs
Mrs M Grace
Greater London Record Office/Middlesex Record Office (R Samways in particular)
Guildhall Library
R W Hale (Commercial Union Group)
Clive Hammond
Charles Hammond
E Hammond
Miss G Hammond
J V Hammond
Mrs V Hammond
J Hearne
Hillingdon Local Heritage Service (Mrs C Cotton, G Jones, Mrs M Newbury and their predecessors)
Mrs E M Howard
India Office Library
Kensington and Chelsea Library
W J Locke
S A J McVeigh
Mr and Mrs Marsden
J Marshall
Lady Meade-Fetherstonhaugh
H S Middleton (Curator, Maidstone Museums)
Mrs A L E Moore
Museum of London
National Buildings Record (later National Monuments Record) (S Croad and others)
Mrs K Osborne
K R Pearce
Pembroke College, Oxford
Miss B Povey
Public Record Office

G L Read
D Rust
The Science Museum
P T Sherwood
Mrs M Sibley
Dr R T Smith
Stockley Park plc
Stockport Central Library
K R Surman
Mrs F Symmons
The (8th) Earl of Tankerville
The A P Taylor Trust
Victoria and Albert Museum (Miss W Hefford)
J Walters
Dr O C White
Mrs C Zouch
Miss J Zouch

Finally, heartfelt thanks to the Hayes and Harlington Local History Society whose Officers, Committee and Members have given long-standing and patient encouragement to the production of 'The History of Dawley'.

PS   It is all too easy to overlook my wife, Janis, and children, who had to put up with me all the time.   I hope that 'Dawley' is not engraved on their hearts - thank you for your forbearance !

CONTENTS

LIST OF ILLUSTRATIONS, WITH CAPTIONS

1. 'A Plan of Dawley in the County of Middlesex.   The seat of the Right Hon:ble Charles Earl of Tankerville and Baron of Ossulston'. Jn; Jenner Delineavit [c1721]   For a discussion of the map itself see Chapter 10, although features shown in it are referred to frequently in the book, particularly in the first 17 chapters.   Note here, inter alia, the Long Walk running up to the tip of the estate;   the trees marking the line of the old road following a roughly north-westerly course to the estate boundary;   the Lanthorn Garden running due west;   the Wood Garden at Pinkwell near the south boundary;   and the extended parterre gardens and avenues of the patte d'oie, with the canal in the central one.   For the buildings in the central area see the detail of Jenner's plan in illustration 9.

    (Courtesy Public Record Office)

2. Iron Age settlement site, Dawley.   This is discussed in Chapter 1. Artist's impression by Derek Lucas.

    (Courtesy Museum of London)

3. Sir John Bennet (III), Lord Ossulston, and his wives Elizabeth Countess of Mulgrave and Bridget Howe.   Portrait busts in the Monument in Harlington Parish Church, dated 1686, although Bennet did not die until 1695. (See Chapter 3)

4. Sir John Bennet, Lord Ossulstone (1618-1695) Portrait, wearing armour, by R Phillips. (See Chapter 3)

    (Courtesy Pembroke College, Oxford)

5. 'Dawly in the County of Middlesex, the Seat of the Right Honble Charles Lord Ossulstone'.   A painting or drawing by Leonard Knyff engraved by Johannes Kip, c1700.   For detail of the buildings see illustration 6, but note here, inter alia, the horizon showing Uxbridge in the west to Harrow Church in the east; also the brick kiln and the deer in the park at the left of the picture. (See Chapters 4 to 8)

6. Dawley - detail of Kip's engraving of c1700.   Note the pigeon house in the orchard;   the old Harlington-Hillingdon road curving round the mansion and flanked by farm buildings;   the parterre gardens with their trellis arbours and twin summer houses;   Tijou's (?) ornamental gates;   the statues on the lawns;   the splendid greenhouse;   and the game of bowls in progress.   The complex of buildings near the mansion includes the 7-bay 'dower house' and behind it the long stables and coach house.   The kitchen garden is at the right of the picture. (See Chapters 4 to 8)

7. Uppark, Sussex. The ancestral home of Mary, daughter of Ford Grey, Earl of Tankerville, and wife of Charles Bennet, 2nd Lord Ossulstone. Although smaller, and built some 20-25 years later, the similarity to Dawley is perhaps more than a coincidence.   (See Chapter 6) This

photograph of the east and south fronts was taken in August 1974 before glazing bars had been restored on all windows, and long before the serious fire which resulted in the need for extensive rebuilding.

8.   Cottesbrooke Hall, Northamptonshire.   Built c1702-1713 and although differing in many points of detail, this view gives a general impression of what the house built by the Earl of Tankerville in 1719-1721 (Dawley III) may have looked like.   (See Chapter 15)

9.   John Jenner's Plan of Dawley c1721 - detail showing the principal buildings.   Note the mansion house of c1670 (Dawley II) with its carriage sweeps on its north and west sides; the 6-bay house, to its east with adjacent service buildings; the church-like water house; and the small mansion built 1719-1721 (Dawley III) with the great courtyard to the east.   The extended parterre gardens are south of the Dawley II mansion; part of the Lanthorn Garden is shown running west; and the kitchen garden to the south east.   (See Chapters 10-17)

(Courtesy Public Record Office)

10.   Chateau de la Source, Orleans, France.   Lord Bolingbroke's home while in exile - a 17th century building showing no obvious inspiration for his 're-modelling' of Dawley.   (See Chapter 19)

(Courtesy Orleans Tourist Office)

11.   Sudbrooke Park, Petersham, Surrey.   Built by James Gibbs c1728 and showing some affinity with his works at Dawley.   (See Chapter 19)

12.   Ditchley Park, Oxfordshire.   Built by James Gibbs c1720-1725, this fine house must have provided inspiration for the 're-modelling' of Dawley for Lord Bolingbroke.   The garden front shown here, apart from the attic storey, has many points of comparison with Dawley. (See Chapter 19).

13.   Ditchley, Oxfordshire - the entrance front, showing the service wings linked either side of the mansion house.   (See Chapter 19)

14.   Dawley.   These engravings of James Gibbs' Dawley (IV) 're-modelled' for Lord Bolingbroke, are based on sketches made, probably, in 1760-1770.   Crude as they are these enable an outline plan to be drawn in conjunction with the insurance details and other evidence.   (See Chapter 19 and illustration 15).

(The Gentleman's Magazine, August 1802)

15.   Dawley c1728 - outline sketch plan of the principal buildings.   Key: 1. The mansion built c1670 (Dawley II);   2. Site of 7-bay 'dower house', demolished before 3. built; 3. Six-bay house;   4. Service building, possibly bagnio; 5. Service buildings, the lower one possibly a coach house;   6. Water house;   7a. Mansion built by Lord Tankerville (Dawley III) 1719-1721, later incorporated into Dawley IV.   7a, b, c. Dawley 're-modelled' and wings (7b and 7c) added for   Lord Bolingbroke (Dawley IV)   c1725-1728.

8. The Great Courtyard (originally rectangular, later octagonal).
9. Laundry, pantry and dairy building, later converted into a dwelling as Dawley V; 10. Probably bakehouse and slaughterhouse building; 11. Stables building; 12. Coach house; 13. Enclosure, later garden, wall (shown on Rocque's map, 1754, and still surviving, today, in part). 14. Dovecote (pigeon house) location (off map). 15. Probable appoximate location of kitchen building. (Not shown are the connecting walls or passages that linked the NE and SE corners of wing 7c with the service buildings on the courtyard). Drawing by the author based on Kip's engraving c1700; Jenner's plan c 1721; OS 25in plans; dimensions given in insurance policy 1753; etc.

16 / 17.   Henry St John, Viscount Bolingbroke (1678-1751).
These two portraits seem to typify the contrasting character of the man - the glittering, devious politician on the one hand and the thoughtful man of letters in retirement on the other. The engraving of Bolingbroke in his coronation robes in 1714 is by T A Dean from a painting by Sir Godfrey Kneller. The medallion portrait in his later years is by L -F Roubiliac and forms part of Bolingbroke's monument in Battersea Parish Church.

18.   Alexander Pope (1688-1744). The highly intelligent, witty and waspish poet who was Bolingbroke's frequent companion at Dawley, and his staunchest supporter. Engraving after a portrait by Sir Godfrey Kneller. (See Chapter 21).

19.   Jonathan Swift, Dean of St Patrick's, Dublin (1667-1745). One of Bolingbroke's correspondents and a visitor to Dawley when, it is believed, 'Gulliver's Travels' was read aloud for the first time. Portrait bust by L -F Roubiliac. (See Chapter 21)

20.   Hand in Hand Fire Office - Insurance Policy for Dawley, 1753. The register entry for the four parts of the policy, giving dimensions of all the rooms and separate buildings. Note the description of the hall 'painted with implements of husbandry'. (See Chapters 19 & 20)

(Courtesy Commercial Union Fire Office)

21.   Rocque's map of Middlesex, 1754 - detail showing the Dawley estate. The formal gardens have largely_been swept away and much of the estate has been put to agricultural purposes. At Pinkwell, all that remains is the reverse L-shaped building and the long canal-like pond. (See Chapter 24)

22.   Henry Bayly, 9th Baron Paget (later 1st Earl of Uxbridge) (1744-1812). Portrait by Pompeo Batoni (See Chapter 27).

(Courtesy the Marquess of Anglesey)

23.   Peter, 3rd Count De Salis (1738-1807) who purchased the site of Dawley house in 1797. (See Chapter 29).

33.   The Rudge Whitworth factory buildings, Dawley Road. An artist's impression, included in a bicycle catalogue issued in 1938 or 1939. The buildings were renamed Dawley 1 (the larger one) and Dawley 2 during World War II. (See Chapter 35).

34.   Pillbox facing the railway line at Dawley. This structure, dating from c1940, is on the south abutment of a bridge that once spanned the line. A circular gun pit (only partly visible in the photograph) is in front of the entrance. This was an outlier to a ring of pillboxes surrounding the Royal Ordnance factory. (See Chapter 35 and Appendix 3).

35.   Vertical aerial photograph of part of the Dawley estate (outlined in black), taken August 1945. The buildings of the Royal Ordnance Factory can be seen just south of the railway at the left hand side of the picture and the well-camouflaged Rudge Whitworth factory (Dawley 1 and Dawley 2) is north of the line at the right. Other landmarks are, north to south, the single gasholder; the Glaxo factory (between canal and railway near the west boundary); Dawley House (near the top left hand corner of a rectangular open space bordering the east boundary). The east boundary marked on the photograph shows how part of the yet-to-be-completed housing estate south of the railway lies partly outside Dawley. (See Chapter 35).

36.   Dawley House (Dawley V) c1935. The entrance (south) front. Note the hedge dividing the front garden of Dawley House west - the left hand part, including the front door - from that of Dawley House east, whose entrance was round the side. (See Chapters 37 and 39).

                                                        (Courtesy EMI)

37.   Dawley House (Dawley V) c1945. Years of wartime neglect are showing. Note the skylight behind the parapet where the cupola used to be. The flanking walls have been demolished. (See Chapters 37 and 39).

                                                        (Courtesy EMI)

38.   Site of Dawley House, February 1983. View looking north over the courtyard area taken during the early stages of construction of the Abenglen estate. In the background is the garden enclosure wall of Dawley V. In the foreground are foundations of some of the buildings of Dawley IV. The ranging pole is marked in 1 foot intervals. (See Chapter 39).

39.   Site of Dawley House, February 1983. Part of an arched brick culvert, approximately 2ft 6in wide, running NE to SW. The garden enclosure wall is immediately behind and it appears that the culvert must have originated on its far side. (See Chapter 39).

40.   Maynards Dock, looking north from the Grand Union Canal. The two gasholders are shown in the distance. Photograph taken July 1969. The dock has since been filled in and the gasholders removed by Stockley plc. (See Chapter 36).

41.   'The Dawley Wall', August 1972. A view looking north, taken from where the old Harlington-Hillingdon road (renamed Bolingbroke Way) diverges to the left. The house is 'The Cottage in the Wall' and the location of the builders' yard (then Wilson and Wylie Ltd) is indicated by the name board. The site of a large pond is behind the wall at the left. Much of Dawley wall has since been renovated and restored to its full height. (See Chapter 36)

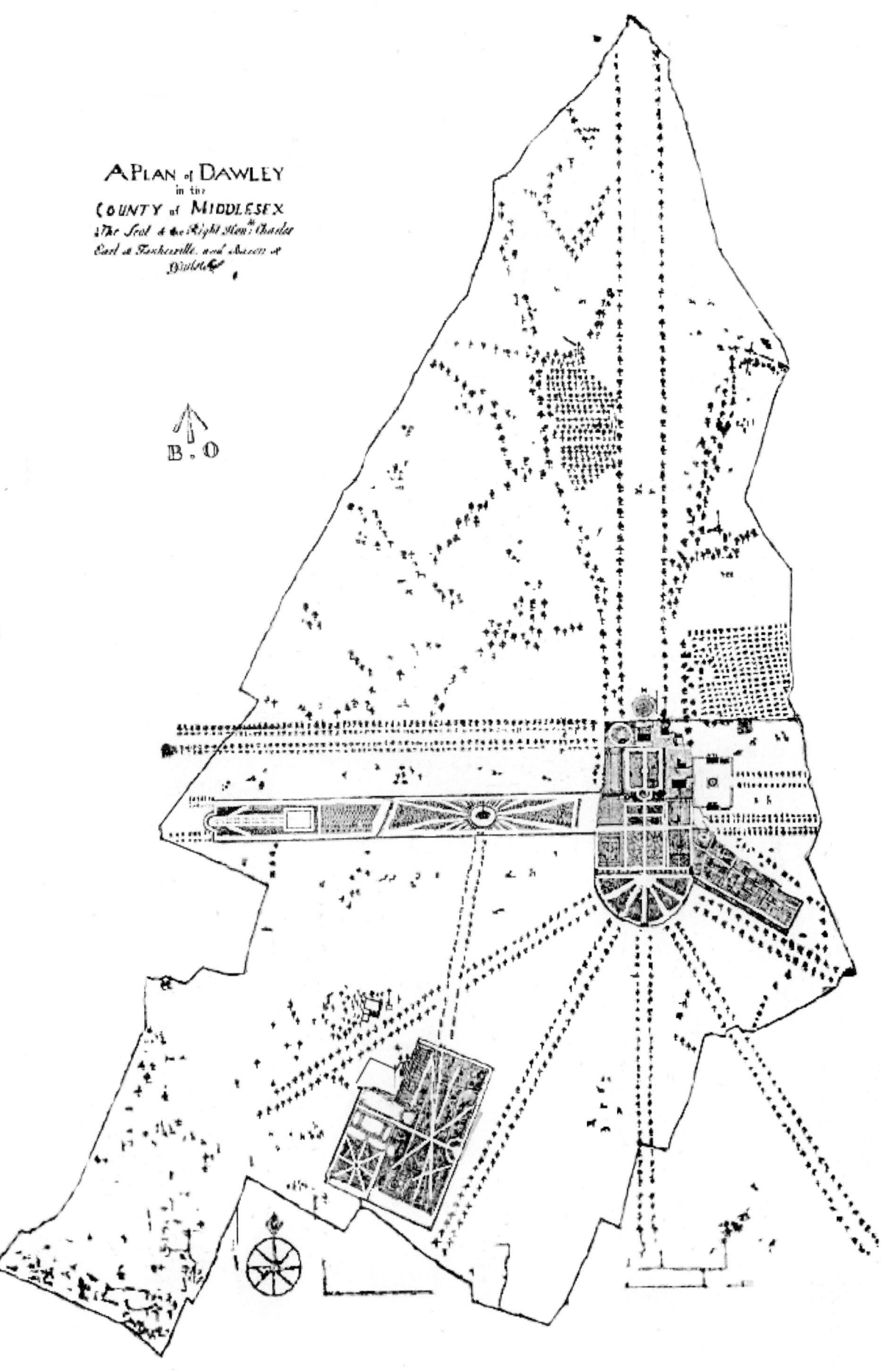

A PLAN of DAWLEY
in the
COUNTY of MIDDLESEX
The Seat of the Right Hon.ble Charles
Earl of Tankerville, and Baron of
Ghisteld

B. O

Plate 1

Plate 2

Plate 3

Plate 4

Dawley in the County of Middlesex, the Seat of the Right Hon.ble Charles Lord Ossulstone.

Plate 5

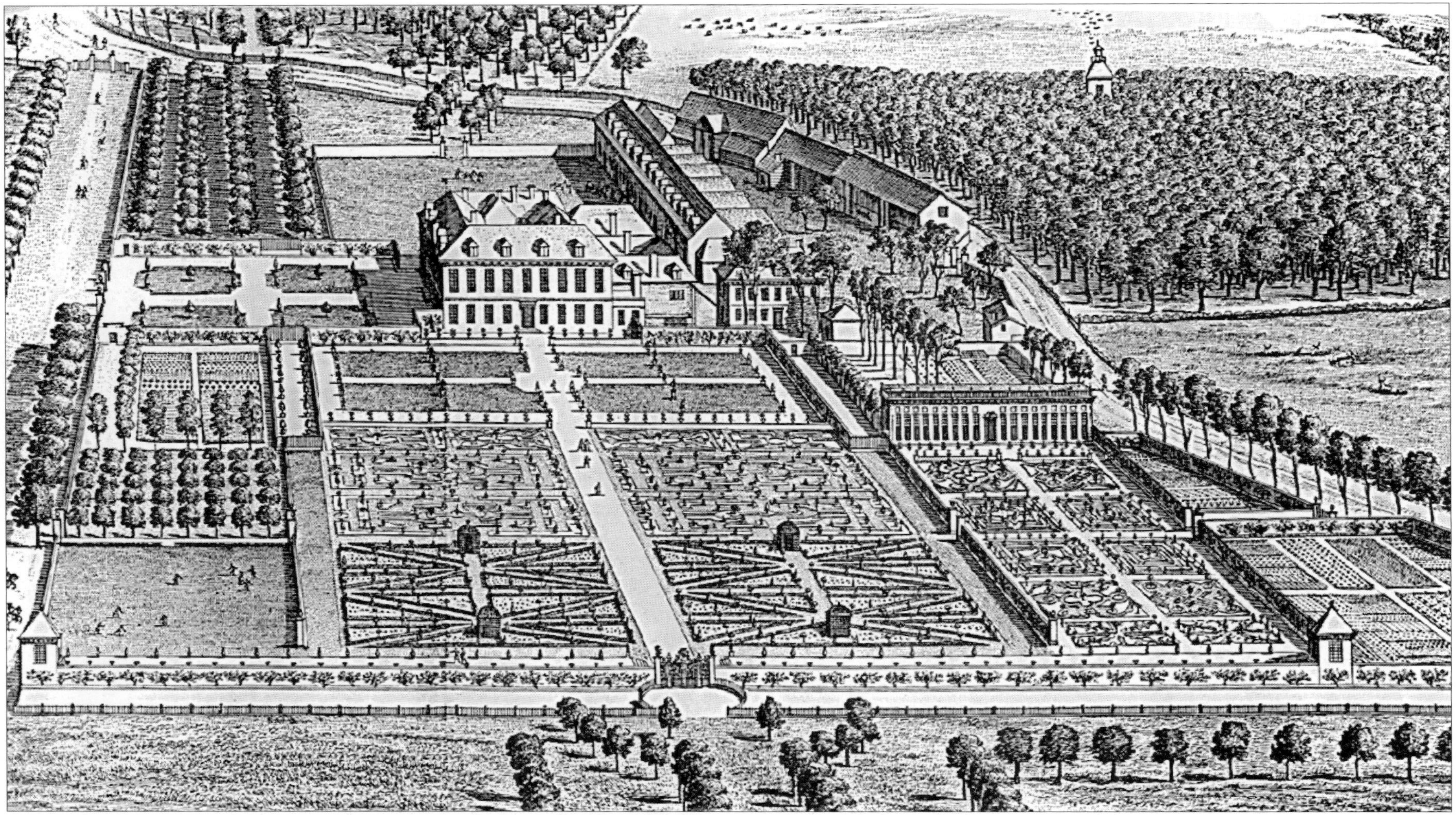

Plate 6

Plate 7

Plate 8

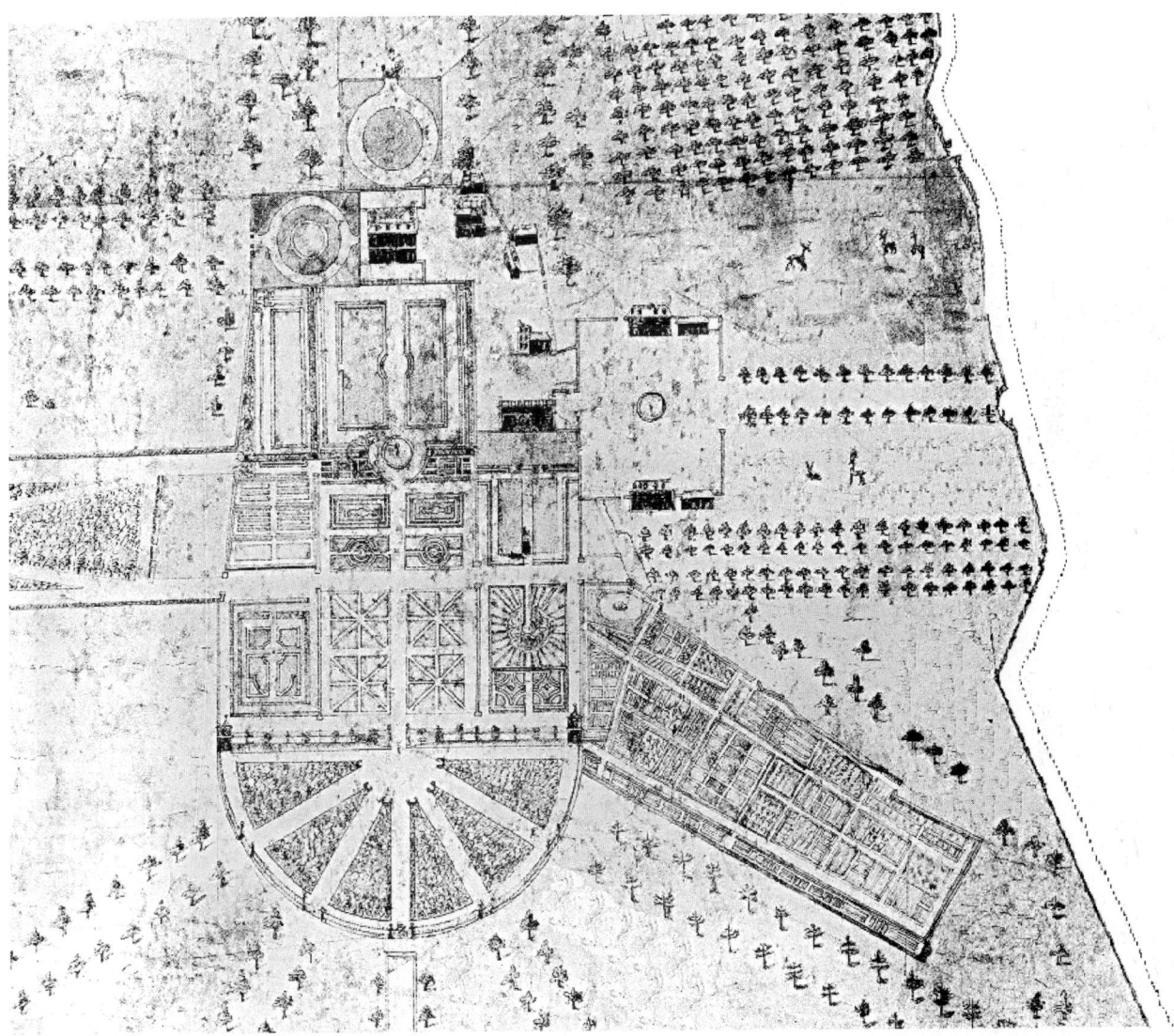

Plate 9

Plate 10

Plate 11

Plate 12

Plate 13

Gent. Mag. Aug. 1802.

1.West View of DAWLEY.

2.South View of DAWLEY.

Plate 14

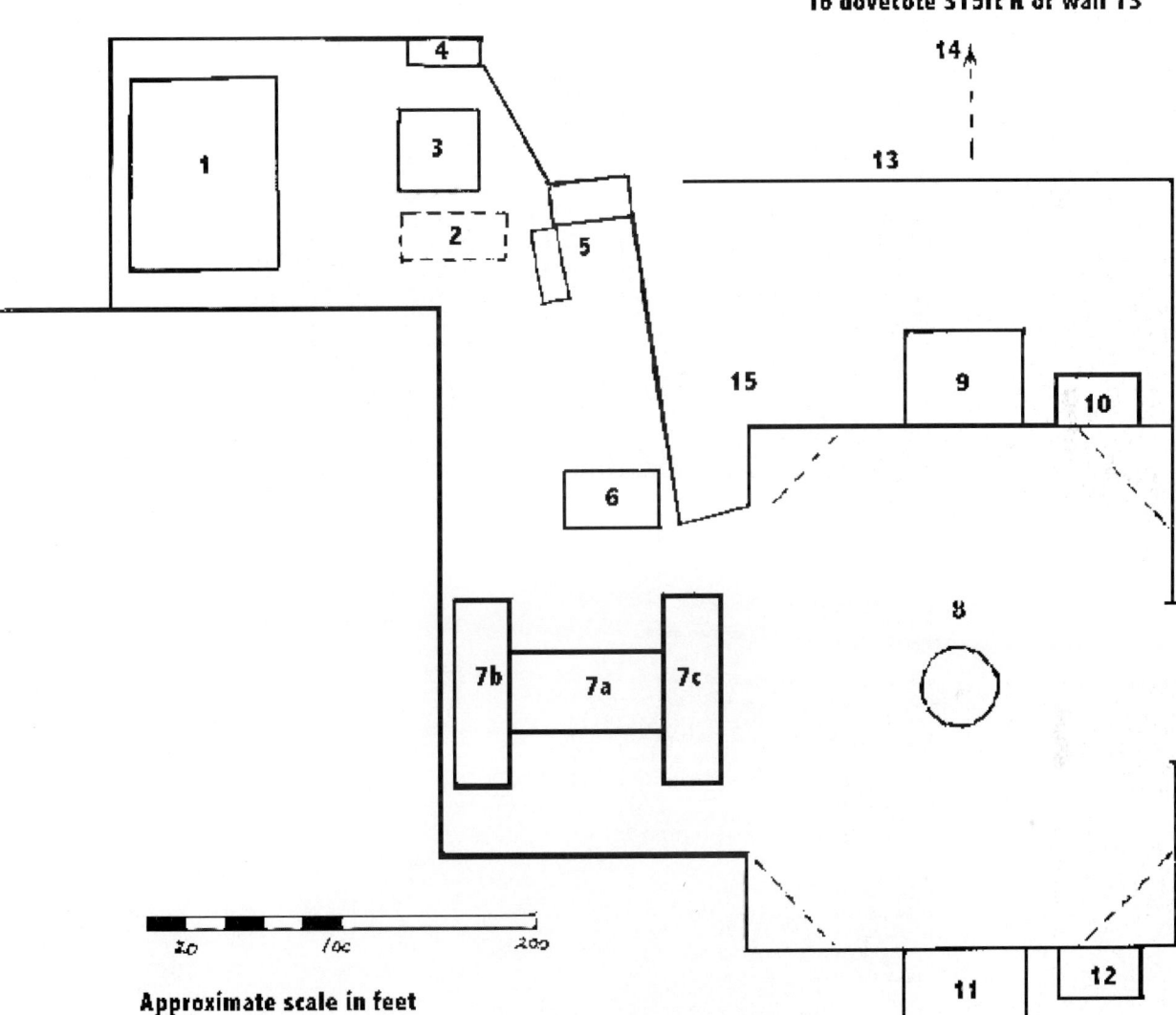

To dovecote 315ft N of wall 13

14

13

1

4

3

2

5

15

9

10

6

8

7b   7a   7c

11   12

20   100   200

Approximate scale in feet
B.T.W. 1998

Plate 15

Plate 16

Plate 17

Plate 18

Plate 19

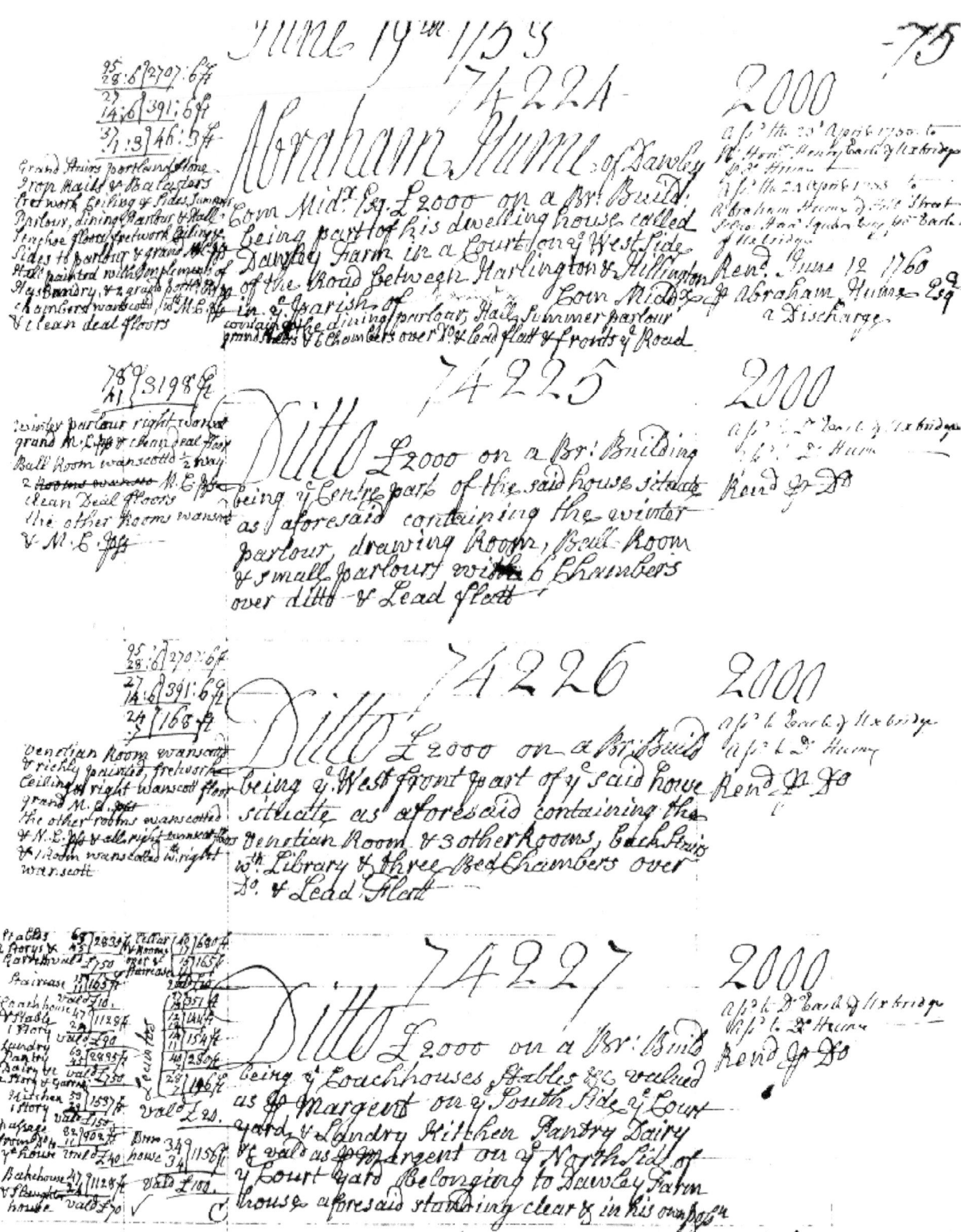

74224

2000

Abraham Hume of Dawley

Com Midx Esq £2000 on a Br: Build:
being part of his dwelling house called
Dawley Farm in a Court on ye West Side
of the Road between Harlington & Hillington
in ye Parish of ————— Com Midx
containing the dining parlour, Hall, Summer parlour
grand Stairs & 6 Chambers over Do & Lead flatt & fronts ye Road

(left margin) Grand Stairs portland stone
Drop Rails & Balasters
fretwork Ceiling & Sides Summer
Parlour, dining parlour & Hall
Stepha floor, fretwork Ceiling
Sides to parlour & grand Stairs
Hall painted with Implements of
Husbandry, & grand part Chamber
Chambers wanscotted, ye N.E. etc
& clean deal floors

95:8 / 2707:6
28:8
27
14:8 / 391:6
3
3:3 / 46:5

(right margin) As pr the 23 April 1750 to
the Honble Henry Earl of Uxbridge
by ye Hume
As pr the 21 April 1755 to
Abraham Hume of Dove Street
John Ann Square by ye Exch
of Uxbridge
Rend 19 June 12 1760
& Abraham Hume Esq
a Discharge

74225

2000

Ditto £2000 on a Br: Building
being ye Centre part of the said house situate
as aforesaid containing the winter
parlour drawing Room, Ball Room
& small parlour with 6 Chambers
over ditto & Lead flatt

(left margin) winter parlour right wanscott
grand N.E. & clean deal floor
Ball Room wanscotted & ¼ bay
2 Rooms wanscott N.E. etc
clean Deal floors
the other Rooms wanscot
& N.E. etc

78:9 / 3198
41

(right margin) As pr — April of Uxbridge
As pr — Do Hume
Rend of Do

74226

2000

Ditto £2000 on a Br: Build
being ye West front part of ye said house
situate as aforesaid containing the
Venetian Room & 3 other Rooms, Back Stairs
wth Library & three Bed Chambers over
Do & Lead Flatt

(left margin) Venetian Room wanscot
& richly jointed, fretwork
Ceiling & right wanscott floor
grand N.E. etc
the other rooms wanscotted
& N.E. etc & all right wanscott
& 1 Room wanscotted & right
wanscott

95:8 / 270:6
28:8
27
14:8 / 391:6
24
3 / 168

(right margin) As pr ye Earl of Uxbridge
As pr ye Do Hume
Rend Do Do

74227

2000

Ditto £2000 on a Br: Build
being ye Coachhouses Stables &c valued
as ye margent on ye South Side ye Court
yard & Laundry Kitchen Pantry Dairy
&c valued as ye margent on ye North Side of
ye Court yard belonging to Dawley Farm
house aforesaid standing clear & in his own poss

(right margin) As pr ye Do Earl of Uxbridge
As pr ye Do Hume
Rend of Do

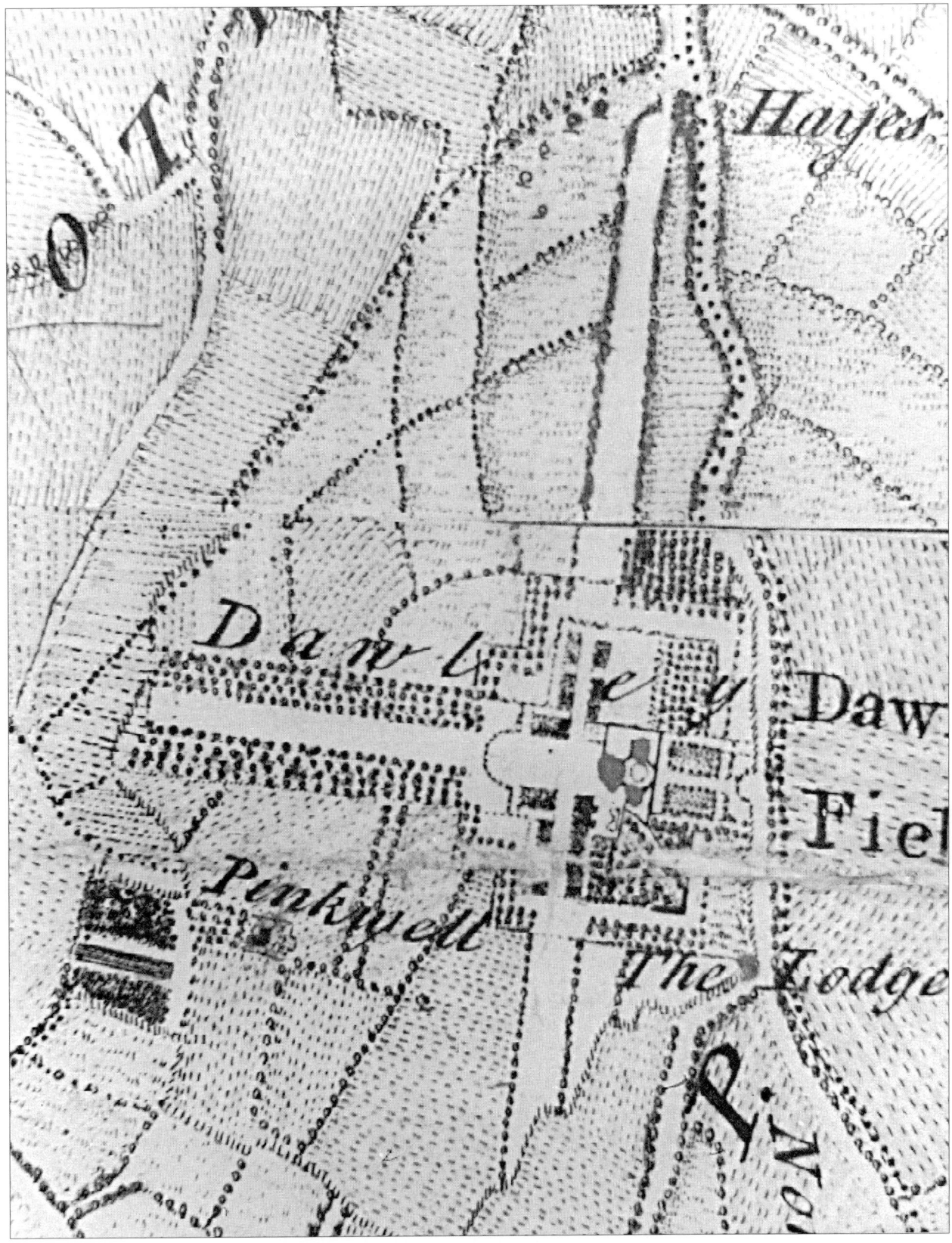

Plate 21

Plate 22

Plate 23

Plate 24

Plate 25

Plate 26

Plate 27

Plate 28

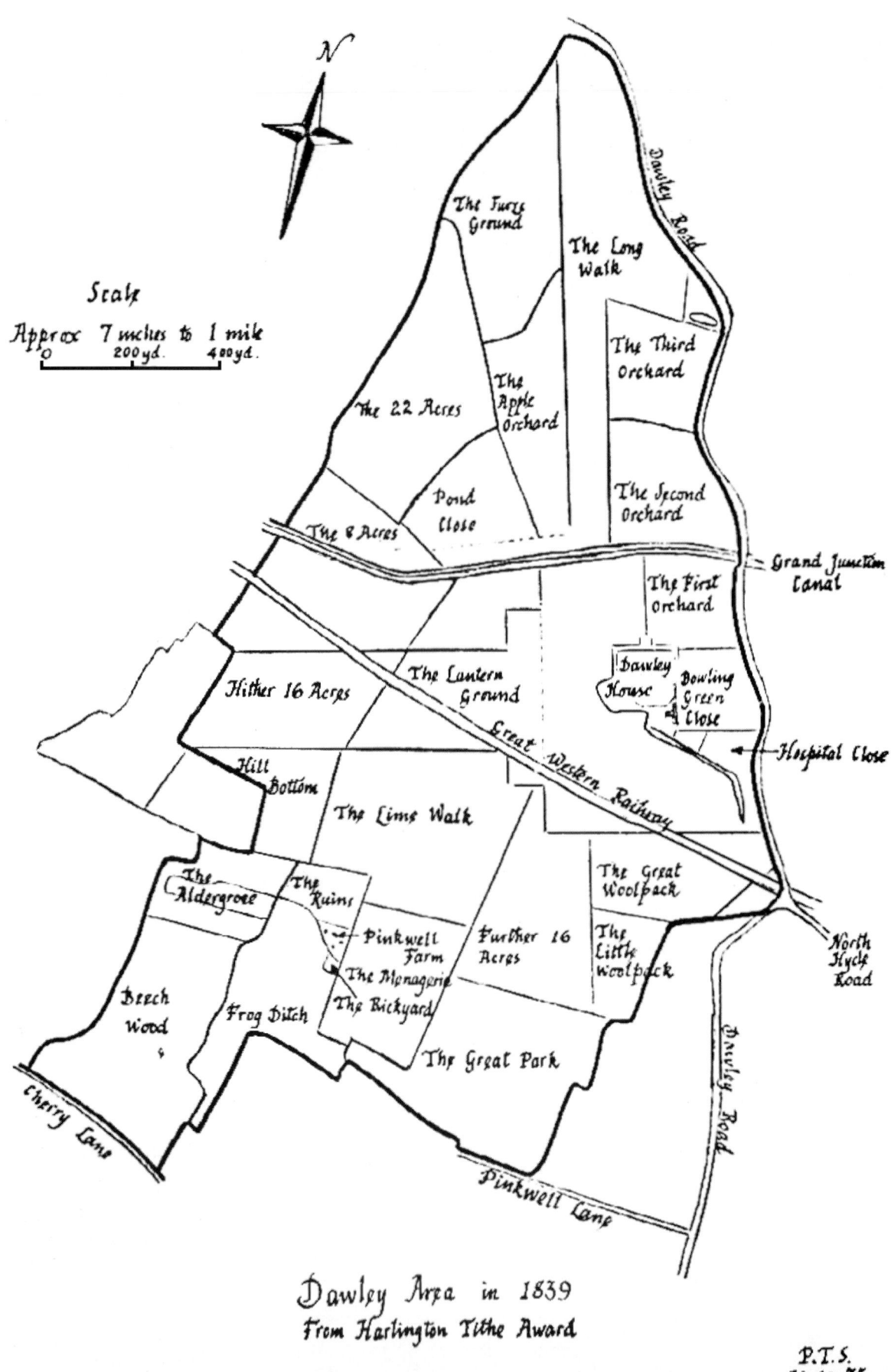

N

Scale

Approx 7 inches to 1 mile
0   200 yd.   400 yd.

The Furze Ground

The Long Walk

Dawley Road

The Third Orchard

The 22 Acres

The Apple Orchard

The Second Orchard

Pond Close

The 8 Acres

Grand Junction Canal

The First Orchard

Hither 16 Acres

The Lantern Ground

Dawley House

Bowling Green Close

Hospital Close

Hill Bottom

The Lime Walk

Great Western Railway

The Aldergrove

The Ruins

The Great Woolpack

Pinkwell Farm

Further 16 Acres

The Little Woolpack

North Hyde Road

The Menagerie

Beech Wood

Frog Ditch

The Brickyard

The Great Park

Dawley Road

Cherry Lane

Pinkwell Lane

Dawley Area in 1839
From Harlington Tithe Award

P.T.S.
30-10-75

Plate 29

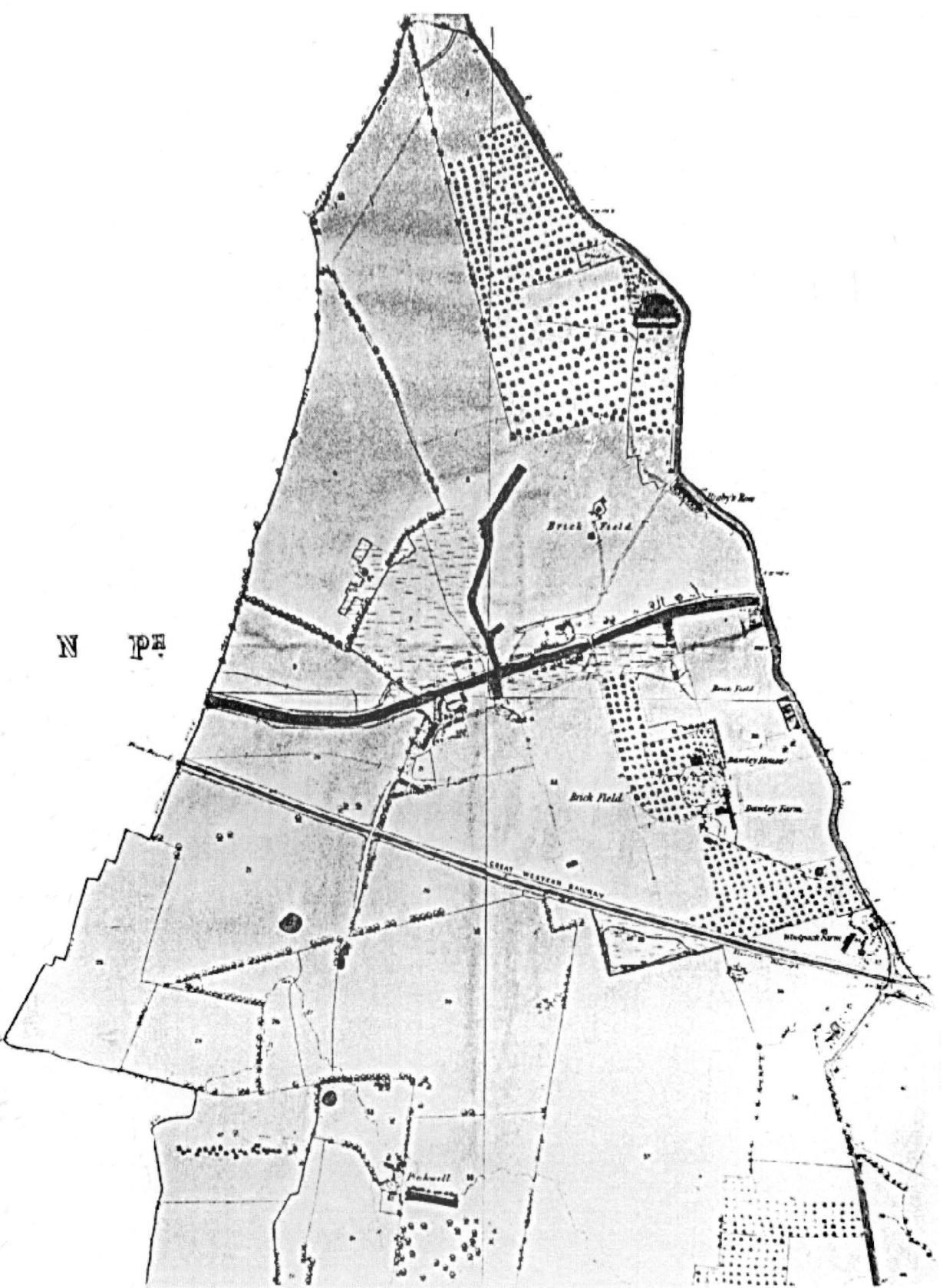

Plate 30

Plate 31

Plate 32

The new home of Rudge - Whitworth Limited . .

THE new Rudge-Whitworth Factories, situate a few miles from the centre of London, have been planned in the light of seventy years rich experience. Here the Hand-built Rudge, with its numerous special features and outstanding quality, is produced in the Factory which represents all that is most modern and best in British Bicycle Manufacture.

RUDGE-WHITWORTH LIMITED
HAYES, MIDDLESEX

Plate 33

Plate 34

Plate 35

Plate 36

Plate 37

Plate 38

Plate 39

Plate 40

Plate 41

CHAPTER 1

GEOGRAPHY; FROM PREHISTORY TO THE TUDOR PERIOD

Dawley is a roughly triangular area of land in Middlesex comprising the northern tip of Harlington. Its only clear boundary today is Dawley Road (A.437) on the east side, (1) still distinguished for much of its length by the 18th century estate wall. The northern apex of the Dawley triangle is just south of the church of St Jerome (Judge Heath Lane). A part of Pinkwell Lane at the south-east and a section of Shepiston Lane (formerly Cherry Lane) at the south-west approximate to the southern boundary. The western boundary of Dawley runs through roughly the middle of the eastern part (east of the Stockley Road - now the Yiewsley By-Pass) of the recently-developed Stockley Park commercial and recreational area. The former Urban District of Yiewsley and West Drayton lies to the west of Dawley together with a small section of Hillingdon parish (once part of Uxbridge Rural District) at the tip; beyond the east boundary down as far as the railway line is Hayes, with Harlington proper south of the railway. The Urban District of Hayes and Harlington (including Dawley) together with the other surrounding local authorities were merged into the London Borough of Hillingdon in 1965.

'Dawley' as described above and in all further discussion in this book is defined by the boundaries of the estate of the Earl of Tankerville delineated in 'A Plan of Dawley' by John Jenner about 1721. (2) This is the earliest reliable source of detailed geographical information and is adhered to for the sake of continuity, although it is known that some adjoining plots of land, particularly at the west, were added to the estate subsequently. Jenner's plan is also, for want of better evidence, taken to be roughly the extent of the Manor of Dawley, although it is known, for example, that at various times some scattered pieces of land in Harlington proper were also regarded as part of the Manor. There was also a small area in Ickenham. These detached areas, although referred to where appropriate, are not otherwise included in this history of Dawley. The exact boundaries of the Dawley estate prior to the Earl of Tankerville's ownership are not known.

For long regarded by many as part of Hayes, Dawley lost most of what identity that still existed in 1965 when the London Borough of Hillingdon was formed. It is now covered partly by Stockley Park (which bears a name derived from a tiny hamlet in Yiewsley) and most of the remainder by a housing estate in which the majority of the inhabitants (as well as the Post Office) consider themselves to be living in Hayes. There is today an ecclesiastical parish known as Dawley, formed in 1935 out of parts of existing parishes, of which its church of St Jerome, together with its main congregation, lies just over the Dawley/Harlington boundary partly in Hayes, partly in Hillingdon.

The terrain in the area is flat, sloping gently from about the 125 foot contour line in the north to somewhere near the 100 foot contour just south of the railway line which roughly bisects Dawley. This gradual slope continues through Harlington down to the Thames flood plain some 9 miles away, due south. The surface soil (where it remains undisturbed) is brick earth, which overlies the gravel beds which formed part of former terraces (most of these known as Stoke Park terraces in our area) of the north bank of the prehistoric river now known as the Thames. (3)

These gravel terraces lying under Dawley are part of a site, including also areas of Yiewsley and West Drayton, known collectively to archaeologists as 'Yiewsley'. Following the construction of the Grand Junction Canal, brick earth and gravel have been removed intensively from Dawley and the adjoining areas from the mid 19th century onwards, and the gravel pits have yielded thousands of palaeolithic artifacts that were lost or discarded by hunter-gatherer peoples over a great span of time. The finds have been chiefly of the types known as Acheulian and Levalloisian (after typical find-sites in France of these patterns of artifact) of the

Lower Palaeolithic era. The great numbers of stone tools and weapons found make the 'Yiewsley' site one of the richest in Britain and, indeed, in Europe. The site is second only to Swanscombe in Kent for the number of hand-axes recorded, indicating prolonged, though not necessarily continuous, occupation of the area by hunters and food gatherers from about 250,000 B.C. until around 70,000 B.C. Pollen analysis shows that for some of the time the area was open meadow, together with mixed oak forest. Some Middle Palaeolithic (Mousterian) stone tools have been found in higher levels, showing that the site was also occupied later during a time, between about 70,000 and 35,000 B.C., when Neanderthal man was dominant in Europe. Sporadic occupation of one sort or another probably continued right through the Neolithic period (New Stone Age, circa 2200 B.C. onwards - marking the introduction of agriculture in Britain) and the Bronze Age that followed it, judging from the scattered finds of stone and bronze weapons from adjacent areas of Harlington.

The succeeding Iron Age has provided the first actual evidence for an occupation site, however, with the excavation in 1985 of a small settlement near the northern tip of Dawley. This site was probably inhabited for about 100 years in total during the period between about 700 and 200 B.C. - the Early to Middle Iron Age. Traces were found of four circular huts and some four-post structures - possibly granaries - together with a lineal earthwork. The site of about one acre represented a farmstead with a community of perhaps two families, who cultivated wheat, barley and oats and carried out weaving. There is also some evidence that they may have smelted metal. (4)

By the time of the Roman conquest of Britain in A.D. 43, the Iron Age tribe (or possibly federation of tribes) controlling our area north of the Thames, including Dawley, was the Catuvellauni, whose tribal capital or 'civitas' was established at Verulamium (St Albans) in Hertfordshire. (5) No trace has been found of any settlement at Dawley during the 400 years of Roman rule that followed, although significant finds have been made at a farming site at Harlington and Sipson a short distance to the south. There is also reason to believe that there was a Roman road running from the Oxford region to London, (6) the line of which would have passed through Hayes, south of the present Uxbridge Road, less than half a mile north of Dawley.

The Anglo-Saxon period that followed the withdrawal of the Roman legions has, likewise, left no trace in Dawley, but the name itself - Dallega - is of Anglo-Saxon origin (from 'dal' meaning dole, part or share, and 'leah' or ley, a clearing), and the area was probably settled by farmers long before its mention in the Norman Domesday survey.

Nothing is known of Dawley in the earliest years of the Norman conquest of England and nothing tangible remains, although the nearby Harlington parish church of SS Peter and Paul dates from circa 1150. The earliest reference to Dawley is, in fact, in the Domesday book, compiled in 1086. This reads as follows (translated from the Latin) :

'Alnod holds Dallega [Dawley] of Earl Roger. It is assessed at 3 hides. There is land for 2 ploughs. In demesne there is 1 plough and the villeins have 1 plough. There are 4 villeins each on 1 virgate and 4 bordars on 5 acres. There is meadow for 6 oxen; pasture for the cattle of the vill; woodland for 15 pigs. In all it is worth 30s; when he received it, it was worth the same; in the time of King Edward 60s. The manor belongs to Colham to which it did not belong in the time of King Edward. Godwin Alfit the man of Wigot held it and he could do with it what he pleased.' (7)

From the entry it can be deduced that the population in 1086 was about 30, which compares with an estimated population of 110 for the main settlement in Harlington.

The name Dallega had evolved into Daulee in 1199 and Dalleye by 1311 (and into the modern form Dawley with variant Doyley by 1600) but little is known about the development of the hamlet and the manor in the Middle Ages. Harlington and Dawley combined mustered 20 men and two under-constables for an array about 1335. There is evidence that a windmill existed, from the place names Windmill Hill and Windmill Hill Close, which was probably west of Dawley Road near Pinkwell Lane. This was probably in the southern part of Dawley manor, rather than Harlington proper, although no trace survives of a windmill mound to prove exactly where it was. (8) No stream suitable for a water mill, incidentally, appears to have existed in the area, with the possible exception of the tiny water course known as Frogsditch. The manor of Dawley was held by members of the Corbet family in the 12th century, and in the following century, in 1220, it is recorded that there were two plough teams - the same number as in the Domesday survey.

By 1307 the manor of Dawley had passed to Joan, wife of William de Barentyn, and by 1316 it belonged to their son, Gilbert. Later in the same century it was acquired by John Lovell, whose family also gained the manor of Harlington. The Lovells kept Harlington manor for some 200 years (there are memorial brasses of Gregory Lovell and his wife, Anne, in Harlington church dated 1545) but their interests in Dawley manor had been sold by 1515 when the manor is known to have belonged to Richard Aubrey. He it was who converted 100 acres of arable into pasture in 1517, so that two ploughs were put down, causing three houses in Dawley to be deserted and twelve people to become homeless. It is probable that Dawley gradually ceased to exist as a separate community (apart from the manor, that is) within the next 30 years or so. Thomas Aubrey held the manor in 1540 and William Aubrey in 1547. John Aubrey died in possession in 1557 and was succeeded by his son, William. The latter, although it cannot be confirmed, may have been the Dr William Aubrey (1529 - 1595) who was the grandfather of the famous antiquary John Aubrey (1626 - 1697). (9) William Aubrey appears to have conveyed Dawley to William Roper, lord of Harlington manor, in 1564, although he (Aubrey) was still living at Dawley in 1571. It is tempting to believe that this is the William Roper (1496 - 1578) who was the biographer of Sir Thomas More and who married More's favourite daughter Margaret. Sir Thomas More's son-in-law held estates in Eltham and Canterbury, Kent, although no record of him also holding property in Middlesex appears to have survived. (10) The manor of Dawley seems to have belonged in 1590 to Richard Reynolds, and in 1595 William Hitchcock conveyed it to Ambrose Coppinger. (11)

CHAPTER 2

'DAWLEY COURTE' - THE MANOR HOUSE AT PINKWELL

Nothing is known of the mediaeval manor house at Dawley - if one existed. By 1571, however, a house in the manor of Dawley was known to be occupied by William Roper, as mentioned earlier. In 1592 there is a reference to 'Dawley Courte' (1) and its location is referred to in 1600 at a manorial court of the Bishop of London, who held the Manor of Drayton or Colham Garden, as it was called, with lands in the parishes of both West Drayton and Hillingdon. At this court, two customary tenements and 2 acres of arable land were surrendered. They both lay in Bidwell's or Bydwell field, in a 'certain shott (2) called Dawley Croft Shott'; one of them with, on its north side, the way leading to Dawley Court called 'Le Greneway', and the land of John Stanborowe in the south. The other one had land belonging to Rabbes Farm on the north and land occupied by Edmund Edlin in the south (3). The 'Greneway' can credibly be identified with the old lane leading from West Drayton to Pinkwell, later known as Porter or Portway Lane (in the Hillingdon Inclosure Award of 1825); the surviving portion in West Drayton today is called Porters Way. Bidwell's Field was probably the one known later as Drayton Field, one of the common fields of the manor. Forty-five acres of this field, with Porter Lane on its north side and the lane to Sipson (Stockley Road) to the east, was on lease by the Bishop of London to Brook Hamilton Gill Esq., at the time of the Drayton Inclosure of 1824. Although the holdings of Stanborowe and Edlin cannot precisely be located, the farm house of Rabbes Farm in 1825, at any rate, was just over a mile away in Yiewsley, to the north-west of Drayton Field, according to the Hillingdon Inclosure map. Incidentally, an indenture of 1683 (4) relating to 1 acre of arable land near 'Dawley Poore' in Harlington describes it as being between land of the late Bartholomew Cowdrey on the north and the Greenway leading towards Pinkwell in the south. This is almost certainly the same 'Greenway', but the fact that only Pinkwell, rather than Dawley Court, is mentioned, suggests that the latter had by then been demolished, as will be discussed later. It was at Pinkwell that the Dawley manor house in the late Elizabethan era was located: a part of the estate that derived its name from a well or spring possibly associated with finches. (5)

Elizabeth Hunt, the historian of Hayes, wrote in 1861 'tradition says ... that Queen Elizabeth used sometimes to stay at Pinkwell and with her unrivalled train of courtiers and statesmen worshipped God in our parish church'. (6) It is important to note that Miss Hunt, who knew the district well, specifically referred to Pinkwell and not Harlington, in which parish Dawley manor lies. No printed or documentary source for this reference to Pinkwell is known and there seems to be no reason to doubt that Miss Hunt derived her knowledge from oral tradition. One likely reason for the Queen to visit the parish church of Hayes (which is only about $1^1/_2$ miles from Pinkwell) is that the Rector of Hayes (from 1601 to 1623) was her Chaplain, Robert Wright. (7)

Ambrose Coppinger, who had acquired the manor of Harlington at the same time as Dawley, is on record as having been host to Queen Elizabeth in 1602 - 'Oct 2. The Quene's progress went not far - first to Cheswicke to Sir William Russell's, then to Ambrose Coppinger's, who, because he had ben a Master of Art, intertained her himselfe with a Latin oration'. (8) Accommodating the Queen and her entourage was an honour, but also could be a considerable financial burden (9) and one that some of her loyal subjects tactfully avoided wherever possible. Many of those who sought the distinction of a royal visit spent large sums of money in refurbishing and enlarging their houses - extra 'lodgings' were often needed to accommodate the large number of courtiers and servants attending the Queen. Coppinger's Harlington manor house was probably a mediaeval building on the moated site, of which slight traces still remain, a short distance north of the Harlington parish church of SS Peter and Paul. This house would almost certainly have been inadequate for the entertainment of the Queen, and the only possible venue for the Queen's visit would have been Coppinger's other nearby manor house of Dawley, at Pinkwell. Nothing is known about the house at this time, beyond the fact that to be suitable for a Royal visit it must have been of a fair size. Sixty years later, in the Hearth Tax return of 1664, it was assessed at 22 hearths - the biggest house in Harlington parish, and the same size, by assessment, as Robert Child's manor house of Hayes Park Hall. Place House, Uxbridge (the remaining wing of which is now The Crown and Treaty Inn), built in the 1530's and 23 hearths in 1664, was also comparable in size if not necessarily in appearance. (10) The varying circumstances of the owners and tenants of Dawley Court who succeeded Ambrose Coppinger, make it seem unlikely that they would have been able and/or willing to add to or rebuild it, and the house appears to have been demolished by the time of the 1674 Hearth Tax assessment. (11) Jenner's plan of the Dawley Estate of c.1721 still shows the site of the extensive enclosed garden at Pinkwell. It was roughly 300 yards by 200 yards, excluding an area in the north-west corner of around 100 yards by 67 yards where the house and its outbuildings must have stood. What were, possibly, some of the remains of the outbuildings are also shown by Jenner. The Elizabethan Dawley manor house will be discussed further later on in this book.

The Queen, in that progress of 1602, incidentally, went on to Harefield where, on arrival and sheltering under a tree in the pouring rain, she was entertained to an address by the Lord Keeper of the Great Seal, Sir Thomas Egerton, who was doubtless accompanied by his wife, the Dowager Countess of Derby.

Ambrose, the third son of Henry Coppinger, of Buxhall near Stowmarket, Suffolk, (12) born about 1546, was sent to St John's College, Cambridge, in 1560, gained his B.A. in 1565 and was made a Fellow in the same year. His M.A. followed in 1568. He was Rector of Buxhall (a living in the gift of his father) in 1569-71 and afterwards trained as a lawyer, at Barnard's Inn and Gray's Inn. He entered the service of the Earl of Warwick, and later the Countess of Warwick, some time after 1571. It has been suggested (13) that this connection was instrumental in his becoming Member of Parliament for Ludgershall, Wiltshire, in 1586 and also gave him the opportunities to acquire considerable estates in Kent and Suffolk as well as Middlesex. The Queen died only six months after her visit to Dawley. Her successor, James I (and VI of Scotland), knighted Ambrose Coppinger in the garden at Whitehall on 23 July 1603, before his coronation. The more certain honour (James created no less than 435 knights on that 23rd day of July alone) of the Lord Keepership (if the rumour was true) eluded Sir Ambrose, since he died on 17 March 1604. His widow, Letitia, (14) held a life interest in the manors of Harlington and Dawley, and probably continued to live at Dawley for about two years, or at least until, as the Harlington parish registers record, the marriage of 'Sir John Maurice and my Ladie Coppinger lic.' (by special licence from the Bishop of London) took place on 27 February 1606. Sir John Maurice (Morrys, Morris) held an estate at Chipping Ongar, Essex, (15) to which the couple presumably returned. Sir John later changed his name to Poyntz (Pointz), that of his first wife's family. Lady Letitia evidently maintained her interest in Harlington because, about 1610, as Lady Poyntz, she founded a benefaction of the interest on £100- to be distributed among poor widows or widowers in the locality. (16) Before this, however, in 1607 she joined with Sir Ambrose's nephew, Francis, (17) to whom the reversion on the manors belonged, to convey Harlington and Dawley to Sir John Bennet. (18)

CHAPTER 3

THE BENNET FAMILY TO c.1670

Sir John Bennet, who acquired the manors of Dawley and Harlington in 1607, was the first representative of a family that was to remain in possession for well over a hundred years. During this time they made significant changes to the estate, created impressive gardens, and built two of the successive manor houses of Dawley. Therefore, because of their importance in the history of Dawley, it is felt appropriate at this point to give a brief general account of the Bennet family, through the fortunes and disgrace of Sir John Bennet to the revival of the family affluence under his grandson, Sir John Bennet (III). (1)

John Bennet (I) came from a branch of a gentry family of no great distinction whose seat was Clapcote, near Wallingford in Berkshire. He was the eldest son (2) of Thomas Bennet and Elizabeth, daughter of the founder of Pembroke College, Oxford. His younger brother, Thomas, became a wealthy alderman of London and Lord Mayor in 1603. Bennet went up to Oxford (Christ Church College) where he was appointed a junior proctor of the university in 1585, acquiring the degrees of bachelor and doctor of laws in 1589. An ecclesiastical career followed, with his appointment as a prebendary of Langtoft in the diocese of York in 1591; he became Chancellor of the diocese by 1599 when he was made a member of the Council of the North. He entered Parliament in 1597 as the Member for Ripon, represented York in 1601 and Ripon again in 1603. This last year was the one in which he accepted a knighthood from James I, on 23 July, just before the King's coronation. (3) He was also appointed a judge of the Prerogative Court of Canterbury about this time and (before 1613) chancellor to James I's Queen, Anne of Denmark. Sir John became M.P. for Oxford in 1614 and again in 1620. In 1617 Bennet was sent on a mission to Brussels to try and induce the Archduke Albert to punish the producers of a book in which King James and his court was satirised. In this he was unsuccessful, without apparently forfeiting the Royal regard for him.

Sir John Bennet's first wife, Anne (Weekes), died in 1601, after having given birth to four sons and two daughters. His second wife, Elizabeth (nee Lowe, daughter of an alderman of London), died in 1614 after having added four more children to his family. (4) She was buried in Harlington Parish Church. Sir John married again (not later than 1617), this time to Leonora, daughter of Adrian Vireendeels of Antwerp, as her third husband. Dame Leonora, outlived Sir John by 11 years and has an elaborate tomb, including her full length effigy, in St Margaret's Church, Uxbridge.

The years from 1603 onwards under the patronage of James I were prosperous ones for Sir John Bennet. They were marked not only by the purchase of the manors of Dawley and Harlington, but by the acquisition in 1612 (5) of what was almost certainly the largest house in nearby Uxbridge - The Place, or Place House, at the west end of the town, near the Colne bridge. The remaining wing of this house is now known as the Crown and Treaty Inn. In 1616, Bennet also purchased the manor of Northolt (6).

However, the true reason for the full extent of Sir John Bennet's prosperity became apparent in 1621, when he was impeached in the House of Commons, as a judge of the Prerogative Court of Canterbury, for the acceptance of bribes (often from the highest bidder !) in the administration of the estates of intestates, and misappropriating money left for charities. This included a legacy of £1000- for the University of Oxford in the will of Sir Thomas Bodley, who had respected and trusted Bennet as a graduate of the university. Sir John avoided being sent to the Tower of London on remand, but was held in his own house (probably in London) in the custody of the Sheriff. He was later discharged on bail of £20,000, the trial eventually being taken over by the court of Star Chamber. This resulted in a fine of £20,000-, imprisonment during the King's pleasure, and permanent disability from holding office. On 16 July 1624, the sentence was remitted, apart from the fine of £20,000- (which he had apparently been able to pay), and he was discharged from the Fleet prison. Bennet was probably already in bad health, and died at his home in the parish of Christ Church, London, in 1627, and was buried in the parish church in Newgate Street.

Sir John Bennet's heir was his eldest son, John (II). Although he succeeded to the estates in Dawley and Harlington (Northolt Manor had been sold), the heavy fine paid by his father only three years earlier without, apparently, the opportunity or strength to repair the family fortunes before he died, meant that there was probably little supporting capital. John Bennet (II) was born in 1589 (7) and educated at Oxford, studied law at Gray's Inn and then went on a tour of the Continent. He married Dorothy, daughter of Sir John Crofts of Saxham, Suffolk, and their eldest son, John (III), was baptised in the parish church of Saxham in 1616, the year in which John Bennet (II) received a knighthood from James I at Theobalds, Hertfordshire. Two years later, their second son, Henry (later to become Earl of Arlington) was also baptised at Saxham. After his father's impeachment, followed by imprisonment in 1622, Sir John Bennet (II) moved with his family to Harlington, where five of their children were to be baptised between 1628 and 1637. (8) A strong Royalist, at the beginning of the Civil War in 1642 when the King's army began a march on London, Sir John Bennet set out to meet the King at Colnbrook, taking with him all the horses from his stables. In a charge of delinquency against Sir John it was recorded (9) 'That the said Sir John Bennet did ayde and assist the late King against the Parliament by sending horses unto the said late King and that he furnished the late King with horses when he came to Colbrooke [Colnbrook] and soe to the fight att Brandford [Brentford] and that he rode with the King to Brandford fight against the Parliament and that he dyned with the King att Auditor Powell's house, wore the King's signall att the fight att Brandford which was a handkercheife in his hatt and rode with the King there with his Armes and sent the King after two Coach horses'. However, despite his Royalist sympathies Sir John accepted the authority of the Commonwealth after the execution of Charles I and in 1652 made his peace with the government according to the Act of Oblivion. (10)   Nevertheless, his support of the Royalist cause during the Civil War must have left him a relatively poor man. In 1643, when endeavouring to escape tax assessment by Parliament, he valued his real estate at £300- a year and his personal property at £500-. In the order book of the committee for assessing the tax of the twentieth part of personal property, Sir John is assessed at £120- which would make his personal property worth £2400-. (11)   The shortage of money probably explains why in 1657 he mortgaged the Dawley estate to Dame Arabella Bryors (widow of Sir William Bryors of Pulloxhill, Bedfordshire, who had been knighted in 1627 and died in 1653). An indenture (12) among the papers in the Greater London Record Office dated 29 May 1657 reads '... the aforesaid Dame Arabella Bryors has lately purchased of the said Sir John Bennet the manor of Dawley and diverse lands in the aforesaid parish of Harlington ...... for the sum of £3400 and there doth remain to be paid by the said Dame Arabella Bryors unto the said Sir John Bennet £1800'. Dame Arabella's first Court Baron of the manor of Dawley was held on 20 September 1657. (13)   The choice of Dame Arabella as mortgagee was, no doubt, seen as a wise move to protect the family's interests, since she was the sister of Sir John Bennet's wife, Dorothy. Dame Arabella was probably at that time in a good position to help, since she had been left half of the property of her husband, who had died some four years previously.

Sir John Bennet (II) died in 1658, and was succeeded by his eldest son John (III).   As mentioned above, he (John III) was born when his parents were living at Saxham in Suffolk, and was baptised in the parish church there on 5 July 1616. The family would have moved to Harlington by the time John Bennet (III) went up to Oxford University, matriculating (viz being enrolled) at Pembroke College as a gentleman commoner in 1635. He went on to study law in February 1636, like his father, at Gray's Inn. John Bennet joined the King's army at the beginning of the Civil War, sharing strong Royalist sympathies with his brother, Henry, and his father. Nothing seems to have been recorded of his participation in any action, although as 'Colonel John Bennet of Uxbridge' just after the Restoration (in August 1660) he petitioned for 'the bailiff's place at Westminster', stating in support that he had served the King (Charles I) from the time of leaving London to the surrender at Exeter. He had been imprisoned at Windsor, Portsmouth and Lambeth, and had also served Charles II at Worcester, and had been in danger of execution by the 'High Court of Justice'. (14) The result of the petition is not known, but John Bennet (III) was created a Knight of the Bath on 23 April 1661 at the Coronation of Charles II. The Monarch was not ungrateful to his loyal supporters, and several official posts for Sir John Bennet, K.B., followed. He was appointed Lieutenant of the Band of Gentlemen Pensioners about 1662 (this lasted until November 1676). In 1663, according to another source, Bennet became 'Treasurer of the money for indigent officers and soldiers' (15), although it is not clear if this was part of his duties as Lieutenant of the Band of Gentlemen Pensioners or a separate post. Appointment as Deputy Postmaster followed in 1666, and this office was held until 1672. In 1671 he was given yet another appointment, as one of the Farmers of the Customs for a five year period. For the greater part of the two decades following the Restoration, Sir John Bennet served in Parliament as the Member for Wallingford (the seat of his ancestors) - from 1663 to 1679.

Sir John Bennet (III) married, on 28 October 1661, Elizabeth, widow of the 2nd Earl of Mulgrave and daughter of Lionel Cranfield, Earl of Middlesex - a very wealthy London merchant and banker. She died in 1672, and Bennet married again, in May 1673, this time Bridget, daughter of John Grubham Howe, an officer of the Royal Hospital, Chelsea. Bridget Bennet kept a notebook (16) with details of her children, and this includes one fact revealing that her husband was evidently on terms of personal friendship with Charles II - 'Charles [her son] was born may ye 15th and christend ye 20th 1674 by the King, Lord Arlington and my mother'.

In an age where a public appointment was often an accepted, if unacknowledged, means of private gain, Sir John Bennet followed in his grandfather's footsteps and, without doubt, used his official posts to the full to his own advantage and to revive the family fortunes. As Deputy Postmaster, for instance, he charged postage on official correspondence that should have been carried free, and in 1686 was ordered to refund no less than £12375-17s-3d to the King. Also, he appears almost certainly to have misused his position as Treasurer of the money for indigent officers. However, as can be seen from the following account of a private transaction, he once got the worst of a bargain. 'Dear Brother ...... I think you will laugh when I tell you that I have sold the old silver minute watch to Sir John Bennet for 4 gines and a new silver watch to boot, but after a weeks trial he found he could not make the minutes and the hours go together, therefore he desired his Sister Carr to get his gold and watch again, and to desire me to take my own again, but I said no, if he had spoiled the watch he had no reason to think that I should pay for that, for I said he might remember that I told him I would not pass my word for the good going of it, but because it was Aspenall's work he was fond of it. But now he thinks he is choust, and everybody tells me that I had great luck to cosen him that he has cheated all the indigent officers.' (17)

Against this, there is some evidence of social conscience, if not generosity, in the fact that Sir John Bennet, at some time between 1682 and 1693 (he was then Lord Ossulstone) gave the sum of £100- to the town of Uxbridge to set up a trust for children to be apprenticed to handicraft trades. The cause of this gift was said to be an accident when Lord Ossulstone, driving through Uxbridge in his carriage, ran over and killed a boy. (18) Earlier, in 1672, he donated a silver flagon and a silver cup with cover to Harlington church, of which he was patron. Lord Ossulstone also took the wise precaution of ordering his own monument to be installed in the church, where it remains today. It carries his head and shoulders portrait bust, under the Bennet coat of arms, and is flanked by busts of his two successive wives, Elizabeth and Bridget, the latter by whom he had a son and two daughters. The monument is dated 1686, although he did not die until 1695. The Harlington Parish Registers record the date of Lord Ossulstone's death as 11 February 1695 and his burial 15 February. (A later Parish Register entry is on 21

8

July 1703, as follows: 'The Rt Honble Bridget Lady Dowager Ossulstone - The forfeiture for being buried in a coffin faced with velvet was pd. to me foar 50s.').

Although he is only peripheral to the story of Dawley, some account should be given of Henry Bennet, Sir John Bennet (III)'s younger brother, because of his much greater place in history as Earl of Arlington. Born in 1618 at Saxham, Suffolk (although numerous authorities, including Samuel Pepys, record him as being born at Harlington) Henry moved with his family to Harlington in the 1620's. According to the diarist John Evelyn, who knew him well, he was educated with a view to becoming a parson and the incumbent of Harlington Parish Church. This limited ambition perhaps signifies the extent to which the family fortunes had fallen at that time. However, the living of the rectory of Harlington with £40 a year does not seem to have appealed to him and he did not take holy orders while he was at Oxford. Henry Bennet was on the Royalist side in the Civil War, as were his father and elder brother. He does not appear to have taken part in any fighting except for a skirmish in which he became involved at Andover, where he received a sabre-cut over the nose which bit deep into the bone and left a scar that he carried all his life. Portraits show him with a prominent black patch over the bridge of his nose. In 1645 he was sent abroad on official business and remained on the Continent until the Restoration in 1660.

On the restoration of the monarchy he entered politics. It is not the purpose of this note to record his political life, which is fully described in his biography, as from this time on he had no connection with Dawley apart from the fact that his elder brother lived there. However, in addition to his other local connections another point of interest lies in the fact that in 1665 he was created a Baron and after some deliberation decided to take the name of Harlington, from the parish where he lived as a boy. Unfortunately, through an error in transcription, this was recorded without the 'H' and despite his objections the College of Heralds refused to change his title from Arlington to what he had intended. The mis-spelled title was retained when Henry Bennet was elevated to an earldom in 1672. (19)

As a footnote, Henry Bennet's memory was not, apparently, highly regarded locally. In 1729, John Saxy, the Harlington parish clerk, wrote in a long poem in praise of the ancient yew tree in the churchyard -

> 'The Doyly of the Norman race
> and nobler counts our village grace,
> Yet higher than them all Yew Tree
> Derives her stock called Pedigree
> And yields to Harlington a fame
> Much louder than its Earldom's name'

CHAPTER 4

THE DAWLEY ESTATE, 1607 - 1670

Sir John Bennet could presumably have moved into the Dawley manor house in 1607 after its sale to him by Ambrose Coppinger's widow and nephew. However, he was a busy judge as well as Chancellor to the Queen at this time and may well have found it more convenient to continue to live in his London house. There is, in fact, no evidence that he ever resided at Dawley, and perhaps regarded the estate as no more than one of his investments. It is much more likely that Place House in Uxbridge, that he acquired in 1612, was intended as a family home, and from this time until his death in 1627 he probably divided his place of residence between Uxbridge and his house in the City - excluding the period between 1622 and 1624 spent in the Fleet prison ! Sir John Bennet's entry in the Dictionary of National Biography describes him as of Christ Church (parish), London, and Uxbridge, and the inscription on the monument in St Margaret's Church, Uxbridge, to Dame Leonora Bennet, his widow, who died in 1638, states that she 'gave order to be here interred, where shee spent the greatest part of her last dayes'. There is certainly a record of her being in Uxbridge in 1623. (1)

Sir John Bennet (II), son and heir of the disgraced judge, moved to Harlington with his family some time after 1622 when his father was imprisoned, and the Harlington parish registers record the baptisms of some of his children on various dates between 1628 and 1637, indicating nearby residence. It is not known where they lived, although Harlington manor house had been conveyed to John Bennet by his father in 1615, together with other lands in the estate (as part of a marriage settlement) so he and his family may have lived there. There is possibly some significance in the fact that Sir John Bennet (II)'s second son, Henry, later chose Harlington (Arlington) for his title when ennobled, rather than Dawley. Perhaps of more significance is a reference in the diary of Samuel Pepys who, returning from a visit to Sir Robert Vyner at Ickenham in 1665, was shown a house 'in a towne called Harlington' where, he was told, Lord Arlington was born. (2) The diarist was misinformed as far as Henry Bennet's birthplace was concerned (it was Saxham in Suffolk, as mentioned earlier), but the house Pepys had pointed out to him, which must have been near the road from Ickenham via Hillingdon to Harlington (and thence to London), could nevertheless have been associated in the mind of his informant with Arlington's early years. Harlington manor house was close to the road and, being just north of the parish church, was indeed in the 'towne called Harlington', in contrast with the Dawley manor house at Pinkwell, which was nearly half a mile from any public road.

After the death of his father's widow (his stepmother) in 1638, Sir John Bennet (II) and his family (apart from his two eldest sons, he and his wife had had at least eight children by this time, several of whom did not survive infancy) may have moved into Place House in Uxbridge. He was apparently living somewhere on the Dawley and Harlington estate at the outbreak of the Civil War, however, when in 1642 he rode out to meet the King's army at Colnbrook, although whether he was using the manor house of Harlington or that of Dawley is not known. During the Commonwealth period that followed the War, Bennet mortgaged Dawley as mentioned earlier to his wife's sister, Dame Arabella Bryors, the widow of Sir William Bryors. This took place in 1657, and although Dame Arabella held her first Court Baron for the manor of Dawley in September of that year, there is no evidence that she chose to live at Dawley, rather than in her own home in Bedfordshire. Sir John Bennet (II) died in 1658 and was succeeded by his eldest son, John Bennet (III).

In 1660, as Dame Arabella Bryors had not paid the outstanding sum of £1800- plus interest in accordance with the agreement, John Bennet (III), together with Elizabeth Bennet (probably his sister, later to become Lady Carr), his brothers Charles and Edward, and Sir Henry Crofts (brother of his late mother and Dame Arabella) re-mortgaged the Dawley estate to John Caryll, of Harting, Sussex. Caryll was acting as a trustee for his distant cousin Philippa, Lady Morley and Mounteagle, widow of Baron Morley and Mounteagle. Lady Morley and Mounteagle wished to make an investment for the benefit of the daughters of her niece, Mary Selby, the wife of George Selby of Whitehouse, Co Durham.(3) Accordingly, £4000- was laid down to take over the 99 year lease on the Dawley estate originally granted to Dame Arabella Bryors. Lady Morley and Mounteagle was to hold a life interest in the estate, with the profits thereafter to go towards the maintenance and upbringing of her Selby grand-nieces. The settlement provided that £600- of the transferred debt of £1800- was to be met as part of Lady Morley and Mounteagle's payment of £4000-, and the balance of £1200- to be paid by George Selby, who was to take up residence with his family in the manor house of Dawley. (4) Lady Morley and Mounteagle's life interest in the estate did not last for long, since she died during the year of the agreement (which was signed on 9 May 1660) or soon afterwards.

John Bennet was described in August 1660 as 'Colonel John Bennet of Uxbridge', which might be interpreted as indicating that he was not living on the Dawley estate or in Harlington at that time. (5)

George Selby Esquire appears in the 1664 Hearth Tax return for Harlington as the occupier of a house assessed at 22 hearths. Although not specified in the return, this can only have been the manor house of Dawley, at Pinkwell, where Queen Elizabeth was entertained by Ambrose Coppinger some sixty years before. Sir John Bennet was also occupying a house in Harlington in 1664 - one assessed at 16 hearths. John Bennet (III) had been knighted (K.B.) in 1661 and had also got married in that year to Elizabeth Cranfield (widow of the 2nd Earl of Mulgrave), so either or both of these facts may have prompted him to move back to the family estate, albeit mortgaged. The only house available to him would appear to have been the old moated manor house of Harlington, just north of the parish church, and this is probably the 16 hearth house referred to in the 1664 Hearth Tax return. The old house may not have been in a good state of repair, because no building of 16 hearths appeared in the Hearth Tax return of 1674, indicating that it must by then have fallen into disuse and was no longer inhabited.

Sir George Selby (he was created a baronet on 3 March 1663/64) (6) died in September 1668, and his only son died within an hour of him, so that the baronetcy became extinct. Dame Mary Selby, his widow, continued to live at Dawley manor house and manage the estate, although with increasing difficulty. Sir George had paid only £700- of the transferred debt on the estate, leaving £500- still due; rent receipts from tenants fell; and the cost of repairs to the house and other buildings was heavy. Accordingly, Dame Mary sought the permission of the trustee to sell the estate and put the proceeds towards the upbringing of her daughters in accordance with the wishes of her late aunt, Lady Morley and Mounteagle. This evidently was agreed and she sought a purchaser and came up with the obvious (and possibly the only) person interested - Sir John Bennet (III).

Sir John made what appeared to Mary Selby the quite generous offer, in the circumstances, of £4000-, less the £500- outstanding debt on the mortgage agreement. Dame Mary wanted a quick sale, so to save the time that would be required to obtain a decree in the High Court of Chancery, she made a written declaration of the circumstances, as outlined above, indemnifying Sir John Bennet from any loss or damage arising from the sale. This declaration (7) was dated 7 May 1670, the lease and release documents for the sale itself being dated 2nd and 3rd May respectively. (8)

Bennet (described as 'of the Parish of St Martin in the Fields' in the above documents) had probably already decided to replace the old Dawley manor house, which had not been kept in a good state of repair by the Selbys, by building a new mansion more in accordance with his status and ambitions. In these aims he was possibly stimulated by his younger brother, Henry, who had already been created a Baron and had acquired a house on an important site in London, where Buckingham Palace now stands. By 1674, the only large house in the Hearth Tax

11

return for Harlington was one of 27 hearths occupied by Sir John Bennet. Neither the old house of 22 hearths vacated by Dame Mary Selby, nor the one of 16 hearths, appeared in the record and they are not identifiable in 1674 with the next largest houses, after Sir John Bennet's, which are only of 11 hearths or less. It is likely that the house at Pinkwell was wholly or partly demolished for materials for use in the construction of the new Dawley House. (9) The building of the new mansion will be discussed in the following chapters.

CHAPTER 5

THE NEW MANSION BUILT BY SIR JOHN BENNET (III) -
THE SITE, ARCHITECT AND BUILDING PROGRESS

Before embarking on a detailed description of the new mansion built at Dawley by Sir John Bennet (III) in the early 1670's, some consideration should be given to the site it occupied. To start with, Bennet, as owner of the manors of both Harlington and Dawley, presumably had the choice of building his new house in either of them. However, although sounding more important, Bennet's Harlington property represented, in fact, only part of Harlington parish (as distinct from Dawley). Its full title was the 'manor of Harlington or Hardington', a name adopted to distinguish it from another manor, with its origins in the Middle Ages, that had been created in the parish, known as 'Harlington with Shepiston'. (1) The latter seems to have consisted of lands mostly in the more southerly part of the parish, including the hamlet of Sipson (Shepiston), whereas the land of the Bennets' manor of Harlington or Hardington (2) seems to have been concentrated mostly in the north, abutting on his manor of Dawley. Dawley, the more compact and well-defined manor of the two, was probably of greater importance to the Bennets and no doubt the reason why Sir John decided to build his new mansion house there, although on a site more central to the manor than Pinkwell.

The site chosen for the house was about 740 yards north-east of the old Dawley manor house at Pinkwell and close to the Harlington-Hillingdon road that at that time curved round it on its east and north sides. Such close proximity to a public road seems a little strange, when there appear to have been no geographical or other limitations on Sir John Bennet's choice of sites on his estate. There may have been factors of which no record survives, but the site was, as mentioned, central to the Dawley estate and possibly he may have intended to divert the public road away from where his house was to be built - something that was eventually done, by his son, against strong local opposition, some forty years later.

The question also has to be raised as to whether there was already a house on the site. Farm buildings, which might from their appearance have existed before 1670, are shown in Kip's engraving of c.1700 of Dawley (discussed in full later) adjoining the road immediately to the east of the mansion, and the same engraving also shows a smallish seven-bay house which looks as though it could just possibly have dated from the early 1660's. (This house is also discussed more fully later). There was also the pigeon house - a manorial perquisite - that could, from its appearance, be dated to either before or after the 1670's. Also, irregularly-placed chimneys at the north-east corner of the new house and the service range could, just possibly, represent part of an earlier building and its appurtenances incorporated in the new. On balance, though, it seems improbable that a house of any consequence could have been on the site before Sir John Bennet (III) commenced building his new mansion.

The date on which work in building the new house at Dawley was started has not apparently been recorded, although there is no reason to suppose that it was not quite soon after Sir John's re-purchase of the estate from the Selbys' trustee in May 1670. A possible incentive for building at Dawley was that John Bennet's younger brother, Lord Arlington, was building his new country house at Euston, Suffolk in 1670. The 1670's were an affluent period in his life demonstrated, for instance, by a generous contribution towards the rebuilding of Pembroke College, Oxford, (his old college) and the endowment of two Fellowships and two Studentships there. About 1672, he donated a silver chalice with cover and a flagon to Harlington church, (3) perhaps in memory of his first wife, Elizabeth, who died early in that year. A building the size of Dawley could take several years to complete, and perhaps the very costly 'great supper and masquerade' Bennet held early in 1673 (at Dawley, it has been suggested) (4) was to celebrate the completion of the new house. Sir John married again in May 1673, this time to Bridget, daughter of John Grubham Howe, (5) and his new, young bride (she was only about 20) may well have moved immediately into the brand-new house. In any event, the Harlington Hearth Tax return of 1674 includes Sir John Bennet as owner of a house of 27 hearths (and omits any indication of the old house at Pinkwell), showing that the new mansion at Dawley must, by then, have been built. The only caveat against full completion of Dawley house by 1674 is that the Hearth Tax return also shows Sir John Bennet in occupation of another house in Harlington of only 3 hearths, suggesting the possibility that he was living there temporarily while, perhaps, interior decorations were being carried out at the new mansion.

Bennet's Dawley house as shown in Kip's engraving (discussed below) is fairly typical in most respects of the style of architecture brought from Holland after the restoration of the Monarchy. This style (of which The Mauritshaus at The Hague, begun in 1633, is regarded as the leading Dutch prototype) is characterised by brick construction, with a limited use of stone for ornament, such as string courses, quoins or pilasters. A triangular pediment usually embellished the principal front (and at the Mauritshaus on other fronts as well) and this commonly surmounted classical pilasters or brought-forward centre bays of the house. Unlike the earlier Anglo-Dutch style of 30-40 years before (typified by Kew Palace and Swakeleys at Ickenham) the roofs were now usually hipped, over a simple eaves cornice, and, frequently, dormer windows lighted the attic.

Hugh May (1622-1684), who had been in Charles II's circle during the King's exile in Holland, was the earliest and most influential exponent in England of the new style. At the Restoration, May was appointed to the senior post of Paymaster of the King's Works - the Office of Works. He was responsible for the financial aspect of the renovation of the Royal palaces that took place after the return of the King. In 1666, May was made acting Surveyor of the Works, in effect chief architect, during the illness of the incumbent, Sir John Denham, who was renowned as a poet but had no more than a gentleman amateur's knowledge of architecture and had been given the post as a reward for services rendered to the King during the interregnum. When Denham died in 1669, Hugh May was not, as he had hoped, appointed Denham's successor - the Surveyorship went to Christopher Wren. The King did not overlook May, though, and granted him a pension of £300- per annum in 1669 and two further profitable posts in 1670. Then, in November 1673, May was appointed Comptroller of the Works at Windsor, with responsibility for the reconstruction of the Royal apartments in Windsor Castle. This amounted to full recognition of the fact that, unlike some of his contemporaries at the Office of Works, Hugh May was a professional architect, and an accomplished one. (6)

One of the earliest houses in England in the new Dutch style was Eltham Lodge, Kent, built by Hugh May in 1663-1664. This house is now widely regarded as the English prototype for others, by other hands, such as Melton Constable, Norfolk (1665-1670) and Ramsbury, Wiltshire (c.1680). All these houses are of a rectangular plan, but the style was also elaborated into an H-plan, such as Sir John Denham's house in Piccadilly, begun in 1664 and possibly designed for him by Hugh May, who certainly completed it after Denham sold it, unfinished, to the 1st Earl of Burlington. Denham's house still exists, much altered, as Burlington House, seat of the Royal Academy. Another, much changed, building in Windsor, Burford House, appears, from a contemporary engraving by Kip, to have been very similar to Burlington House. As Burford House was built for the Duke of St Albans (Earl of Burford), Charles II's son by Nell Gwynne, it is tempting to believe that it was designed by May when he was Comptroller of the Works at Windsor Castle.

Returning to Dawley, no record survives of the name of the architect responsible for its design. It may even have been the case that Sir John Bennet designed the house himself with the aid of a master bricklayer or other experienced craftsman, since knowledge of architecture was considered to be an appropriate accomplishment for a gentleman of the period. (It has to be said, though, that Sir John Bennet claimed to have 'little skill in building' - but this was during Chancery proceedings in 1676 against the architect/bricklayer of his London house in St

James's Square). (7)   Some large as well as many small country houses were built in this way, although professional architects came increasingly to the fore during the 17th century, particularly for the design of the more grand houses.   It is likely that a professional was employed at an important house like Dawley, and among possible candidates the finger of probability points at Hugh May.   The house shown in Kip's engraving is compatible with May's restrained style and was in all likelihood built during the period when the architect was carrying out commissions for country houses in and around London.   Apart from those already mentioned, Hugh May carried out works at, for example, Cornbury Park, Oxfordshire, between 1666 and 1677, and Cassiobury, Hertfordshire, from 1674.   Sir John Bennet (III) was close to the King - as witnessed by the Royal favour at the christening of his (Bennet's) son in 1674, (8) so what is more likely than that the King should recommend one of his leading architects, Hugh May, Paymaster of the King's Works ?   (Wren, Surveyor of the Office of Works from 1669, was almost exclusively engaged on official works and public buildings for the rest of the century and very few country houses can with any certainty be ascribed to him).   There is, however, another reason why Hugh May might well have been chosen to design Dawley.   The younger brother of Sir John Bennet's grandfather (the first Sir John) was Thomas Bennet, an Alderman of London, who married Dorothy May - Hugh May's aunt.   Such a family connection cannot be ignored, particularly in the closely knit society of the 17th century. (9)

Nothing is known about the actual building progress of the 17th century Dawley house, since no building accounts or other relevant records are known to survive.   One can be reasonably certain, however, that many of the bricks for the house, which may have taken around two years or more to build, were made on the estate.   It was the practice to use local materials where possible; the area had a plentiful supply of brick-earth (most of which at Dawley was worked out commercially in the 19th century) and a working brick kiln is shown a short distance away to the north-east of the house in Kip's view of c.1700.   Also, for the foundations, at any rate, and possibly some internal walls that would be plastered or concealed from view, it is likely that materials were taken from the old house at Pinkwell which, as mentioned, had disappeared from the Hearth Tax return by 1674.

CHAPTER 6

THE NEW MANSION - THE EXTERIOR;
RELATIONSHIP WITH UPPARK, SUSSEX

Only two views are known to exist of the house at Dawley built by Sir John Bennet (III). The one most vital to the study of Dawley in the 17th century is the detailed engraving by John (or Johannes) Kip (died 1722). This, a view from the south, was taken from a painting or drawing by Leonard Knyff (1650-1722), of which the original is not known to have survived - in fact, less than a dozen of his paintings of country houses are known to exist and no definite examples of his drawings. (1) Kip's engraving of Dawley, which is inscribed to Charles, Lord Ossulstone, Sir John Bennet's son, who inherited the estate from him in 1695, was first published in 'Britannia Illustrata' in 1707. Knyff, a Dutchman, is not known to have worked in England before about 1695, so it would seem, therefore, to be a reasonably accurate assumption that the engraving shows the house as it was about 1700, and Kip's view of Dawley will be referred to here henceforth as of c.1700.

The only other known view of the house built by Sir John Bennet is a tiny coloured drawing included in a plan of the Dawley estate drawn about 1721 by John Jenner for Charles Bennet, by then Earl of Tankerville. (2) The view is also from the south, and the colouration shows that it was a brick building, the details of which (as far as they can be made out) broadly agree with those in Kip's engraving, although the service wing on the east side has been removed. The Jenner plan, and the evidence for its date, will be discussed more fully later.

What we have no means of knowing is how the house may have been altered (if indeed it was) in the thirty years or so between the time it was completed and the date of Kip's engraving. It is a reasonable assumption, however, that no major changes were made to the basic structure of the main building, although there are solid grounds for believing that the gardens were evolved, and various out-buildings were added, in this period, during which (in 1682) Sir John Bennet was created 1st Baron Ossulstone.

Sir John Bennet's Dawley mansion, then, was a two-storied brick-built (3) structure with a hipped (except at the north-east corner), tiled roof containing an attic in which there were four gabled dormer windows, regularly spaced on the south side. This south elevation was about 75 feet long (4) (excluding the single storey extension at the east end) and consisted of nine 'elements' or bays - nine windows on the upper floor and a door and eight windows on the ground floor. The west elevation, from what can be seen in the Kip engraving, would have been about 90-95 feet long and was of eleven 'elements' (windows or doors) and included the principal entrance, approached by steps, within a portico surmounted by a triangular pediment which would probably have carried in its tympanum the coat of arms of the Bennets. This would have been similar in style, in all probability, to the stone coat of arms of Ford Grey at Uppark (now transferred to Combe Farm in the village of Rake, about 7 miles north of Uppark). The centre bays of the west front were probably projected forward and/or were decorated with pilasters supporting the pediment. There were also four dormer windows on this side, spaced in pairs either side of the pediment. The gateway in the drive leading from the Harlington - Hillingdon road facing the house on the west side had four pillars, as if to emphasise the importance of this approach. Nothing is known of the north elevation, although it is likely broadly to have corresponded with the south front, on the opposite side of the house. The end of the roof nearest to the stables, however, appears to be gabled, if Kip's drawing is accurate here, rather than hipped as on the other sides. The inner side of the north roof has two gabled wings projecting into a courtyard in the centre of the house. At the east side of the house, completing the enclosure of the courtyard, is a complex of domestic service buildings with hipped roofs lower than those of the main block. The chimneys of the house itself are all on the inner slopes of the roof and seem curiously insubstantial and unimposing.

The windows on the first floor of the house are taller than those on the ground floor, indicating that the principal rooms were on this upper floor. Having the 'piano nobile' on the first floor is a feature shared with, for example, Eltham Lodge (where the windows of both floors are the same height, however), Althorp House, Northants (remodelled 1666-68), and the splendid east front of Hampton Court Palace, built by Sir Christopher Wren from 1689 onwards.

The south elevation of Dawley, the only side of which a clear view exists, is very simple, with no trace of quoins or window adornment, the decorative effect being confined to the modillion eaves cornice, a projecting string course between the upper and lower windows, and an ornamented doorway, approached by two steps. Even the doorway is fairly simple, carrying a flat architrave on consoles, but no pediment. The eaves cornice and the string course would have been carried round the west and north sides of the house. A small single-storey extension, with two windows and a chimney, adjoins the east side of the south front, and behind this can be seen in the engraving the south end of the service range which has diamond-pane casement windows, and dormers in the roof.

In two respects, Dawley was unusual, compared with most contemporary houses of the same style. Firstly, it was apparently _not_ built over a basement, if the Kip engraving is accurate in this respect. Basements were usually used in mid-late 17th century houses to accommodate the service rooms, which at Dawley were, as we have seen, under separate roofs, although joined on to the house at the east side. This fact, together with the somewhat more archaic appearance of the service range, could be taken as evidence that the new house was built partly over old foundations. This is not considered very likely, however, and the absence of a basement, apart from any architectural preference, may have been dictated by soil drainage problems. (5)

The second unusual - and very rare - feature of the Dawley mansion is the windows which, if the Kip engraving of Knyff's view is to be believed, were exceptionally narrow in proportion to their height. They are shown as six panes high but only two panes wide, with narrow glazing bars. (6) It is not clear from the engraving if these are casement (outward opening) or sash (sliding) windows. The normal type of window in large houses in England in the first half of the 17th century was the mullion and transom in the form of a cross, with one casement opening. After the Restoration, the vertically-sliding sash window was introduced from Holland and gradually superseded the casement, both in new buildings and as replacements for existing windows. This was an easy conversion, since the proportions of sash windows could readily be made to fit the openings filled by 17th century casements. The first sash windows started to come into use in England after the Great Fire of London and the earliest recorded in a country house are those installed in Chatsworth by the 3rd Earl of Devonshire from about 1676 (they have now been replaced in later alterations to Chatsworth). Since the Dawley windows are quite unlike the usual proportions for casements, it is assumed that they are sashes and the original ones put in when the house was built; not replacements substituted by the time the engraving was made about 1700. Since the Dawley windows would appear to be very early ones of their type, their proportions can perhaps be put down to experiment before the larger sash windows settled down to the almost universal norm seen on 17th and early 18th century houses today of three or four panes wide. Practically no exact parallel with the Dawley windows can be found. The Mauritshaus at The Hague in Holland (mentioned above) does have windows two panes wide, but they are of quite different proportions from those at Dawley. Mompesson House, Salisbury, Wiltshire, and Trumpeter's House, Richmond, Surrey, for example, both have windows two panes wide (in the former only either side of the entrance, specifically to fit a restricted area) but in each case they are only four panes high, and both houses were built about 1701, much later than Dawley. Another interesting house in this connection is the south wing of Dingley, Northamptonshire, built about 1680 (probably by Hugh May, incidentally) where the windows of the south wing, although three panes wide by seven high and more widely spaced, are similar in proportion to those of Dawley.

It is perhaps appropriate, at this point, to discuss the possible architectural connection between Dawley and Uppark, Sussex. Charles Bennet married Mary Grey, daughter of Ford Grey, Earl of Tankerville, in 1695, shortly after he (Bennet) became the 2nd Baron Ossulstone, following the death of his father. Uppark - still existing, although reconstructed after serious fire damage in 1989 - is believed to have been built about 1690-1694, and William Talman is claimed to be the architect, with George London as the garden designer. (7) Although later in date by twenty years or so, Uppark is very similar to Dawley in many respects. Ford Grey is likely to have visited Dawley with his daughter prior to the marriage and could well have been sufficiently impressed with the Bennets' house to instruct William Talman to build him a similar mansion to replace his old house at Uppark. Talman was familiar with Dawley, having (as will be discussed later) almost certainly worked there, together with George London, on the gardens and associated buildings. (8) A commission of this kind would account for Talman's relatively restrained design for Uppark, compared with his normally more flamboyant style. In any event, the likelihood of the cross-fertilisation of ideas between Dawley and Uppark is very strong, since Charles Bennet became the owner of both when his wife, who was the sole heir of her father, inherited Uppark. Ford Grey had been created Earl of Tankerville by William III, a title that was revived in favour of his son-in-law in 1714. The possibility of the Uppark courtyard and service buildings layout influencing the design of the new Great Courtyard at Dawley is discussed later.

CHAPTER 7

DAWLEY HOUSE - THE INTERIOR (1679 - 1722)

No interior views of Dawley are known to exist, although some idea of the location and appearance of the rooms can be gained from inventories that have survived. The earliest of these is headed 'a note of the beding at Dawley', in a notebook (1) compiled by Bridget Bennet (second wife of Sir John Bennet (III)) on 8 January 1678 (1678/79) and therefore lists only the rooms containing beds. These include the Gold Room, the Scarlet Room, velvet chamber, green chamber, 'my own chamber', Charles' bed (Charles Bennet, her son, born 1674), Nana's bed (probably Annabella, born 1675), Roly's bed (possibly a pet name for her younger daughter Dorothy, born 1676 and just over one year old), the servants room next to ye gold chamber, the servants room to ye scarlet chamber, the servants room to ye green room, and so on, down to 'the gardeners bed'. There is also the 'hal [hall] chamber' and, more surprisingly, a bed 'in the hal'. The bedding at Dawley was again listed, room by room, towards the end of 1690. Unlike the earlier one, this list was evidently compiled by a servant. Some rooms are identifiable with those named in 1678/9, but with most one cannot be certain. As this inventory is the one closest in date to Kip's engraving of the house, it is quoted in full below.

'An Accompt of Dawley beding Nov ye 7 1690'. (2)
In my Lords roome
Ladys chamber
In the scarlet roome
little room within
the young Ladie's roome
Drawing Roome by my Lady
Mrs Rowett's
Maggdelines bed
Mr Magdaniell's roome
Mr Charles' old Chamber
Mr Trifframs
Mrs Fairechilds room
ye Landrey
Mr Beards roome
The Bed by ye pantrye
In the Hall chamber
ye Shepards roome
the room att ye foot of ye Great Stairs
ye maids Chamber by ye store house
Mr Greens roome
the roome by ye Wool chamber
Mrs Bavey's chamber
the stables
ye Carter roome

(Unrelated but interesting information is that in the back of the same book is a separate list headed 'A note of The Cloathe in the greatt heave Trunk at Dawly March ye 27th 1691'. It begins 'My Lords & my Lady coronations robs'. There is also 'A catalogue of books of Lady Bennett Feb 25 1680' and a similar list dated Nov ye 17 '92').

The next inventory for Dawley - the first full one known to exist - is dated 12 February 1712 (1712/13) (3), when Charles Bennet, 2nd Lord Ossulstone, had succeeded his father. His wife, Mary (Grey) had died some 18 months earlier, in 1710. The inventory is a complete list of the furniture and other moveable items at Dawley. The following is the list of rooms in what is believed to be the main house and attached offices, and some outbuildings. Some of the more interesting or unusual items are noted in brackets here, and where there is indication that a room had a fireplace (e.g. mention of a chimney glass, hearth, fire dogs, tongs, and/or bellows etc) this is indicated by (H) (for 'Hearth'). Starting with the top floor, the rooms are as follows:

The cooks room

Christian's room

The footmens room

The Gentleman of the horse room (the Gentleman of the Horse was, by 1722 at any rate, the highest paid servant)

'The   Room called   Mr Bennett's' (this may originally have been the bedroom of Charles Bennet, who by 1713 had inherited the house and estate: then used, possibly, by Charles (II), his heir)

The inward wardrobe (this room was used for storing old furniture)

The outward wardrobe (also used for storage)

The Nursery maids room (this included a half-headed bedstead and 'a picture without a frame')

The Gentleman's room ('hanged with printed paper' - it contained tables and a 'matted chair' but no bed. It had an iron plate lock)

2 closets (11 pairs of bowls and a jack were among the items stored here)

The great staircase passage (a press bed with a sacking bottom, 8 chairs, 2 pictures in gilt frames and a map in a black frame were kept here)

The next rooms were probably on the first floor - the principal floor of the house, or 'piano nobile'. They comprised:

The corner room (5 chairs and a 'cabinet of walnuttree upon a frame') (H)

The Great Dining Roome (this, one of the most important rooms in the house, had a painted ceiling mentioned in later (1716 and 1722) inventories. There were 2 large pictures in gilt frames, 3 smaller pictures, a looking glass in a gilt frame over the chimney, 4 glass sconces (candle holders) in brass sockets, 2 little hanging stands for candlesticks, a pair of brass dogs (for holding logs) in the fireplace and '10 black Jappan chairs covered in blue linen', but no tables) (H)

The bed chamber next the dining room (this was another important room - it may once have been Lord and/or Lady Ossulstone's room and contained,   inter alia, a 'very large picture in a gilt frame', probably (as deduced   from later inventories)   their portrait.   It had a fretwork (decorated plaster) ceiling, specially noted as such in 1722. There were 7 'armed' chairs but no beds. It seems likely that Lord Ossulstone ceased to use it after his wife's death in 1710). (H)

The young ladys chamber (a canopy bedstead with sacking bottom, the furniture of yellow flowered Damask fringed with black silk, and 2 'little standing bedsteads with sacking bottoms' furnished with grey cloth and yellow camblet (4) respectively.   This may have been the bedroom of one of Lord Ossulstone's two youngest daughters, Annabella or Mary). (H)

The closet (containing a close stool and pan - one of only four mentioned in 1713 for the whole house)

The Little Masters Room (black Jappan Table, a standing bedstead with sacking bottom, etc. This may have been the bedroom of one or both of Lord Ossulstone's younger sons, Henry and Grey). (H)

The closet (used for storage - 5 pictures in gilt frames, 4 pictures without frames, 2 prints in black frames, 7 shelves and a row of cloak pins)

The passage room (a press bedstead with sacking bottom, a painted screen with 4 leaves, etc)

The Ladys Womans Room (presumably lady's maids room - 'a little pallet bedstead', etc)

The dark closet (presumably without a window - one Iron chest empty, a black Jappan box)

The Ladys Bedchamber (standing bedstead, 6 black Jappan chairs, 1 easy chair and 2 stools all covered in the same cloth as the bed, screen with 6 leaves, etc. This may have been the bedroom of Lord Ossulstone's eldest daughter, Bridget.) (H)

The stair head and dark passage (it may be assumed that the latter was on the east side of the main block of the house, where the service range joined on and cut out direct lighting - one iron chest, 2 black sconces candlebra attached to mirrors), 12 large pictures in panels).

The closet by the great stair case (one very large picture in a black frame, etc)

It is at this point, probably, that the inventory starts on the ground floor rooms, which comprised:

The stewards room (one round table, 2 square tables, 18 oak chairs, 5 pictures over the chimney in a panel) (H)

The closet (a writing table, 'a case of paper shelves', a chair, 3 deal shelves, a row of cloak pins)

The Servants Hall (one long table, 2 forms, 2 benches fixed, a bell, a deal clothes prop, etc) (H)

The porters room (a half headed bedstead, 'a Parcell of Armour', etc)

His Lordship's Wardrobe (a Walnuttree Table, 'a fine Ebbony Cabbinet Inlaid', 17 Mapps in black frames, etc)

His Lordships Dressing Room (a 'Cannop Bedstead with Sacking Bottom the furniture of Scarlet Cloth fringed with Green Silk', a total of 7 chairs, 4 different tables, 6 cups, 6 saucers, sugar box with cover and teapot - all of china, etc) (H)

The Stone Hall (4 oak ovill (oval ?) tables, 2 sideboard tables, 12 Turkey workd chairs, 10 pictures in frames, a grate fixt, fender poker & brush) (H)

(The hall was probably on the west side of the house, directly accessible from the main entrance)

The closet next his Lordships Dressing Room

The Parlour ('one large peer of Glass in a black Jappand frame' (this would have been a mirror between the windows), one glass over the chimney in a black frame, 49 prints in black Jappand frames, one long folding table,

21

one side board table, slated, 12 cane chairs with bannister backs, 3 other chairs, 'a clock in a standing frame', 'a stool for the cistern to stand on' (the cistern would be for wine cooling), etc) (H)

The drawing room (6 Dammask Chairs fringd with Green & Silver, 1 black & green velvet armd chair, 6 China saucers, 4 cups, basin, sugar pot and cover, tea pot, milk pot & dish for the spoons, etc) (H)

The bedchamber (a canopy bedstead ..... the furniture Crimson Damask, hangings of the same, counterpane, 2 feather beds, 4 quilts, 1 bolster, 7 pillows, 6 blankets, 8 chairs 4 of them armd all covered in Damask the same as the bed, 'a large Peer of Glass in a black frame' (a tall mirror, hung between windows), a clock in a hanging case, 35 pieces of China, etc) (H)

The little room next adjoining (a field bedstead with sacking bottom, a Red Leather Close stool case and pan, etc) (H)

Mr Challoner's room (H)

The closet (a row of cloak pins, etc)

The room adjoining (H)

The following rooms (and possibly some of those preceding, such as the servants hall) were probably in the service wing attached to the east side of the house:

The small beer cellar

The outward pantry (a Leading (=leaden ?) cistern)

The inward pantry (perhaps leading from the outward pantry - a copper cistern, 7 china plates, 14 Delfe (Delft) Ware plates, etc)

The washhouse (one copper fixt, etc)

The Maids chamber (2 half headed bedsteads, etc)

The room next adjoining

Mr Levett's Room (one Peece Tapistry hangings, one peece printed paper, etc)

The Laundry (one long Deal dresser, a drying horse, a little step ladder, 6 clothes baskets, 9 smoothing irons, etc) (H)

The Room late the Housekeepers (H)

Major Parson's room (one standing bedstead, 'one Oake table with a Drawer', etc) (H)

The Inward Still Room (a store cupboard for sweetmeats, 6 wainscot boxes for sweetmeats, 2 copper preserving pans, a pair of Wafer irons, a pair of brass scales and weights, 21 Delfe ware plates, etc (from a long list of equipment))

The outward Still room (one large Deal folding table, and a long list of furniture, equipment, bed linen and table linen, etc)

'The pastrey' (one long Elm dresser with a drawer, 12 tinn Fat (?) pans, etc)

The kitchen (3 long dressers, 'a very large jack with cords and weights', a grate fixt for a range, an iron crane with 2 hanging hooks, 1 gridiron, 2 frying pans, 1 iron cheese toaster, a lead cistern, 1 iron mortar & pestle, 1 marble mortar, 2 mincing knives, 1 iron dripping pan, a large copper fish kettle) (H)

The larder (2 dressers, 1 chopping block, 2 powdering tubbs, 1 leaden salting cistern, 2 shelves)

The Store room (1 candle box, etc)

The scullery (a copper fixt, a brass fish kettle, etc)

Joans chamber (a half headed bedstead, etc)

The flower roome (flower (flour) tub & cover, bran tub, kneading trough, 'wyre cive' (wire sieve), etc)

The following rooms (and possibly some of those preceding) were probably contained in buildings not attached to the house and standing to the east of it:

The bake house (large kneading trough & cover, etc)

The darey (dairy) (churn, 2 milk trays, 3 tubbs, milk pail, a pair of brass scales & weights, one pair wooden scales, 1 milk cive (sieve)).

The brew house (one large brewing copper fixt, 1 mashing tubb, 1 under back (?), 2 coolers fixt, 1 leaden cistern, 3 working tubbs, 4 tapp tubbs, 3 bareing (?) tubbs, 2 tunn dishes, 1 piggin, 1 hopp basket, a coall rake & poaker, a side press, a pair of - (?), 2 iron screw hoops, 9 empty pipes.)

The bagnio (the bath house - although it did not have a bath tub and seems to have been furnished as a bedroom since it contained a cannopy bedstead, also 2 black frame stools, 1 walnuttree inlaid card table, 3 cane dressing chairs, 9 Indian pictures in panell frames, a hearth, doggs, fire shovell, tongs & bellows, etc) (H)

It will be noted from the above that for 20 rooms a hearth is mentioned or implied from the contents, and if the bagnio, scullery, bakehouse and brewhouse are added, a total close to that of the 1674 Hearth Tax return of 27 hearths is reached.

Further inventories of the contents of all the buildings at Dawley were taken on 17 January 1716 and again in June 1722, (5) by which time many additions and changes had been made, but they still included the (by then) 'old house'. The rooms in the 'old house' were, as before, numbered in sequence but unfortunately the same numbers or sequences were not used, so the later inventories cannot readily be compared with that of 1712/13. Some rooms, however, have the same names and others can be identified positively or probably by features or contents mentioned on both occasions. Some of these are (1712/13 names where different are given in brackets): The Gentleman of the Horse his room; the Room called Mr Bennet's; Corner Room upon the Great Stairs head (Corner Room); Room where my Lord and Lady's picture is (bedchamber next the dining room in 1713 - called the Fretwork Ceiling Room in 1722); the White Room (the Lady's bedchamber); the Red Damask Room and Little Room by the Red Room (Bedchamber, probably next to the Drawing Room, and 'Little Room next adjoining'); Drawing Room; Dining Room (possibly 'the Parlour' of 1712/13); the Marvel (marble) Hall ('the Stone Hall' in 1712/13 and simply 'the Hall' in 1722); the Great Dining Room (referred to as such in 1712/13 and 1716 but described as 'the Painted Ceiling Room' in 1722). A bagnio is not included in the 1716 inventory, whereas one is in 1722 - this was presumably a new building. It contained, inter alia, a 'bathing tubb'.

23

CHAPTER 8

DAWLEY c1700 - OUTBUILDINGS, GARDENS & THE ESTATE

Although the mansion house itself, it may be assumed, remained much as it was when built, the formal gardens and various outbuildings at Dawley had been laid out and added to and improved over a period of 30 years or so until they presented the appearance shown by Kip about 1700. Certain of these other buildings and architectural features at Dawley provide some clues to the progressive development of the environs of the house up to the end of the 17th century.

The small seven-bay, two-storied house just to the east of the Dawley mansion shown in the Kip engraving is something of a puzzle. The slight possibility, mentioned earlier, that it might have been a farmhouse pre-dating the mansion cannot entirely be discounted, although if so it cannot, at the most, be more than about ten years earlier in date. It has a south frontage of about 55 feet (1) and with its hipped roof, dormer windows, modillion eaves cornice and string course between upper and lower windows, it is like a miniature version of the mansion. The central doorway shown (the main entrance was probably on the opposite (north) side) is similar to that of the south front of the mansion, if slightly simpler, and although the windows are of the older mullion and transom 'cross' pattern, casements of this type were still used for smaller houses long after sashes had been introduced, so this house could easily have been built at roughly the same time as the mansion and by the same architect. If later than the big house it was perhaps erected as a dower house by Sir John Bennet (III), in anticipation of his demise, for his second wife, Bridget (who was some 37 years younger than he was) after their son was born in 1674. (As it happened, Bridget Bennet survived her husband by only eight years; she died in 1703). For convenience, this building will be referred to henceforth as the 'dower house', although it has to be emphasised that there is no documentary evidence to support this description. It was later replaced by another building of similar size a little further north, as shown in Jenner's plan of c.1721.

Among the other buildings near the mansion shown in the Kip engraving is a long stable block, forming the east side of the grass courtyard north of the house. A coach house is incorporated in its south end. These stables evidently had extensive accommodation for servants in the attic: the roof has no less than fourteen dormer windows on the west side. On the east side there are six gables and, at the north end, a double-pile roof arrangement. Beyond the stables, across a triangular farm yard, is a row of farm buildings lining the Harlington - Hillingdon road. From north to south, these are a barn with a porch; a smaller wooden building having an outshut at one end with a chimney; and a brick-built structure with pillars at the front - possibly a cattle shelter. These three buildings all have gabled, tiled roofs, and are joined end to end. A little further down the road, past a pillared gateway giving access to the farm yard, is a small brick cottage with a gabled roof. It is very difficult to date these buildings from the engraving, although there appears to be nothing to suggest that they are earlier than the 17th century. A little distance away to the north-east of the house, in the middle of an orchard, a dovecote with a flock of pigeons above it is shown in the Kip engraving. This is a square structure with a window shown in the upper floor and a pyramidal roof surmounted by a cupola or lantern with a balustrade round it. The cupola suggests a 17th century date, but it is difficult to be certain. From later information (2) the pigeon house appears to have been about 25 feet square in plan, so by analogy with existing dovecotes it could have accommodated 500-600 pigeons. More will be said later of the dovecote, which outlasted nearly all the other buildings at Dawley. Finally, mention should be made of a small, square, detached building with a pyramidal roof located close to the south-east corner of the 'dower house' at Dawley. The purpose of this little structure, which appears to have no windows, is not known, although it may possibly have been a bagnio, or bath house, since one was mentioned in the Dawley inventory of 1713, although we cannot be sure that this particular building still existed at that date. Alternatively, it may have been a well-head building, since the later water house was located close to the site of this pyramid-roofed building.

The formal gardens at Dawley as they were about 1700, and their architecture, as shown in Kip's engraving, must next be described. The gardens were designed to complement the architecture of the mansion, and were centred on the middle of its south front, although they extended also to the west of the house. On the edge of the gardens, sited to the south- east of the mansion with its east end adjoining the public road, was what was then perhaps one of the most important architectural features of Dawley, the green house, or orangery: orange trees in pots are shown standing in front of it in the engraved view. This splendid structure had a frontage of about 145 feet - much wider than the south front (excluding service buildings) of the house itself. The central doorway with a scrolled pediment had a glass-panelled door, and there were eighteen tall, narrow windows (two panes wide), and a flat roof with a balustraded parapet. Some actual dimensions of the green house were recorded (on 3 June 1719) when it was to be dismantled for some of its materials to be used for the new house then to be built. (3) Among these, there were listed nineteen window shutters (actually for 18 windows and one door of similar size) 9ft9in x 4ft10in; 189$\frac{1}{4}$ feet of modillion cornice; and 28$\frac{3}{4}$ square of rough deal board under the lead (roof). Mr John Harris (4) believes that this green house bears the stamp of William Talman's style. Talman (1650-1719) was a leading professional architect who, it has been suggested, (5) was a pupil of Hugh May, whom he succeeded as Comptroller of the King's Works from 1689 to 1702. The formal gardens, as they were in 1700, are attributed with certainty, (6) however, to George London, (? - 1714) the garden designer. Talman and London were both associated with the Royal Gardens, of which they were Comptroller and Deputy Superintendent respectively, and also collaborated closely on the designs for buildings and gardens of many country houses. It has been claimed that wherever Talman went, London followed, and vice versa.

The other main architectural feature of the gardens is the pair of summer houses, or gazebos, at the south-west and south-east corners: they are connected by a raised terrace reached by steps where interrupted in the middle by a pair of ornamental gates. These buildings (referred to as the 'west summer house in the garden' and the 'east summer house in the garden' in the inventory of 1713 (7), when they each contained a table and chairs) are square in plan with a modillion cornice surmounted by a pyramidal roof with a ball finial, have a window on the south side (and presumably others on two further sides) and are each entered via three curved steps through a door facing the terrace. Almost identical summer houses were to be found at Hampton Court, Herefordshire, where Talman and London are known to have worked together on the house and gardens between about 1692 and 1699. (8) If Talman designed the summer houses at the Herefordshire mansion, it seems more than likely that he was responsible for those at Dawley (and also its green house) when cooperating with George London there.

The showpiece of the Dawley gardens in 1700 was the magnificent pair of wrought iron gates, set midway in the walled terrace between the pair of summer houses and in line with the wide walk leading through the middle of the parterres to the centre of the south, garden, front of the house. The stone or brick gate piers bear the lions rampant that are the supporters of the Bennet coat of arms, and the centre of the iron over-fly to the gates themselves carries the Bennet arms. The wrought iron work of the gates is slightly different on each side, although the sides balance each other. This was a characteristic of the late-17th century master of this art form, Jean Tijou (late C17 - circa 1712). An authority on Tijou's work (9) believes that the Dawley gates were indeed designed by the master himself. Tijou's best known work was carried out at the Royal Palace of Hampton Court (Middlesex), not far away. Tijou is believed to have arrived in England in the retinue of William III and Mary, so the work on the Dawley gates is most unlikely to have been carried out before 1689.

Turning to the formal gardens themselves, (10) these are completely enclosed

25

by walls, which are terminated at the south-west and south-east corners by the summer houses referred to above.   Internal north-south walls divide the gardens south of the house in a ratio of 1:2:1.   The walls are interrupted on all sides by gates or doors;   on the south, where they enclose the raised terrace walk, by the gates, already described, bearing the Bennets' coat of arms.   The wide walk leading from these gates to the centre of the south front of the house divides the east and west parts of the gardens;   those parterres immediately adjacent to the walk being identical either side of it.   Outside the terrace on the south side are what appear from the Kip engraving to be two wide gravelled walks, enclosed by railings which, where they meet the gates, form an inward-curved approach to them on either side. The portion of the gardens nearest to the house on the south side consists of a large lawn, divided by the central walk and cross paths into four parts, embellished with statues (the inventory of 1722 (11) mentions 'seven large figures of lead, eight boys do. smaller, four large flower pots do.') and bordered with potted shrubs.   To the south of the lawn, forming the middle section of the gardens, are twelve small parterres with patterns made up of various coloured substances.   Nearest the ornamental gates are more parterres laid out as two flower gardens either side of the main walk.   These are in four identical diagonal patterns, with grass walks, resembling in plan 'Union Jack' flags.   In each side of this arrangement are two wooden trellis arbours, facing each other and linked by grass walks wider than the others.   Enclosed in the south-west corner of the garden walls is a bowling green and adjoining it is a small square orchard, with regularly-spaced trees.   North of that are some rectangular flower beds with, beside them, a gravel walk lined with shrubs in pots.   At the opposite (east) side of the gardens in front of the orangery is a space reserved for the orange trees, placed outside during the summer, and a small garden, divided by a wall from the rest, with ten miniature 'parterres de broderie', with flowers and shrubs, no two the same.   Outside the formal gardens on the east side, enclosed by more walls, are two kitchen gardens, separated by a path leading to an iron gate, hung between square piers with finials, opening on to the public road.   A further kitchen garden, including a glass growing-frame, is north of the green house or orangery.   Facing the west side of the house are four small lawns, embellished with formal shrubs, in the walled courtyard which forms the main approach to the house on its principal front.   The courtyard walls on their north and south sides have each set in them a door and a length of iron railings, the latter apparently located so as to provide a north-south vista.   This area is entered through gates with four piers topped with urn finials.   The gates may have been as impressive as those on the south side, but no details are visible in Kip's engraving, where they are shown end-on.   An avenue, possibly gravelled, runs north-south in front of the four-pier gateway.   For visitors coming from the north, this avenue is entered through a two-pier gate (with ball finials) on the public road from Hillingdon. The formal approach for visitors coming from the south must have been via a road entering the estate at a point somewhere along its south boundary, since a coach and six with outriders is shown by Kip approaching the aforementioned north-south avenue from this direction.   The north side of the house has a simple grass courtyard, walled except on the east side where it is flanked by the stable block, and is entered through a gateway (with pillars and finials) not far from the public road, which curves round to the north.

To summarise, Dawley and its gardens as drawn or painted by Leonard Knyff about 1700, and engraved by Kip, was probably evolved over the last thirty years or so of the 17th century.   While it is likely that a start was made in laying out the gardens immediately the house was completed, they were probably enlarged, particularly on the south east side, later.   This was most likely when Talman built the green house and the two summer houses.   More likely than not, this was in the 1690's, when Tijou would have been brought in to design the culminating glory of the gardens, the gates proudly surmounted by the Bennets' armorial achievements. The likely dates of the various works suggest that, apart from the house itself, the major part of them was carried out by Sir John Bennet (III) after he had been created Baron Ossulstone (in 1682), but it is probable that the schemes up to 1700 were completed by his son Charles, the 2nd Baron, after he succeeded to the title and whose name appears on the Kip engraving.   As we shall see later, Charles Bennet had even grander designs for Dawley.

The Estate c1700.   Kip's engraving of c.1700 gives some information about the Dawley estate in general, in addition to a more detailed picture of the house and gardens.   A deer park existed there at this time and deer are shown in some numbers, but only in the area west of the house. It can be assumed, though, from the absence of any barriers, that they ranged also all round the south part of the estate, being excluded only from the immediate environs of the house, formal gardens and kitchen gardens.   It may also be assumed that they were denied access to the formal gardens of the old house at Pinkwell, not shown by Kip. The deer were also kept out of the land in the north-west part of the estate, including the field where a large haystack and a smoking brick kiln are shown (and beyond them, near the north-west boundary of the estate, a small unidentified building) and all the land east of the public road (then still running on its old course).   The main farming activities were then apparently confined to the area east of the public road, served by the farm buildings already described.   Long-horned cattle are depicted in the field east of the orangery on the other side of the road.   North of this field is an orchard with the dovecote in the middle of it and north of this orchard is a field containing, apparently, sheep.

The full extent of the estate about 1700 cannot, of course, be assessed from Kip's view, which shows only a part of it, but a survey of the whole of the Parish of Harlington was made by the parishioners on 2 March, 1692. (12)   This records that Lord Ossulstone held 101 acres of arable and 175 acres of meadow land in Dawley, together with 205 acres of arable and 70 acres of meadow elsewhere in Harlington (the latter was described as Lalams grounds, Birds grounds, Godmans ground, Bishops farm and Woolfords farm - the names of Godman and Woolford being listed elsewhere as having separate holdings of 13 acres and 4 acres respectively).   These figures - a total of 276 acres of farm land at Dawley - would seem to indicate that about 100 acres or so was given over to the deer park at this time, if the total estate in Dawley alone was then around 380 acres, as it was known to be a decade or so later.   Lord Ossulstone had received licence in 1690 to impark 300 acres, (13) although it seems that he did not take full advantage of this until a few years later. A record of the extent of the park, undated, although it is assumed that it must be later than the above survey (1692), gives its total area as 373 acres 1 rood (Lord Ossulstone's total holding in the whole parish was 602 acres).   There were then 750 head of deer in the park, valued at 40 shillings per head. (14)   The first accurate record of the estate that can be associated with definite boundaries is Jenner's plan of c.1721 (to be discussed fully later) which, by comparison with later maps, represents 396 acres.   Jenner depicts deer ranging over the whole of the estate, excepting only the area of the house and gardens, and the formal gardens at Pinkwell.   The type of estate fencing shown in Kip's engraving on both sides of the public road and also along the north boundary of the deer enclosure consists of close-boarded vertical planks with pointed tops.

Finally, a point of general interest before leaving the Kip engraving, which is a low oblique 'aerial' view, (15) is that beyond the estate on the horizon are shown, from left to right, some buildings representing, presumably, the town of Uxbridge; Hillingdon church tower;   the hamlet of Wood End Green;   a large house to the north-east - possibly intended to represent the manor house of Hayes Park Hall; the tower of Hayes church and, in the far distance, what must be the spire of Harrow church on its hill.

27

CHAPTER 9

THE LATER BENNETS AT DAWLEY

'Charles was born may ye 15th and christend ye 20th 1674 by the King: Lord Arlington and my mother ....'. Bridget, second wife of Sir John Bennet (III) recorded in her note book (1) this auspicious beginning in life for their son and heir. (Charles' sisters, Annabella, born 8 May 1675, and Dorothy, born 30 November 1676, were not similarly honoured with a Royal godparent). Charles Bennet's years of childhood were not uniformly happy, particularly bearing in mind that some relatively minor illnesses of today were sometimes fatal in the 17th century. His mother recorded elsewhere in her notebook: 'Charles had the meazels April 1677 at Dawley'; 'Charles had the smal pox Sept 1678 at Euston' (Lord Arlington's house in Suffolk); 'Charles had the feaver and ague May 1679 at Dawley and London'; 'Charles went to Schoole at Eaton May ye 30th 1681'. Of his earlier adult life little seems to have survived on record, beyond rumours of his matrimonial aspirations: it was believed (July 1694) that he was to marry 'Mrs Thomas of Wales, the greatest fortune in England'; then in September 1694 it was said he was to marry 'Mrs Crew, one of the heiresses of the Lord Crew'; and in April 1695 (after his father's death, and his succession as the 2nd Lord Ossulstone) it was claimed that he had married 'a young exchange woman'. (2) Whatever truth there may have been behind these stories, Charles did marry Mary, the only daughter and heir of Ford Grey, Earl of Tankerville, on 3 July 1695. He maintained his father's close interest in Dawley, as will be discussed later. It must have been when travelling to or from Dawley that he had the misfortune to be robbed by a highwayman on Hounslow Heath on 18 June 1698. He was in good company, 30 to 40 persons, including the Dukes of Northumberland and St Albans being attacked that day. (3)

For the years from mid-November 1703 to near the end of December 1712 we have some insight into Lord Ossulstone's life and thoughts because he regularly kept a diary which, for this period of his life, has survived. The diary, in five volumes (referred to here, for convenience, as A, B, C, D and E), has been preserved in the Public Record Office among papers for a Chancery action in which he was involved (4). It is not the purpose here to go into any detail, but to summarise Ossulstone's activities, particularly those at Dawley. There are also some valuable clues as to the building work at Dawley and the development of the Park and gardens there - these will be discussed separately later. Many of the entries are prosaic and repetitive, but Lord Ossulstone led an active life and was fond of company. He made frequent trips to London on legal affairs and attended Parliament when it was in session. Although he sometimes stayed overnight or longer in his Town house, (5) he quite often came back to Dawley (only some 15 miles away), to which he was evidently very attached, on the same day. He went to his Chillingham estate in Northumberland periodically, and also visited Up Park in Sussex - both inherited through his wife - and, with his family, stayed at Bath in the Season. Lord Ossulstone kept a barge at Brentford on which he occasionally dined, and used for journeys on the Thames. At Dawley, he frequently entertained the Walkers of Little London, Hillingdon, or visited them: they were the Ossulstones' closest friends, it seems. The Berkeleys at Cranford, who were his wife's relatives, were also seen regularly. Among other nobles and gentry at Dawley or visited were the Jennings, Lords of the Manor of Hayes, and the Palmers of Dorney Court, related to the Jennings by marriage; the Duke of Schomberg of Hillingdon House, Lord Paget, Mr Child, Mr Cooke of Harvill (Harefield) (6), Mr Vyner of Ickenham, and the Duke of St Albans. Major Parsons was a frequent companion and (from 1713, if not earlier) had his own room at Dawley.

Ossulstone was fond of his wife (although they disagreed at times - he recorded his sorrow over an argument on one occasion) and family - particularly the three girls (Bridget, Annabella and Mary) with their pet names of Bid or Biddy, Nanna, and Moll or Molly, and his eldest son and heir, Charles or 'Charley' (born in 1697). (Ossulstone's second son, John, had died in June 1703, followed in July by his mother, Bridget, the dowager Lady Ossulstone - both before the commencement of the earliest extant diary.   The birth of Henry, his third son, also predated this diary).   The record of Grey, Ossulstone's fourth son, being born in April 1703/4, is included in the diary.   Ossulstone mentions when Charles fell off a new horse, luckily with little harm, and when he was sent to successive schools and returned at holiday times.   He was anxious when he found Molly 'not very well' at Dawley - with small pox, it transpired.   This was in April 1710, and she was lodged at 'Collins at Hayes', where she evidently made a good recovery.   His wife, whose health was often poor, became very ill at this time and on Thursday 30 May 1710 he recorded in his diary 'This evening she dyed and left me six poor children.   My Lady Tankerville [his wife's mother] came but did not see her, I went immediately away for London'.   This strange occurrence can probably be put down to a combination of shock and deep sorrow, rather than heartlessness.   He did not return to Dawley until 23 July.   Later that year, in November, he mentions having arranged a puppet show at Dawley for the children.   Lord Ossulstone himself, incidentally, seems to have enjoyed fairly good health, apart from occasional attacks of gout.   Perhaps referring to his lengthy absence from Dawley following his wife's death, Ossulstone wrote in his diary on 8 March 1710/11 of seeing 'Mr Woolford who I had taken to look after my affairs at Dawley'.   Woolford may have been one of his principal tenant farmers - 'Woolford's farm' of 103 acres was second only to Bishop's farm (c.145 acres) in 1692. (7)   There are many references in the diary to sporting activities - particularly hunting, type unspecified except on one occasion 'we hunted today a deer' (27 October 1705).   He probably had a pack of foxhounds, like his neighbour the Earl of Berkeley at Cranford, and mentions buying 5½ couple hounds in December 1711.   In September 1716 he purchased about a dozen beagles - the latter usually used for hunting hares.   As well as kennels there was a warren in Dawley Park.   Hawking was popular in 1707 and 1708 (there is a reference to 'The faulkner's room' at Dawley in the inventory of 1713 and to 'mews' in a builder's account of 1714, although this term was often synonymous with 'stables').   On 12 October 1705 Ossulstone notes 'Did not hunt but went out setting with Mr Stallard's dog' - this was apparently a one-off activity as was, perhaps, fishing, also mentioned only once - with Mr Walker in September 1710.   The bowling green in the formal gardens at Dawley was removed, it would seem, as early as 1703 and there is no evidence that its replacement, 'staked out' by the road, as was mentioned in the diary, was ever made.   However, 'fifteen pair of Bowls and two jacks' are mentioned in the 1722 inventory of Dawley.   Ossulstone mentions playing bowls only once, and that was at Up Park in 1709.   He went to a horse race at Hounslow Heath on 23 August 1708.   Lord Ossulstone, as would be expected, was involved in local affairs.   He attended Harlington church regularly, sometimes twice in a day, and he had the Rector, Robert Cooper, (8) to dine on a few occasions.   He also attended Hillingdon church with the Walker family now and again.   The proposed closure of the road through the Dawley estate, mentioned in 1707 and 1708 and discussed fully later here, caused local dissent, but the matter was apparently settled amicably.   Good relations were, no doubt, maintained by such events as when a 'great many farmers and their wives dined here [Dawley] and danced in the evening' - on 30 December 1709, and on the 4th January following.   The Manorial Court was held in January 1712, but few attended, and again in May.   'Mr Bennet' acted as Steward on both occasions.   Lord Ossulstone paid the salary of the charity schoolmaster at Harlington.   This was £20- per annum, paid quarterly.   The schoolmaster in 1720-1722 (and probably earlier) was Thomas Beldham. Ossulstone also contributed directly to charity - for instance, he records that in the hard winter of 1711/12 he gave on 25 December to one Mr Wolf 2 guineas for the poor of Harlington, had 'a great many poor people' at Dawley on 26, 27 and 28 December, and on 1 January of the New Year entertained 500 poor people.   He gave them meat and drink on each of these days, and a total of £75-13/- in silver. Charles Bennet's interest in architecture and gardening, inter alia, is demonstrated in the catalogue (9) of his books.   His library included folios of Tijou's drawings 1693, Camden's Britannia 1695, Campbell's Vitruvius 1715, Palladio's Architecture 1715, Loggan's Colleges of Oxford 1675 and Noblemen's Seats 1675; also Speed's map of 1611.   In octavo are Bradley's Art of Gardening 1718, 'London and wife' Compleat Gardner 1704 and Pictr'd Gardner (2 vols) 1706 (both by Mr and Mrs

George London, it is assumed), and Mollett's Garden of Pleasure 1670. Other books, some in French, include Bishop Wilkins' sermons and others 1678-1694; and 'Foes' works 1703 (by Daniel Defoe, presumably). The latest date of publication recorded for a book is 1719.

Charles Bennet, Lord Ossulstone, was granted his late father-in-law's title on 19 October 1714, being created Earl of Tankerville. Various posts and honours followed: he became Chief Justice in Eyre, South of Trent from 14 November 1715 for the rest of his life; was made a Privy Councillor on 6 July 1716; and a Knight of the Thistle on 27 February 1721. (10) Evidence of his continued interest in local affairs is his contribution of £10-10/- towards the cost of re-casting the bells of St Margaret's Church, Uxbridge, in 1716. (11) Proof of continued Royal favour is the brief note by Thomas Robertson (Master of the Horse) dated October 9, 1718 'My Lord dined with the King'. (12) Charles, the first Earl of Tankerville (of the second creation) was attended by an Uxbridge physician, Dr William Thorold (13) in what turned out to be his last illness and he died at Dawley on 21 May 1722 and was buried at Harlington on 26 May. He was in his 48th year.

Charles, the second Earl of Tankerville, appears to have led in some ways a more adventurous life than his father. He was baptised at Harlington on 21 December 1697. His first schooling began in September 1704 with 'Mr Bush minister of Harmsworth' (14) and later in London, apparently. He was then sent to Eton (like his father) and for a reason unknown, transferred to Winchester. When his father was created an earl, young Charles assumed the, then, secondary title of Lord Ossulstone, and as such he courted and married Camilla Colville, daughter of a butcher in Co. Durham. (15) (This anticipated a similar case towards the end of the 18th century when the 5th Earl of Berkeley married Mary Cole, the daughter of a butcher, grazier and farmer, though there were complications in this affair that were absent in Lord Ossulstone's) (16). Lord Ossulstone became a soldier, and was a Captain in Major-General Pepper's Regiment (8th Dragoons) by 1716. As he sold Dawley within a few years of his father's death, the many and varied offices he held after this time are of less interest, so it is sufficient to list them here: a Lord of the Bedchamber of the Prince of Wales (1729-1733); Knight of the Thistle (1730); Master of the Buckhounds (1733-1737); a Lord of the Bedchamber (1737-1738); a Doctor of Law of Cambridge (1749) (17); and Lord Lieutenant of Northumberland (Chillingham Castle, Northumberland, then being his main seat) from 1740 until his death in 1753.

CHAPTER 10

DAWLEY - A SUMMARY OF CHANGES
BETWEEN c1700 AND 1722: THE JENNER PLAN

Charles Bennet, the 2nd Baron Ossulstone, carried out extensive building works at Dawley, including a new small mansion house, and made ambitious additions and alterations to the gardens. These changes modified considerably the appearance of the estate and its buildings as they were shown in Kip's engraving of c.1700. All these activities took place at various dates up to about 1721. Charles Bennet, by then Earl of Tankerville (of the second creation) died on 21 May 1722, and his son, the 2nd Earl, for reasons discussed elsewhere, does not appear likely to have instigated further major works at Dawley before selling the estate in 1725.

The evidence for the many changes that took place during these years is both documentary and pictorial. First among the latter is, of course, Kip's engraving, which shows the old mansion and its surroundings and part of the estate as they were about 1700. Lord Ossulstone's surviving diary for the period from November 1703 to December 1712 gives some useful first-hand information, although many references are tantalisingly vague. Various household, garden and estate account books for the period, held in the Public Record Office, likewise provide valuable details, although these are also, at times, liable to various interpretations. An exception is the detailed estimates and dated craftsmens' accounts for the building of the new mansion, 1719-1721. Detailed inventories of Dawley for 1713, 1716 and 1722 are, of course, invaluable, although even these, in places - such as the meaning at a given time of the term 'new buildings' - are liable to misinterpretation. Best of all, for a single source of information, is 'A Plan of Dawley in the County of Middlesex drawn by John Jenner for the Earl of Tankerville about 1721. (1) This plan, held in the Public Record Office (2), is coloured and is to a scale of 3.45 inches = 10 chains, or roughly 1:3000. For a reason that cannot now be explained it was included in the records with a collection of War Office maps, and bears the Board of Ordnance initials, together with its broad arrow mark. The Jenner plan of Dawley is the earliest (and, indeed, the only) precise information we have on the extent and boundaries of the estate before the 19th century. As far as can be judged by comparison with later maps, the plan is fairly accurate (and the eastern boundary, in particular, is strikingly close to that of the line of Dawley road shown on modern Ordnance Survey maps) although the compass orientation given by Jenner does not, of course, correspond with that of today. However, for convenience of presentation, all the later maps included in this book follow Jenner's orientation and also, for want of better information, cover exactly the same area. As the boundaries shown by Jenner can quite easily be correlated with field boundaries shown in the Harlington Inclosure and Tithe Award maps, for which precise acreages are available, the extent of Tankerville's Dawley estate in c.1721 can be calculated as 396 acres. All the buildings on the estate are shown in little sketches, some in elevation and some in low oblique views, but none in plan. Included is an elevation of the new mansion that is known to have been completed in 1721. In the inventory of Dawley, carried out, following the 1st Earl's death, in July 1722, the contents of the Great Parlour of the new mansion included a 'plan of Dawley'. On the not unreasonable assumption that this was the plan drawn by Jenner showing the completed new mansion, it has been dated to 'circa 1721'. John Jenner, as will be discussed later, was the master bricklayer for the new mansion, and apparently its principal contractor.

Establishing the sequence of the changes that resulted in the appearance of the estate as shown by Jenner presents several problems, the first being that only rather less than half of the estate is shown by Kip c.1700 and while some confidence can be placed in his depiction of the buildings, the accuracy of the area shown north of the house is more doubtful. Jenner's plan is quite accurate although his thumbnail drawings of the buildings are very small and as they are shown variously in oblique views or elevations their precise location is sometimes uncertain. This said, we are fortunate in having two such good pictorial sources of information as a basis for considering the development of the Dawley estate during the first quarter of the 18th century. Of the documentary references, some are difficult to interpret. For example, the use of the adjective 'new', which could mean recently built or new as compared with old - say, something erected one year ago rather than 10 ? Also, contemporary terminology can sometimes be imprecise, such as the term 'mount' for a garden feature, either something like a castle mound or simply a raised terrace. The term 'wood' used at Dawley during the period in question caused confusion until it was realised it was interchangeable with 'wilderness', the name more widely used in the 18th century for a formal tree-planted area. The suggested chronology, then, for the changes at Dawley is summarised below.

Minor changes in the formal gardens south of the mansion probably took place continuously, with alterations to the parterres and so on, and there is some evidence for this in the early years of the period under consideration. The circular carriageways west and north of the house also arrived early, before the public road diversion in 1708. Some new coach houses were also built at about the same time, in 1704, probably in the area immediately east of the mansion. The Long Walk, the tree avenue leading north from the house, may also have been started in 1704, perhaps in anticipation of the road diversion. The major extension of the formal gardens, including the patte d'oie, ('goose foot') was also possibly started before the road diversion; it was not dependent on it. Work perhaps started in 1706 and continued to 1712 or later. Various works to improve the water supply to the house and gardens started with pipes being laid down the Long Walk in 1708. The formal gardens west of the house shown by Jenner, but outside the area of Kip's engraving, may have been started before 1709, when a mount is mentioned. By 1716, at least, they were known as the Lanthorn Gardens, and work on them continued until at least 1721 or later. Important building works were commenced by about 1712, perhaps near the new coach houses mentioned above, and possibly included the new small house of six bays east of the mansion, although it is difficult to be certain. It must be concluded that around this time the seven-bay 'dower house' and the old stables were demolished to make way for the new buildings in this area. The major building work around the courtyard, over the site of the old public road, now diverted, was certainly under way by 1717 when the 'Great Stable Court' was being paved. The domestic buildings on the north, and stables etc on the south side of the courtyard, were in existence before the new house on the west side was commenced in 1719. Before the house could be started, the orangery had to be demolished. Materials from the service wing of the old house and/or the 'dower house' may have been used in the new buildings. The garden at the site of the 16th century manor house at Pinkwell may originally have been maintained in its old style by the Bennets, but certainly a lot of new work was in progress there by 1718 to create a 'wood garden', and its maze was constructed in 1719. The new mansion on the Great Court, started in 1719, was completed in 1721, and the inventory of 1722 shows that it was the principal residence of Lord Tankerville at Dawley. The old mansion was then used for accommodation of some of the senior servants; some of the principal rooms were run down, with broken mirrors and damaged chairs mentioned in the inventory.

From the foregoing, it will be seen that a discussion in detail on a chronological basis of the Dawley estate and its buildings would be impossible. Therefore, a breakdown by geography and topic has been adopted, beginning with the road diversion because of its importance for later developments. This is followed by an overview of the Park and estate as a whole, with its gates, ponds, timber and other features. The three distinct areas of formal gardens - the 'parterre gardens', the Lanthorn Garden, and the Wood Garden are examined next, followed by the buildings. The buildings at Dawley can be divided into four groups for detailed consideration. These are the stables, barns etc at Pinkwell; the Lodge and the pigeon house, both too isolated to be considered with others; the buildings near the old mansion and changes to the house itself; and, finally, the buildings around the Great Court, including the new mansion.

CHAPTER 11

DAWLEY - THE ROAD DIVERSION

The public road or common highway between Harlington and Hillingdon, running as it did diagonally across the Dawley estate, must often have been something of an irritant to the Bennets. The thought of diverting the road away to the east boundary of the estate must have occurred, in particular, to Sir John Bennet (III) when, about 1672, he built the new Dawley House nearer the middle of the estate, but much closer to the public road. Part of the road can be seen in Kip's engraving, curving away behind the house and heading to the north-west. Sir John Bennet, by then the first Baron Ossulstone, died in 1695 without, apparently, having taken any action to divert the road. His son and heir, Charles, the 2nd Lord Ossulstone, had wide-ranging plans to embellish Dawley in many ways, for some of which the existing road would be an obstacle. However, it was not until the end of 1706 that he first applied for permission to enclose the road. The Middlesex Quarter Sessions issued on 19 December 1706 a Writ to the Sheriff to summon a jury for an enquiry of ad quod damnum to look into the matter. (1) What Ossulstone proposed was to enclose that part of the public road from Hillingdon Common to Harlington that traversed his Dawley estate, and provide a new road further east. The old road was described more precisely as a road with a breadth of 30 feet running (north) from Little Park Gate (a point almost certainly where a lodge is shown on Jenner's plan) to Allen's Pond in Gold's Green. The latter was probably outside the Dawley estate and was perhaps the pond at Goulds Green designated as a public 'watering place for cattle' on the Hillingdon Inclosure map of 1825. The length of the stretch of road in question was given as 388 poles (2134 yards). The section actually to be enclosed was between Little Park Gate and the Gate in Bridewell Lane in Hillingdon, a shorter unspecified distance, but was about 290 poles, or 1600 yards. Bridewell Lane can be identified with 'Allright Lane' shown running between Goulds Green Farm and Barnes Farm on the Hillingdon Inclosure Map. The replacement road proposed by Lord Ossulstone began at Allen's Pond and ran down to Botwell Heath Gate: it was 385 poles (2117 yards) in length and wider, at 34 feet, than the old road. The location of Botwell Heath Gate has not been identified, but seems from measurements to have been a short distance north of the Lodge or Little Park Gate, although no part of Botwell Heath adjoined the Dawley estate in this area. (2) The inquisition into Lord Ossulstone's application was held at Dawley House on 6 January 1706/7. He wrote in his diary 'there was here to day a Jury of ye gentlemen of ye Neighbourhood that agreed to a write [writ] ad quod damnum to turn ye way by my house ....'. Agreement by Ossulstone's neighbouring landowners to allow his request was not surprising, but an appeal against the decision, allowed under an Act of William III of 1697, immediately followed. The humble petition of Richard Price, gentleman, Matthew Nicholas, Henry Turner, Robert Russell and John Turner was heard on 17 January 1706/7 and the appeal was apparently upheld. Lord Ossulstone must, in turn, have appealed against this decision because a further inquisition was held on 17 April 1707, this time on the more neutral ground of the home of Joseph Attlee at Colham Green. The jury was headed by Sir William Benson, Kt and Sir Ambrose Cowley, Kt and consisted of 25 other local men, two of whom were baronets and all the rest designated as 'Esquire' or 'Gent'. Among them were John Walker, John Jenyns and George Cooke who were certainly friends of Ossulstone - their names occur frequently in his diary. Another interesting name is that of Robert Heddin Esq, who would appear to be the nurseryman cum gardener who was later employed in connection with the gardens at Dawley. This jury reached the same verdict as before, to the effect that the road diversion proposed would not be of any damage to the Queen or any of her subjects. Some of the Queen's more humble subjects certainly did not share this view and on 24 April 1707 a further appeal against the enclosure of the road was again headed by Richard Price, gentleman, this time supported by no less than 26 others, including his previous four supporters. (3) The outcome of this appeal is uncertain, but the original Sheriff's Writ is endorsed (in Latin) 'Writ discharged because the old road was not enclosed'. (4)   Lord

Ossulstone must have given up his road plans for the time being and turned his attention to other matters until January 1707/8, when on the 15th he notes in his diary 'I was this day at Hines Hall [in London] where Pric of Bottwell [sic] entered an appeal against turning the way, his appeal was dismissed it being not in time'. On 24 April 1708, the diary shows that Ossulstone conferred with Mr Cooke and Mr Jenings at Dawley regarding the 'new way', and on 27 April he was again at Hines Hall. The precise outcome of these matters is not known, but as Jenner's plan shows, the road across the estate was closed, although its line across the estate was still marked by trees. The new road as drawn by Jenner is almost identical with Dawley Road today, apart from a modern 'by pass' section that cuts off an inward-curving length of the estate boundary. This eastern boundary of the Dawley estate is also for much of its length the boundary between the parishes of Harlington and Hayes, according to 19th century Ordnance Survey maps. From near the north tip of the Dawley estate down to where Botwell Common Road joins, the parish boundary line is along the west side of Dawley Road, whereas continuing south to just short of the junction with (the present) North Hyde Road, the line is on the east (Hayes) side of Dawley Road. This is believed to have been a sensible way of allocating responsibility for road maintenance between the two parishes, rather than dividing the road down the middle. Harlington had the longer stretch of road at Dawley to maintain, presumably because most of the original way through the Dawley estate was in Harlington parish anyway.

CHAPTER 12

DAWLEY PARK & ESTATE GENERALLY
c 1700 - 1722

The Dawley estate is roughly triangular in shape, the east side forming part of the boundary with Hayes Parish, and the west bordering Hillingdon, Yiewsley and West Drayton. On the south, the estate boundary is, it must be assumed, the dividing line between Dawley and Harlington proper, in the same parish. Jenner's plan of c.1721 has been used here to define the boundaries of the Dawley estate. It is known that additions of adjacent lands were made at the perimeter of the estate from time to time, although their location cannot always be established with any precision. However, 9 acres of meadow and 3 acres of woodland called Long Mead 'sometime in the tenure of Sir George Selby' and $3^1/_2$ acres arable 'in the West Field of Dawley in a shott called Pinkwell Gate Shott and abutting on a meadow called Long Mead' appear to have been acquired by Lord Bolingbroke. These lands must have been near the south-west corner of the estate. Lord Ossulstone bought 6 acres of land 'lying by Lalams' (ground) in 1706 from 'Yeoman Attlee' and in April 1708 a 'little piece of ground with part into ye common at upper end of Walk'. This land at Gould's Green may have been acquired in connection with the subsequent diversion of the Harlington-Hillingdon road. Also in 1708, three pieces of land totalling 12 acres, known originally as Dawley close and Longheath close, later as Dawley Closes, together with a pightle, were leased to Lord Ossulstone for 50 years. By 1712, Lord Ossulstone was renting a house in Colham Green. (1) There were also, by the time of the Harlington Inclosure Award of 1821, at least, some detached portions of the Manor of Dawley in Harlington proper, but it has not been established when these were first acquired. The whole estate is shown by Jenner to be enclosed by a solid wooden fence, most of it composed of alternate long and short vertical boards or flat stakes. This gives a castellated effect which, it is supposed, makes it difficult for deer to judge the height of the fence and leap it to escape. Deer are depicted by Jenner all over the parkland of the estate. A surviving, but far less substantial, paling fence of this kind can be seen enclosing the deer park at Charlecote, Warwickshire - where William Shakespeare is alleged to have been caught poaching deer. A brief survey of features of the estate - boundary gates, trees, ponds and enclosures - follows, but excludes the gardens and buildings, which will be discussed separately later.

There were at least seven gates in the estate boundary by about 1721, as far as can be ascertained from Jenner's plan. These are as follows, going clockwise:

1.   Gate, with two iron piers and iron railings either side, at an inward-curving point in the boundary where a two-tree avenue leads to the new mansion's courtyard. This would have been (later on, if not then) the principal approach to the house.

2.   Gate (? - delineation on the plan is not clear) at east end of four-tree avenue some 230 feet south of 1.

3.   Gate at the Lodge at the south-east extremity of the estate. This adjoins the Lodge building on its west side and has four iron(?) posts with flame-shaped finials.

There appear to have been no gates at all along the south and lower part of the west boundary of the estate (the Pinkwell Gate has disappeared) until, going north:

4.   Gate at west end of the four-tree avenue leading west from the old mansion. This has four iron piers with flame-shaped finials. Lord Ossulstone's diary reference in September 1708 to 'ye new park gate next to Collum Field' could mean this one, or possibly No 5.

There is no trace of a gate at the boundary where the old public road once crossed the estate, and the next entrance is:

5.   Gate with four pillars with pointed finials at the north end of the Long Walk - a wide two-tree avenue leading from the old mansion.

6.   Gate - probably a farm-type gate, with tall inward-curving posts, on an isolated position on the Dawley road, some 400 yards south of the tip of the estate.

7.   Gate (?): two tall wood or brick piers with ball finials, although no gate is actually shown, on the Dawley road at the south-east corner of the orchard where the dovecote is.

A bill submitted by a painter, Anthony Davis, dated 10 July 1721 (2) itemised 26 days work (at 3 shillings per day) on painting various gates (most specified as iron) and railings.   Some of these gates are in the gardens and elsewhere, and are discussed separately, but the exact location of most of them cannot be identified.   However, 'priming the new gates at the road' is mentioned as well as two pairs of gates with 'the coat of arms in them'.   One pair of the latter was no doubt the gates by Tijou at the patte d'oie in the garden, but the other pair may well have been at an entrance to the estate.

Trees were scattered widely over the Dawley estate.   Apart from the formal avenues, which will be described with the gardens of which they were an extension, many of the trees were in single or double irregular lines.   Certainly, the double line running diagonally across the estate from approximately south-east to north-west is the trace of the old public road and another, more or less straight, line may possibly be the overgrown remains of an avenue shown earlier by Kip in his engraving running north-east from the old mansion.   The other irregular lines of trees may possibly be traces of old enclosures.   The rectangular area of closely planted trees surrounding the dovecote, shown by both Kip and Jenner, is almost certainly an orchard.   A similar looking area, but more irregular in outline, north-west of the dovecote, shown by Jenner (and roughly the same by Kip) may also be an orchard.   Cherry trees certainly are mentioned ('Morells' - probably marinellos) by Lord Ossulstone, (3) and they were grown commercially in the area many years later.   Lord Ossulstone ordered a total of 200 fir trees from Robert Heddin, a nurseryman and gardener, in January 1704/5 and in March 1705/6 bought dwarf ball hollies from Mason, another gardener. (4)   Heddin, between 1715 and 1719, provided 100 birch trees and 49 cherry trees (also pear, quince, and peach or nectarine trees, probably destined for the kitchen garden) and among plants as cuttings or slips to produce quickset hedges were a total of 5000 'whitthorn' (whitethorn - hawthorn).   A total of 693 striped holly trees was also supplied by Heddin. (5)   It is impossible to say where all these plants ended up - some may, of course, have gone to land owned by the Bennets in Harlington or elsewhere outside the Dawley estate.   In a lease of land to Ossulstone in 1708 (6) the trees are specified and are predominately elms (also as hedges) with some oak and ash. These are likely to be the varieties of 'native' tree growing naturally in Dawley.   The many references in the Dawley papers from about 1717 onwards to 'the wood' refer to the formal 'wilderness' planted in the area of the old gardens at Pinkwell, to be discussed later.

There were numerous ponds (aside of ornamental waters, described later) scattered round the estate, most of them probably maintained for the benefit of deer and cattle.   Some of these, indicated on Jenner's plan, are not coloured in there as water, although from later maps are known to have been ponds.   Following a clockwise progression, these are as follows:

1.   A pond at the south-west corner of the courtyard at the east side of the estate, at the west end of the four-tree avenue.   This is about 150 feet long and is of an irregular 'leg-of-mutton' shape.   It was railed off on its east side but was accessible from the courtyard and may have been used to water the horses in the

nearby stables.

2.   A small oval pond with an island in the middle, just south of 1. and probably linked to it.   This is in the north end of the kitchen garden and may have been where ducks were kept for domestic use.

3.   A long rectangular pond a short way west-south-west of the 'pink well'. Over 200 yards in length, this runs roughly east-west to a point close to the estate boundary.   Although apparently kept only for watering livestock in 1721, by its very shape this seems once to have been an ornamental 'canal', perhaps forming part of an earlier garden scheme for the manor house at Pinkwell.   Alternatively it might have been a domestic fish pond.

4.   A small roughly diamond-shaped pond, about 140 yards from the west boundary, at the south end of a prominent square re-entrant angle shown on Jenner's plan.   This was the 'pink well' that gave its name to the area.   It is marked as Pinkwell on a farm estate plan of 1767. (7)   The 'Frogs Ditch', a small stream that flows south and east to eventually join the River Crane, originates here.

5.   A very small, roughly oval, pond near the L-shaped building (stables ?) on its east side.   Probably for watering animals kept nearby.

6.   A small round pond appears to be shown near the centre of the estate, about 200 yards north-west of the old mansion.   Just north of this is a roughly rectangular fenced enclosure.   As this, and the pond, are in an area where a brick kiln is shown in Kip's engraving of c.1700, it is possible that both these features were associated with brickmaking on the estate.   Alternatively, was this the site of a warren, one of which existed at Dawley ?

7.   A D-shaped pond close to the west boundary palings about 330 yards south of where the old road (diverted later) left the estate.   This is fenced except on its south side.

8.   A rectangular pond just north of where the old road used to leave the estate.

9.   A pond near the Dawley road in a projecting angle of the estate (this is near where the northern end of what is now known as Bolingbroke Way, the original road, diverges from the present by-pass stretch of Dawley Road).   This large pond, which contained a long rectangular island, existed until quite recently, when it dried up or was filled in.

10.   A rectangular pond adjoining the east side of the dovecote in the orchard north-east of the mansion.

Of these ponds, Nos 1 and 2 are post c.1700 and are not shown on Kip's engraving, and No 10 does not appear to be.   There is no information on the age of the others, although No 4 (the 'pink well') could well be ancient and No 3, if it was a fish pond, might have had mediaeval origins.

CHAPTER 13

THE GARDENS AT DAWLEY -
CHANGES BETWEEN c.1700 AND 1722

The many and varied additions and changes to the pleasure gardens at Dawley carried out by Charles Bennet, Lord Ossulstone, latterly, Earl of Tankerville, during the last 20 years or so of his life will be discussed next.   It is, however, important, for the purposes of this study, to be able to distinguish readily between the three distinct sets of pleasure gardens that existed at Dawley by c.1721 as shown in Jenner's estate plan. Unfortunately, many of the contemporary references are imprecise, and the name of only one of the gardens is spelled out.   This is the Lantern Ground or Lanthorn Garden (1) - the pleasure ground stretching west from the old mansion.   The garden at Pinkwell - believed to be the site of the formal garden attached to the old manor house there - was known as 'The Wood' when work there was in progress in 1718-1719.   By 1720, Lord Tankerville employed a 'Wood gardener' (John Robertson - later John Gotobed).   It seems reasonable, therefore, for the present writer to allocate the name 'Wood Garden' when discussing this site.   The formal pleasure gardens south of the old mansion (built c.1672), largely consisting of parterres, to which the patte d'oie ('goose foot') was added, were probably known contemporaneously just as 'the gardens'.   However, they will be referred to here, to avoid confusion, as 'the parterre gardens', while emphasising that there is no known historical reference to them as such.   The 'parterre gardens' will be discussed first, because of their pre-eminent importance, followed by the kitchen garden, the Lanthorn Garden and the 'Wood Garden'.

The Parterre Gardens.   Changes to the gardens adjoining the mansion at Dawley   were quite likely an on-going process,   perhaps starting with minor alterations to the parterres and leading ultimately to the spectacular extension with the patte d'oie.   The most notable development, overall, during the period between c.1700 and c.1721 is the introduction of several water features.   One of the earliest of these was a round pond in the centre of the new circular carriage drive, or sweep, at the west front of the house.   Another circular drive (without a pond) was built at the north face of the house.   One of these, probably that on the west front, was referred to in Lord Ossulstone's diary on 4 September, 1704 'I began ye sweep in ye Park today', and again on 14 December, more certainly referring to the west front pond, 'ye fountain in ye Marble hall court began to play'.   A round pond was also introduced in the middle of the gravel walk running south from the centre of the south front of the mansion, and it is this, shown in Jenner's plan, to which the diary entry of 16 September 1710 refers - 'ye Statue was this day fixed in ye fountain'. The third addition of water to the original gardens was a rectangular pond near the north-west corner, just south of the carriage sweep with the round pond.   This was aligned north-south and was about 200 feet long and 40 feet wide.   Of other changes in the original gardens, perhaps the first alteration of all was the removal in 1703 of the bowling green shown by Kip at the south-west corner.   On 19 November of that year, Ossulstone wrote in his diary 'I stak'd out of bowling green by ye road'. It was replaced by a parterre divided into four unequal parts, according to Jenner's plan.   The location of the new bowling green near the road has not been identified (it could, of course, have been removed by c.1721) but it may have been just south of the orangery where Jenner shows two lawns, replacing four small parterres, which might possibly, if sunken, have been 'boulingrin' - not necessarily for playing bowls.   Four more small parterres further south were replaced by a square feature with a radiating pattern of plants or shrubs and a path leading to its centre: it is just possible that this might be a mount.   Finally, two small parterres near the bottom right hand corner of the gardens may have survived from the original ten at this side.   The centre section of the gardens, separated by walls from those on either side and bisected by a long gravel walk leading from the south door of the mansion, had fewer changes made to it since c.1700 than other parts.   From north to south, firstly, the earlier four lawns, two either side of the path, are now two only, the east-west path having been removed.   Also, surprisingly, missing are the numerous statues shown by Kip (if Jenner is correct in omitting them) since statues are mentioned in the inventory of 1722. The pond with its fountain and statue already referred to, came next, then, in an area formerly consisting of two squares, one each side, each comprising six smallish parterres, is in about 1721 two areas of shrubs in small rectangular parterres, either side of the pond. South of these are four larger parterres, two either side - the upper two with a rectangular pattern, the lower ones with a circular pattern. Below these parterres is a wide transverse path, with openings in the enclosing garden walls at both its east and west ends. It appears from Jenners' plan that this was designed as part of a long vista right across the estate - from the public road through a four-tree avenue, through the parterre gardens, along the path at the south edge of the Lanthorn Gardens, and through a short two-tree avenue to the boundary - about 3/4 mile in length. The four 'Union Jack' parterres, next to the south, are apparently unchanged since c.1700, except that the four wooden arbours have gone. The raised terrace, terminating the south boundary of the original gardens is still there, with the two summer houses, although Jenner's sketch seems to indicate that they now have ball finials on their roofs and extra doors at ground level on the south side. The Tijou gates have gone from their original location, and the top of the terrace behind them is now approached by slopes either side instead of the steps shown previously. The west section of the gardens can be described briefly in that, between the new pond and old bowling green site already mentioned, the serried rows of trees and closely planted rectangles have been replaced by a more homogenous area of small plants.

The Kitchen Garden. A kitchen garden is shown by Jenner which approximates to that of c.1700 as Kip depicts it, but it appears to have been curtailed at the north end and extended and widened elsewhere. A new oval pond, already described, is at its north tip. Some of the contents of the kitchen garden are given in a list of plants supplied by Robert Heddin, a nurseryman and gardener, to the Earl of Tankerville between 1715 and 1719. (2) These comprised (totals for the whole period) 57 quince trees, 36 peach or nectarine trees, 43 standard or dwarf pear trees, 60 white currant bushes, 100 raspberry canes and 850 asparagus plants; also 200 honeysuckle plants - the latter, no doubt, to encourage the bees (there was a Beehouse and beehive on the estate) (3) as well as for their aesthetic value. The enlargement of the kitchen garden may date from about the end of 1711. One John Stanboro was paid £2-4-0 on 2 January 1711/12 for 'ye two Kitchen Garden gates', according to Lord Ossulstone's diary, and again nine days later 22s.6d. for 'boards for caps' (capitals for the gate posts ?). On 7 February 'Stanboro ye carpenter' was contracted to erect 'pailing against ye new south wall in ye Park in ye kitching garden' and he began work on the 25th. Stanboro was probably a local man: a Henry Stanborogh occupied a 'little house' listed in the Harlington Parish Survey of 1692. (4)

Before coming to the most dramatic addition to the formal gardens at their south side, the northern tree avenue known as the Long Walk must be mentioned. Kip's engraving shows a two-tree avenue running north from the mansion and a four-tree avenue running north-east. The exact location and/or orientation of these may not have been shown accurately, and Jenner's plan, which seems to have been carefully surveyed, shows neither avenue in the same location. The Long Walk, shown c.1721, a four-tree avenue exactly lined up with the centre of the north front of the mansion may, however, have incorporated the earlier two-tree avenue as its western half. Lord Ossulstone mentions in his diary on 2 November 1704 'We began to plant ye first walk on ye right with elms', followed by further references to tree planting on 6, 7 and 13 November. Without a point of reference, it is difficult to know what he meant, but this may refer to part of the Long Walk - well before the road was diverted - or perhaps part of the avenue leading west from the mansion, or even an avenue of the patte d'oie, although the date is considered by the present writer too early for this to be likely. The great parterre added on to the south of the formal gardens was, in fact, probably conceived in 1709. In June of that year, Lord Ossulstone, as he noted in his diary, visited several houses and gardens, all within a reasonable distance from Dawley, almost certainly to get ideas for re-working his gardens and, possibly, for new buildings. He saw 'Cliffden' (Cliveden,

Buckinghamshire ?), 'Bowyer's' and 'Sr Hill's' (almost certainly the seats of Sir William Bowyer at Denham Court and Sir Roger Hill at Denham Place - both nearby in Buckinghamshire, just outside Uxbridge) (5), and 'Moore Park' (Moor Park, then Lord Cornwallis', near Watford, Hertfordshire).   Then, on 6 August, 'we went to Hampton Court in ye evening only to see ye gardens'.   This was followed, two months later, by the diary entry on 6 October 'There came down eleven of Palatines to work in ye garden'; on 9 October 'a great many workmen at work'; and on 19 October 'I was (in) my garden most of ye day about alterations ..... there was about 19 or 20 of ye Palatins come here this evening to work'.   All this activity is best explained by Ossulstone having extensive changes made to the gardens after getting ideas from existing gardens, including, above all, those of Hampton Court Palace.   A definition of 'Palatines' or 'Palatins' in this context has not been discovered, but the most likely explanation is that it referred to a group of gardeners from the Royal Palaces, and Hampton Court in particular.   (Latin 'palatinus' - 'of a palace'. Workers from the German or English palatinates is not considered likely by the present writer). (6)   The likelihood, however, of assistance from Hampton Court in at least laying out the garden extensions is considered credible when examining what actually took place at Dawley, as demonstrated by Jenner's plan of c.1721.

The great garden extension south of the mansion, consisting of a great parterre, radiating avenues and a canal, was probably started in 1709 (as suggested above) and was certainly completed by about 1721, if not some time before.   It appears that the digging of the canal at Dawley followed the planting of the radiating avenues, rather than preceding it, as at Hampton Court.   The earliest evidence found is Lord Ossulstone's diary entry for 23 June 1712 - 'Mr Wallker was here about digging ye canal in ye park'.   The only other reference discovered among the papers at the Public Record Office is the following entry (7) for a payment of £1-1-6 made on 16 November 1717 - 'Paid the fisher men at Brentford for fishing the canale at Dawley'.   Very puzzling !   The parterre was a giant semi-circle with five radiating gravel paths which were continued beyond it by tree avenues running out to the boundaries of the estate: the central avenue contained the canal.   The Royal Palaces of Hampton Court, St James' and Greenwich all had gardens of this type, but few private houses.   There can be little doubt that the chief inspiration for Dawley was the gardens at the east front of Hampton Court, begun for Charles II and improved and completed under William and Mary.   The stages of their evolution at Hampton Court were as follows. (8)   The Great Canal, with a double line of trees either side, was designed by Andre Mollet (who had worked for Louis XIV in France) and constructed in 1661-1662, and was intended to be viewed from the east front of the old palace.   Nearly 30 years later, Sir Christopher Wren was called in by William and Mary to completely reconstruct the palace.   This work was eventually confined to the south and east fronts, and to complement the latter a new Great Parterre was designed.   This was enclosed in the semi-circular area from which the Great Canal and its tree avenue, slightly shortened at its near end, ran.   The original avenue had added to it two new ones radiating out from either side of it, the similarity in plan to a goose's foot leading to the French name coined for this feature.   The new scheme was designed and probably carried out in 1689 and 1690, although the ironwork by Jean Tijou to enclose the semi-circular parterre was added later. (9)   The Dawley patte d'oie or 'great parterre' was, befittingly, smaller than that of the Monarch's and less elaborate - the fate of overmighty subjects and their building works in the reign of Henry VIII was, perhaps, not entirely forgotten !   It had only closely-planted shrubs instead of the complicated broderie flower beds and round ponds in the semi-circular area.   Dawley did, however, possess no less than five radiating avenues, compared with the three of Hampton Court (geese have only three toes !).   The central canal at Dawley was only about 290 yards long, compared with Hampton Court's canal of over 1000 yards. (10)   As shown in Jenner's plan, the semi-circle from which the Dawley tree avenues begin runs in an arc of 90 yards radius from the west summer house on the terrace round to the east one.   It is enclosed with iron railings which have ornamental wrought-iron screens where the radiating paths join the avenues, except at the centre.   Here are wrought iron gates, almost certainly those by, it is believed, Tijou, transferred from the centre of the terrace, although Jenner's sketch is too small to be positive on this point.   If the avenues of Dawley's patte d'oie were to be described in clock-face notation, they are (from east to west) at 4, 5, 6 (the centre one), 7 and 8 o'clock. The one at 4 o'clock terminates at the Lodge at the junction of the Dawley, Botwell and Harlington roads; those at 5 and 6 run well beyond the estate boundary (although possibly over Ossulstone's tenants' lands), the former being well over 700 yards long. The avenue at 7 o'clock ends just short of the estate boundary; and that at 8 terminates obliquely well within the estate at what appears to be an internal division where it meets a rectangular area at the estate's south-west corner. This '8 o'clock' avenue also cuts across what was the site of the old 'Dawley Courte'. These last two facts suggest that the old house had been demolished before the avenue was planted and possibly before the south-west rectangular area was added to the estate. One avenue of the Hampton Court patte d'oie was aligned on the tower of Kingston church, something under 1½ miles away, making a focal point of interest from Queen Mary's study in the centre of Wren's east front of the Palace. None of the Dawley 'goose foot' avenues appears to have a corresponding aim, Harlington church tower (about 1 mile south) being about 5 degrees west of the line of the central (canal) avenue. The Dawley avenues do not, in any case, converge on the south front of the mansion, which is some distance away, but on the centre of the raised terrace, terminating the original south end of the formal gardens. Nevertheless, the vista from the centre of the south front of the mansion would comprise the path through the centre of the formal gardens, with the round pond with a fountain in the middle, the gap in the raised terrace, the centre path through the patte d'oie shrubbery to the Tijou gates, to the canal with its avenue, and across the fields of Harlington to Hounslow Heath in the distance. The trees forming four of the five avenues of the 'toes' of the patte d'oie are all shown in the same way by Jenner and probably represent common deciduous trees, such as elm. The avenue at '4 o'clock' is the exception, and the 32 trees depicted there are evidently firs. The design of the Dawley patte d'oie was ultimately derived from French sources via Hampton Court, although neither of the leading French landscape designers, Andre Mollet, who died in 1666, or Andre Le Notre, who died in 1700, could have been directly involved. However, any of the leading English gardeners of the time, such as George London (who had already worked at Dawley but died in 1714), his partner and successor Henry Wise (1653 - 1738), or Charles Bridgeman (who will be mentioned later in connection with Bolingbroke) were all capable of such work, and any one of them may have been involved, although no documentary evidence has come to light. It is perhaps significant, though, that one Andrew Mollet was listed in 1722 (11) as the Earl of Tankerville's 'principal or head gardener'. He had been employed at Dawley from at least 1707. No genealogical evidence has been traced to prove it, but it is a reasonable assumption that Andrew Mollet was a descendant (possibly son or nephew) of Andre Mollet and thus derived his professional inspiration through family ties from Louis XIV's Versailles. (12)

The Lanthorn Garden. Kip's engraving shows the beginning of a four-tree avenue running west across the Park from the mansion, for which it must have provided a vista. South of this, parallel to it, and roughly in line with the centre of the formal gardens, is shown a second (two-tree) avenue - also the east end of it only. Jenner's plan of about 20 years later shows that the four-tree avenue extends to the west boundary of the estate, where the paling fence is interrupted by some formal gates, and a little way beyond it. This probably gave access to Porter Lane, leading to West Drayton. The two-tree avenue, on the other hand, has by c.1721 been replaced by a long garden, enclosed by hedges on its north and south sides, stretching almost to the west boundary. The lines of the garden are continued right to the boundary by two short two-tree avenues, the southerly of which may have been vestiges of the original long avenue. There is no evidence to suggest that this garden existed in Kip's time, and deer are shown in the area at the west edge of his engraving. The garden, about 220 feet wide, was in three main parts. The section nearest the mansion consists of a mount, surrounded by a round moat, about 100-130 feet across, contained in a long rectangle or rhomboid in plan about 340 yards long, closely planted with shrubs divided by paths radiating from the mount. The mount is surmounted by a small, possibly hexagonal, brick building with a window or windows, presumably a summer house. Access to it was gained by a

41

bridge over the moat on the north side and steps up the mount: a painter's bill of 10 July 1721 is for (inter alia) painting the 'Greate Laddar and the Reles at the Lantern'. (13)   A lantern (or lanthorn) in architectural terms is a cupola with windows all round to give maximum light and vision.   This feature of the summer house gave its name to the garden in which it was located: the name was perpetuated in later field names.   Henry VIII had had a mount built at Hampton Court to give a view over the river.   Families with old titles often owned the sites of former castles with defensive mounds: families with less ancient lineages sometimes built artificial mounts for prestige as well as to provide a view over their gardens or deer park.   In the Bennets' case, the Dawley mount would have fulfilled all three functions.   The next section of the garden is an irregular rectangle closely planted with shrubs.   The third, west, section consists of a rectangular pond, with 36 fir trees, planted in two rows, leading from it, all surrounded by closely-planted shrubs terminated in an apsidal shape in plan at the far end.   The hedge surrounding the whole garden is replaced by iron railings, also in an apsidal plan, at the west end only.   The Lanthorn Garden is open to the Parterre gardens at its east end, and the only other break in the enclosure is on the south side opposite the mount, where some iron gates, with brick pillars with square capitals, open on to an avenue leading to the Wood Garden.   The dates of all this work are uncertain, although there are some possible clues.   Two hundred fir trees were purchased from Robert Heddin, the nurseryman, in January 1705, according to Lord Ossulstone's diary, and some of these may have been planted in the Lanthorn Garden.   He also records many workmen in 'the garden' (location unspecified) in this month.   Then, on 27 October 1707, he says Mollet (his gardener) was 'laying out of gardens', which may refer to the new area.   However, the first positive reference is in the diary for 30 November 1709 - 'The hurdle man came here to finish ye seat upon ye mount' (even so, it cannot be ruled out that the mount existed in isolation before the gardens were made).   The seat was replaced by the lantern building much later, evidently, because in September 1716, the 'summer house on the mount' had sashes and wainscot installed and chairs were brought from London in the following month to furnish it. (14)   The 'Lantern in the Garden' in 1722 contained a large pierglass, a table and seven chairs, according to the Inventory.   The pond was a late addition to the Lanthorn Garden, for the gardener's account book (15) records a payment of £9-9/- on 4 November 1721 to 'Mr Gates for the new pond in the Lantern Ground in Park'.   The garden was still being enhanced in February 1722, when a payment was made for 140 trees in the Lanthorn Garden.

The Wood Garden.   The third, quite distinct, garden at Dawley c.1721 is the garden at Pinkwell.   Nothing is known about this earlier, nor had it apparently been recorded by an artist, because it is outside the field of Kip's engraving.   However, for reasons previously explained, it is believed to be the site of the garden enclosure of the old 'Dawley Courte'.   It is away in the south part of the Park, isolated from the other gardens and main buildings at Dawley, although it is connected to the Lanthorn Garden by an avenue of trees, with gates at each end.   From later information (16) these trees were probably limes.   The garden, in plan as shown by Jenner, is a rectangle, orientated roughly north-east, about 650 feet along the bottom edge by 930 feet north - south.   There is a rectangular cut-out at the north-west corner where, it is believed, the old house stood.   The garden may well have been allowed to degenerate into a true wilderness, even during the later tenure of the Selby family, and the earliest references that have been located that might possibly relate to new work in this area are in Lord Ossulstone's diary   for November and December 1711.   'A great many labourers here'; 'workmen about ye park';   and 'a gret many labourers'.   From February 1717 onwards, however, particularly between November 1718 and November 1719, there are frequent references in the account book (17) to workmen digging in the wood, which some make clear is the formal 'wood' or 'wilderness' being created at Pinkwell. (18)   Up to as many men as 34 at a time, paid 1 shilling a day, were working there, and up to six cart horses and eight coach horses were used at different times.   It seems that the men were preparing the soil and draining it (the Smith was paid for pumping on several occasions in June 1719) for the large numbers of trees and shrubs that were planted there.   As Jenner's plan demonstrates, roughly half of the whole east side was closely planted with mixed trees and shrubs. It was divided laterally by a wide path running right across the site from a semi-circular feature (an arena ?) at the east edge of the garden. Most of the other paths are narrower and run diagonally from the centre to the north or south boundaries of the garden; the compartments formed by the paths are planted with trees and shrubs. The east part of the south edge is occupied by a long rectangular pond, about 350 feet long and 50 feet wide. Immediately north of the west end of this pond is a fairly simple maze. The gardener's account book entry for 24 December 1719 is - 'Paid Mr Yates for digging by his own hands in the Maze'; and again on 7 April 1720 'Paid Mr Gates 2 gns for .... remainder of digging and growing the Maze in the wood and raking'. Mr Gates (or Yates) was also paid in full on 21 October 1721 for the 'triangle pond in the wood. Measured 544 yards'. (19) This cannot be identified on Jenner's plan, and may post-date it, although a triangular configuration would certainly fit well in to the area of radiating paths. The western part of the Wood Garden is occupied, from south to north, by, first, a feature 200 feet square with shrubs divided by a sort of spider's web pattern of paths with a brick building, presumably a summer house, in the centre. This has a pointed roof with a (pineapple-shaped ?) finial. North of this feature are three rectangular ponds, varying from 210 to 270 feet long, two of them divided into three compartments each, and the third, most northerly, with, apparently, an enclosure at the east end. A payment was made on 18 February 1717 'for digging the pond in the wood' but which pond this refers to is not known (20). North of these ponds is the cut-out area, which has three buildings, to be discussed later, and at the east side of it is an elongated plantation of, possibly, fruit trees or hops in nine very straight rows, adjoining the 'wilderness' described earlier. (A walled 'little old hop garden where ye Morrells cherries grew' was mentioned by Ossulstone in his diary in November 1703. Was it here?) The perimeter of the 'Wood Garden' on its north side has iron gates, with ball finials on the gate posts, where the avenue from the Lanthorn Garden meets it, and a gap (no gates are shown by Jenner) at the east side where the arena (?) feature is. A brick building is at the south-west corner: this will be discussed more fully with other buildings in the area. In the Harlington Tithe Award of 1839 the field on the site of the Wood Garden is called The Menagerie. An 18th century 'menagerie' did not necessarily mean a collection of wild animals, and was often no more than some exotic species of birds. The name menagerie has not been traced in documents of the Bennets at Dawley, although pheasants were reared on the estate, and peafowl were also kept, possibly with other unusual birds, and waterfowl on the ponds. The ponds in the Wood Garden, however, were almost certainly stocked with fish for the table.

CHAPTER 14

THE BUILDINGS AT DAWLEY -
CHANGES BETWEEN c.1700 and 1722

The addition of new buildings at Dawley in the period c.1700 and 1722 will be considered next; also the alterations to others and the demolition of some. Comparison of Kip's engraving with the comparable area in Jenner's plan is the prime source of information on the buildings shown by both draughtsmen. Jenner, however, is the sole pictorial authority for the Pinkwell area, where documentary clues plus some guesswork have had to be used to arrive at the most likely sequence of building construction. The same also applies, largely, to the other areas in trying to establish a chronology for building and demolition during the 20 or so years in which Charles Bennet improved his estate. The buildings of Dawley considered here generally exclude those closely associated with the gardens, such as summer houses and the green house, since these have already been discussed together with the gardens themselves. It is felt most convenient to deal with the Dawley buildings in the geographical groups into which most of them fall. First, the buildings at Pinkwell; then the Lodge and the pigeon house, associated here only because both are relatively isolated from the other groups; third, the buildings immediately east of the old mansion and changes to the house itself; and, finally, the buildings round the Great Court, including the new mansion, which was virtually the culmination of the Bennets' building work at Dawley.

The buildings at Pinkwell. It is not known when the old manor house at Pinkwell was demolished, but it had certainly ceased to exist by c.1721, although the rectangular 'cut-out' in the garden where it stood can be seen clearly in Jenner's plan. What is shown in this area is a paling-fenced enclosure, with a farm gate in its north side, occupying nearly half of the 'cut-out'. There are three buildings in this enclosure, two at right angles to each other in the south-west corner and one in the north-east. All three have thatched roofs and, from Jenner's colouring, are apparently of brick construction. Since none of them appear to have windows, it may be assumed, with other factors, that they are barns or shelters for animals. Eight animal pens are, in fact, shown on the south side of the enclosure, adjoining one of the buildings. A 'barn in ye Park' (almost certainly here) was referred to in April 1715. (1) A barn (perhaps the same one) was moved in that year from 'Burd's' (Bird's Farm) to Dawley by Richard Sparkes of Harlington, one of Lord Tankerville's tenant farmers. A 'new stable at ye dog kennel' is mentioned in the accounts for 4 August 1715 when a payment was made to one James -- (surname indecipherable); the 'stables and cart house at the dog kennel' are referred to in connection with a payment made to Richard Sparkes for 'work and timber' on 21 November, then on 26 November 1715 William Sutton was paid £21- on account for 'marble paving before the New Stables at Dawley'. These stables were presumably for the farm horses: they are probably the 'Long Stables' - as opposed to the 'Great Stable' - listed in the 1722 Inventory. (2) Dog kennels certainly existed at Dawley as early as 1705, and later references indicate that they were at Pinkwell. Tankerville certainly owned dogs in 1716 (he bought some beagles in September). (3) None are listed in the 1722 Inventory of Dawley, but under the heading 'At the Dog Kennel' (a description probably comprising all the barns etc at Pinkwell) is a long list, including 2 old waggons, 5 old carts and one water cart, as well as, for example, 36 loads of hay, 22 quarters of wheat, 20 loads of straw and 'Dung in Harlington Lane', which was probably nearby and, no doubt, one of the lanes at the south of the estate leading to Harlington village. Listed separately elsewhere, among non-agricultural effects, are 18 bird baskets, presumably used by John Sharpe, the bird man. He and his wife probably had accommodation in this area. Sharpe would have been responsible for the peafowl and any other exotic birds on the estate, and also, it must be assumed, raised pheasants, because he was paid for 46 of them at 2s6d each on 30 July 1719. (4) Outside the enclosure, about 250 feet north of it, Jenner shows a single-storey brick building, in plan like an L facing the wrong way round, with attached to it a brick-walled courtyard having two smaller enclosures, also brick, at its south-west corner. The south-facing part of the building has a large central door and four windows and a cupola on the roof, although no windows are visible on the outer part of the building forming the upper part of the 'L'. This building was most likely the new stable, built about 1715. It probably included accommodation for grooms and any other servants employed in or around Pinkwell. The only other building (apart from the summer house in the Wood Garden) in the area is the small brick structure with a pyramid roof and ball finial at the south-west corner of the Wood Garden. It may just have been another summer house or gazebo, but there is the possibility that this is the 'Guarding House in the Wood' listed in the 1722 Inventory, containing a bed and bedding, other furniture and, among other items, a gun. It was, perhaps, the house of John Gotobed, the Wood Gardener, or the Park Keeper, or even John Sharpe, the bird man, and his wife. A fuller discussion and summary of problems concerning the old manor house at Pinkwell, and 'Pinkwell House', which appeared after the Bennets' tenure of Dawley, is included in a later chapter.

The Lodge and the Pigeon House. A gate lodge building is shown on Jenner's plan at the south-east corner of the estate, at the junction of the roads from Harlington and Botwell. Its date of construction is not known, although it was presumably before 1708, when the public road between Harlington and Hillingdon entered the estate at this point before it was diverted to its present route. The lodge must thereafter have ceased to serve its original purpose, although 'Lodge' is still marked in this location on Rocque's map of 1754. (Incidentally, no lodge appears to have been provided at the new approach to Dawley from the east to the new courtyard). Jenner's little sketch shows the brick-built lodge adjoining the east side of the gateway. It is composed of two single-storey bays side by side with a window in each of the south-facing gabled ends, with a smaller wing, also gabled, at right angles on their west side. It is difficult to be certain with such a tiny drawing, but the east bay may have a shaped gable. The Lodge, although still described as such, does not appear to have been permanently occupied in July 1722, since a bed is not mentioned in the Inventory. Its contents were listed as 'a pair of large smith's bellows, an anvil and a block', so the building had apparently been turned into the estate forge. The pigeon house, or dovecote, is not mentioned as such in any of the inventories of 1713, 1716 or 1722, or indeed elsewhere prior to the 19th century. Although it is obviously a dovecote in Kip's engraving, its function may have changed subsequently and become, for instance, a summer house or a gardener's or Keeper's house. Certainly, if both Kip's and Jenner's drawings are to be taken at face value, it was altered slightly between c.1700 and c.1721.

Buildings near the Old Mansion. The changes to the buildings in the vicinity of the mansion at Dawley that took place between c.1700 as depicted in Kip's engraving and c.1721 as shown in Jenner's plan can be summarised very briefly. In 1700 the mansion with its attached service wing and nearby stables and 'dower house' were all concentrated in a compact area immediately west of the Harlington-Hillingdon public road on its old course. By about 1721 the mansion had been shorn of its service wing, the stables and 'dower house' had gone and a number of new buildings, including a new small house, all distanced a short way east of the mansion, had taken their place. If the 'dower house' had indeed been one, the death of Bridget, the dowager Lady Ossulstone, in July 1703 may have been the reason for its removal, creating scope for re-development in the area. South-east of the mansion, an entirely new range of buildings, culminating in the new mansion, built 1719-1721, was created. These will be discussed separately and in full later.

Lord Ossulstone's extant diary, covering in four volumes the period 12 November 1703 to 19 December 1712, has no mention whatsoever of alterations to the mansion house, as surely it should do, since many relatively trivial building works are recorded. This leads to the conclusion that such work was either completed before November 1703 or started after late December 1712. Support for the early date is that the desire to create a more impressive approach to his house with the, then, fashionable carriage sweeps (one of which was built in September

45

1704) may have gone with plans to clean up the north front and remove the service buildings and stables etc. New coach houses were evidently under construction on 2 April 1704, according to Ossulstone's diary, in which a London carpenter called Delavell appears to have been involved. (5) Work in the area in question may well have been carried out piecemeal, from c.1700, of course, but an important project was discussed at Dawley in January 1712 with 'Pric ye builder of Richmond'. Then, on 25 August 1712, Lord Ossulstone wrote in his diary 'I was busie all day about ye drought [draught - plan] off new building I agreed this day with Mr Pric' (6). The man in question was almost certainly John Price of Richmond (died 1736), architect and builder, who had already designed major alterations to Isleworth parish church, carried out in 1705-1707. (7) The work at Dawley to Price's plans presumably went ahead shortly after the agreement: workmen are mentioned 'about ye building' in September; 'tradesmen were here about ye new building' in November; and 'Johnson ye cabinett makers men to sett up glasses in ye new building' are mentioned on 18 December 1712 - the penultimate entry in Ossulstone's surviving diary. The next volume, if one existed, should have given valuable information. Unfortunately, one cannot be certain if the references to 'building' above are meant to be singular, or plural in the sense of 'building works'. If the former, the most likely candidate would be the six-bay small house that at some stage replaced the 'dower house'. It cannot be ruled out though, that the work also represented possibly the first phase of the much wider scheme including the new great courtyard buildings. John Price of Richmond (later 'of London') was certainly competent to undertake such work: in his later career he was employed by the Duke of Chandos at Cannons, Middlesex, following such distinguished architects as William Talman, John James and James Gibbs. (8) Further speculation is unrewarding, so instead it is better now to describe the old mansion and the new buildings in its immediate vicinity as they existed in about 1721.

The old mansion - Dawley house - as depicted in the small drawing on Jenner's plan is now a simple rectangle in plan, without the service buildings formerly attached to the east side. The roof is now hipped on all four sides, although the chimneys on the new east roof are shown on its outer slope, rather than the inner slope as on the west part of the roof. About 60 feet east of the old mansion occupying part of the old stables site is a new small house, very similar in style to it - brick, string course between upper and lower windows, and hipped roof. Its south front is about 45 feet, as measured from Jenner's plan. It is, at first, tempting to suppose that Jenner's drawing is no more than an inaccurate representation (both in appearance and location) of the 'dower house' shown by Kip. This is unlikely, however, because 'Jenner's' house is of six bays, rather than seven, and lacks the dormer window (or windows) and the south doorway of the 'dower house'. It was not a service building, but a dwelling, and an important one. This must be the 'New Building' of the inventory of 12 February 1712/13 which had a dining room ('next the bagnio'), hall, Library, chamber ('over the hall'), lodging room ('near the bagnio'), middle room, dressing room and closet adjoining it. The next inventory, of 17 January 1715/16, makes it clear that Lord Ossulstone, by then Earl of Tankerville, preferred the new house to the old mansion, because rooms are now 'My Lords bedchamber' and 'My Lords dressing room'. The hall is now 'the little hall', presumably to avoid confusion with the hall in the old mansion.

Three other, much smaller, brick buildings are in the irregularly-shaped courtyard surrounding the new small house, one to the north and the other two, at right angles to one another, south-east of it. The most northerly building is somewhat like a chapel externally, with a 'nave' and a smaller 'chancel' attached to it at the west end - both parts with doors on the south side. There is no suggestion whatsoever that this was a chapel, although it may have been the bagnio (bathing house) which, from the 1712/13 inventory description, was next to the dining room of the new small house. This location could also be taken to refer to the middle one of the three buildings, which is roughly the same distance from the small house and gable-end on to it. (9) The most southerly building of the group of three might have been one of the coach houses built about 1704, since it has a largish door facing west into its courtyard; also a window on the south gable end. Some, at least, of the domestic services displaced from the east wing of the mansion must have been accommodated in one or other of these buildings, or at any rate until the service range on the new big courtyard was built.

We will now turn to the most unusual and interesting building of the group near the old mansion, not part of the great courtyard complex. This building, about 200 feet south-east of the old mansion, by measurement from Jenner's plan, resembles a church in its external layout. It has a three-storey tower, shown as grey by Jenner so is presumably stone-built or, at least, rendered. It has on its south side six windows or openings in pairs, with horizontal rustication lines level with their centres. The top of the tower is higher at the west side. Joined on to the tower at the east is a brick 'nave' with a pitched roof, hipped at the east end. This part of the building has four largish windows shown on the side facing south. The function of this structure, somewhat early to be a 'folly' and not in a likely location for one (10) remained a puzzle until several clues suggested an answer - a water house, to provide a head of water both for domestic use and for the fountains in the gardens. Carshalton House, Surrey, has a somewhat similar building, with a battlemented tower, built in 1719-1720, which must have been almost contemporary with the 'church' at Dawley. The Surrey building contained an orangery, a bathroom, and other rooms round the base of the tower; the water was raised to a cistern in the top of the tower by means of a water-wheel. Even steam power by the beginning of the 18th century (11) was used to raise water in country houses, although water-wheels or horse powered 'engines' were more commonly used. None of the Dawley inventories mentions a water house or water tower, but a 'water house mare' was listed among Lord Tankerville's horses in 1722. A water tower building would have required sufficient ground area to allow a circle of between 14 feet and 18 feet in diameter in which the horse would move. The Dawley building is about 50 feet long, with the 'nave' about 30 feet (if Jenner's sketch can be accepted as being approximately in scale) so this should have provided adequate space for a pivoted horizontal shaft of up to 10 feet radius to which the horse would have been attached. The Dawley 'church' building is located in the optimum position for a water house to serve all the main Dawley buildings as well as the fountains. It is interesting to note, in passing, that Uppark in Sussex (also owned by Tankerville) had a pumped water supply, and Euston Hall, Suffolk, country seat of the Earl of Arlington (Tankerville's late uncle) also (as early as 1671) had water supplied by an 'engine' for house and fountains. Improvement of the water supply to the mansion at Dawley was under discussion as early as 9 December 1707 when Lord Ossulstone records in his diary 'Mr Hollond came from Amesbury about ye Engion'. (12) A year later, on 3 December 1708 - 'We made an end this evening with [?] ye pipes wch brings ye water from ye upper end of ye Long Walk'. Then, in what seems a leisurely process, between 9 and 19 December 1709 one reads in the diary 'The men were diging of ye well for Mr Holland's engine'; '.... the workmen are very busie about ye well and Engion house'; and '.... gave Mr Holland 5G [guineas]: £5.7.6 as a gift for being here and assisting about ye Engion'. Eight months later, on 27 August 1710, Mr Holland is again at Dawley, perhaps staying until 10 September or later, and he is further mentioned on 23 September - 'Mr Holland .... who is here about setting up an Engion'. It is not clear if the latter is the same engine or a replacement, or a second, separate, one. Further work took place in 1718. A payment of £24- was made on 30 December 'in full of wooden pipes and all manner of workmanship about the engine at Dawley'.(13) (The pipes may have been replacements for those laid ten years earlier.) Then on 19 March 1719 a bill for £90- for 'the New Water Engine' at Dawley was settled, partly by an allowance of £30- for the materials of the old water engine. (14) Finally, a payment for a cistern in 'the summer house' on 31 August 1719 probably relates to an improvement to water supply in the gardens - location unknown. (15)

All the foregoing work necessitated the demolition at different times not only of the service wing of the old mansion, but of the old stables and coach house, the 'dower house', all of the nearby farm buildings (which were, or substitutes for them, transferred to the Pinkwell site, in all probability) and the orangery.

The Buildings at the new Great Court.   The new great courtyard as shown in Jenner's plan - presumably completed - has five buildings round it, including the new mansion.   The latter, to be described fully later, is end-on to the courtyard at its west side, set back from it about 50 feet behind a rectangular area about 70 feet wide.   The courtyard, about 220 feet east-west and 250 feet north-south, as measured from Jenner's plan, is enclosed by a wall, with a gap at the east side facing the avenue leading to the public road, and has a round pond in its centre.   Jenner shows a dot in the middle of the pond which may be intended to represent the nozzle of a fountain.   On the north side of the courtyard are two brick buildings, a large one nearer the mansion and a smaller one.   Facing these, on the south side, are two other buildings of comparable size and construction.   Although there is no direct evidence, it is assumed that the north side buildings are domestic offices, such as laundry, dairy etc, and those on the south are the stables and coach house.   The reason for this assumption is that a Dawley insurance policy of 1753 (16) itemises service buildings in these locations and, even if entirely rebuilt by this time, it is likely that the stables, laundry etc would have occupied the same relative positions as before.   The large service building on the north side is of three storeys and an attic with four gabled dormer windows on the south-facing side of the hipped roof.   It has five bays (four windows and a central door at ground level; five windows each on the first and second floors).   The smaller building to its east is single storey with a hipped roof and on its south side, from west to east, it has a door, a window, and three large doors or openings.   The large stable (?) building on the south side of the courtyard is shown by Jenner as being the same overall size as its counterpart on the north, with three storeys and an attic.   It is of six bays (the ground floor, south side, from west to east, having a window, door, two windows, door, window; and there are six windows in each of the upper storeys.)   The hipped roof is shown with six gabled dormers on the south side.   The smaller building beside it (coach house?) is depicted as identical to its fellow on the north side.   Although these buildings, particularly the larger ones, appear old-fashioned and stylistically akin to the old mansion, they cannot be earlier in date than 1708, when the old public road (which crossed the future courtyard site) was diverted.   A clue as to the date of these buildings is that one Charles Capell received a final payment in full for paving the 'Great Stable Court' on 2 February 1717.   Earlier, he had, from 7 August 1714 to 4 July 1715, received payments totalling well over £400- for 'paving the New Court at Dawley' or 'paving the mews at Dawley'. (17)   Some of these earlier payments may have been for work on the buildings immediately east of the old mansion, discussed above, but one cannot be certain. In between Capell's first and last payments, one William Sutton was paid for work in 'ye Mews at Dawley' in February 1715 and for 'marble paving before the New Stables at Dawley' on 26 November 1715. (18)   If this work also refers to the new Great Court, rather than at Pinkwell, the marble paving, at any rate, would presumably be for special aesthetic treatment of one particular area. (19)   However, the January 1716 inventory of Dawley includes 'New Stables' that are presumably those on the Great Court, but not, apparently, the new domestic service buildings which, it must be assumed, were built soon afterwards.   Although, as suggested earlier, there is the shadow of doubt that the new Great Court service buildings were really intended to complement a new mansion, the erection of service buildings well in advance of the house they serve is by no means exceptional.   The service wings of Easton Neston, Northants, for example, were completed in 1682, 20 years before the house itself. (20)   The possible influence on Dawley architecture of Uppark, Mary Grey's ancestral home, rebuilt about the time she married Lord Ossulstone (in 1695) can be considered briefly.   The new service buildings at Uppark (subsequently rebuilt, but shown in Pieter Tillemans' painting and a Kip engraving) (21) were grouped either side of a courtyard leading to the original main entrance to the rebuilt house.   These buildings - stables and coach house on the one hand, domestic services on the other - were all two-storied with hipped roofs, not dissimilar to those at Dawley as shown in Jenner's plan.   The idea cannot be dismissed that Ossulstone might have adopted the Uppark service buildings and courtyard as a model for Dawley, although by the second decade of the 18th century a different style of house would have been called for.   (The much stronger likelihood of the Dawley mansion influencing the design of the new Uppark house has already been discussed. The possibility of cross-fertilisation between the two estates, in general, is very real, even if evidence is lacking.)

CHAPTER 15

THE NEW MANSION AT DAWLEY, BUILT 1719-1721

Before discussing the Earl of Tankerville's new mansion in detail, several questions should be asked. First, was the new great courtyard ever intended, in the original planning, to be the approach to a new mansion ? It could have been merely a re-location of the stables as part of a scheme, including the carriage sweep, to improve the prospect of the north facade of the old mansion: a move facilitated by the re-routing of the old public highway. This step may have been followed (if it was not in the original plan) by a decision to re-locate also the domestic service buildings on to the same courtyard. Some buildings, described above, may possibly represent an intermediate stage by moving certain services a little to the east of the old mansion. The courtyard layout, omitting the new mansion, shown by Jenner has analogies with Uppark (before the rebuilding of c.1750), as discussed above, and even the scale and appearance of the 'great court' service buildings are to some extent comparable. Second, what was the motivation of Charles Bennet to build a new mansion on his Dawley estate only a hundred yards from the mansion erected by his father less than fifty years previously ? The need to demolish a particularly fine greenhouse in order to use the site chosen must have been weighed in the balance, one supposes. The reason has not been recorded, but the intention to undertake new building on this scale may already have been there in 1706 when Charles Bennet, then Lord Ossulstone, first attempted to divert the public road. Positive steps to plan a new mansion and service buildings may have followed the death of his wife in 1710, when he perhaps felt disinclined to make much further use of Uppark in Sussex, her ancestral home (very few furnishings were there when he died in 1722). The re-creation of his late father-in-law's earldom in his favour in 1714 may have provided Charles Bennet with the final incentive to create a modern house in accordance with the new status conferred on him. The planning of the new buildings may even have been in anticipation of the honour to come, since noblemen, certainly of high rank, were at that time expected to maintain a standard of living in accordance with their status. Third, once a new mansion had been decided on, and the courtyard site chosen, one might reasonably have assumed that an arrangement like that of a well known building such as Buckingham House (built c.1704) in London might have been adopted. The principal facade of this house (long since altered and enlarged and now Buckingham Palace) formed the central feature of the approach across a courtyard with a central fountain and flanked by stables and domestic service buildings given full architectural treatment. Whether something like this was originally planned, or was planned and then changed or curtailed, we may never know. What was built, and is shown in Jenner's plan of Dawley, is a house of modest dimensions, facing north-south and presenting a virtually blank end wall to the courtyard. The answers to these questions are a matter for speculation, and one can only suspect changes in mind by the noble builder - and, no doubt, some frustrated and aggrieved architects !

Some consideration should be given next to the question of the architect of the Earl of Tankerville's new mansion. John Price of Richmond, the architect and builder, was consulted by Charles Bennet in 1712, plans were produced and agreed, and building work at Dawley followed. (1) This is discussed earlier here in connection with new buildings immediately east of the old mansion. There is no evidence that those plans included buildings on the new great court (although this cannot entirely be discounted) and a new mansion. Lord Ossulstone's extant diaries cease at the end of 1712, and no other references to John Price in relation to Dawley have been traced. However, Price may well have been invited to submit further plans. He was undoubtedly qualified to carry out such work, and the new mansion at Dawley as built looks like a scaled down and simplified version of the centre of John Price's Baroque elevation, drawn in 1720, of a projected (but not built) house for the Duke of Chandos in Cavendish Square, London. (2) Barnsley Park, Gloucestershire, is a country house with a possible attribution to

John Price. (3)   Captain Nicholas Dubois was involved, there is reason to believe, in at least some degree with the design and/or building of the new mansion at Dawley. Dubois (1665-1735) was of French birth;   after a military career he was appointed sub-engineer on the Board of Ordnance (4) in 1718, and in November 1719 was given another official appointment as Master Mason in the Office of Works.   He was the translator into English of Giacomo Leoni's 'The Architecture of Andrea Palladio', published in 1715, a book which helped further to popularise the Palladian style in England in the 18th century.   (The Earl of Tankerville subscribed to this book). Nicholas Dubois' only complete surviving country house is Stanmer Park, Sussex, built between 1722 and 1727:   a plain, well-proportioned Palladian building which appears to have no external features in common with the Dawley house completed in 1721. (5)   His London home at the time the new Dawley house was being built was No 41 Brewer Street.   This house, built by Dubois himself, is known to have been completed by the Christmas of 1718 and was occupied by him in 1721.   It was a plain building of three storeys and attic, again with no external features that can be detected in Dawley: it was demolished this century.   One of its more unusual internal features was a circular staircase, a pattern which Dubois repeated in interior work at Chevening House, Kent, carried out in 1722. (6)   It is recorded in the account book of Thomas Robertson, the Earl of Tankerville's Gentleman of Horse, that a servant was sent, on 28 June 1719, to bring 'Captain Dubois' to Dawley, and again on 19 July.   On the first visit, Dubois appears to have stayed until 30 June, when he probably returned to London with Tankerville, who had to 'prorogue the Parlement'.   On the second occasion, it is specifically recorded that Captain Dubois was taken back to London on the next day, 20 July. (7)   These dates would coincide with the work on the foundations for the new house.   It is a reasonable assumption, therefore, that Dubois visited Dawley for consultation on architectural matters, and may possibly have been involved earlier in the design of the new mansion.   This said, John Jenner, who drew the estate plan of Dawley about 1721 and was the master bricklayer in building the house, was probably quite capable of making the design for it.   A 'Mr John Jenner', it is interesting to note, was later one of the subscribers to James Gibbs' 'A Book of Architecture' (published in 1728), and he may have been one of the old breed of master craftsmen builders who were, in effect, architects.

The small elevation sketch on the estate plan drawn by John Jenner is the only known picture of the Earl of Tankerville's new Dawley mansion.   The south (and principal) elevation of the house, which faces the garden, is shown.   It is seven 'elements' wide, with two storeys above a basement;   the ground floor having six large windows and a centrally-placed door, and the first floor having seven much smaller windows.   The wall is crowned with a parapet (apparently with alternate brick and stone panels, although the sketch is not clear on this point) concealing the flat roof.   A cornice is just below the parapet and a string course runs between the ground and first floor windows.   'Giant' pilasters (probably of the Corinthian or Composite orders - see below), nearly the full height of the building, terminate the elevation at either end.   Steps lead up to the entrance, with three basement windows at each side of them.   Four existing buildings may help to give a better idea of the appearance of the new Dawley house, and their internal layouts give some clues to that of Dawley's (as will be discussed more fully later). Cottesbrooke Hall, Northamptonshire (built c.1702-1712) is of roughly the same size and style of Tankerville's Dawley, and its largely unaltered south front, in particular, gives a good general impression of what Dawley must have looked like. (8)   Marlow Place, Buckinghamshire, also has a seven bay (or 'element') front (the entrance front) with some features in common with Dawley.   It was built c.1720 for John Wallop, Viscount Lymington, who in 1716 had married the Earl of Tankerville's daughter, Bridget.   Was there some architectural, as well as social, cross-fertilisation here ? (9)   The Walton Canonry, 69 The Close, Salisbury, built in 1720, is, like Dawley, a seven bay, two-storey house, although smaller. It shares Dawley's features of having smaller first floor windows (although not markedly so), and steps leading up to the ground floor over a basement.   The parapet is plain, however, and it has only token 'giant' pilasters. (10)   Finally, Deans Court, Wimborne Minster, Dorset, rebuilt around a mediaeval building, has a seven-bay facade of c.1725 that gives a fair external idea of the Dawley house built a few years earlier, although the details differ. (11)   Although the visual evidence for Dawley is limited, therefore, fortunately many details of its structure are preserved in the builder's estimates and craftsmen's progress payments kept among the Earl of Tankerville's papers relating to Dawley in the Public Record Office. (12)

Among these papers, 'An Estimate of the New Buildings Designed at Dawley with the value of Old materials there made 3rd June 1719' lists the cost of materials under the headings: Carpenter's, Joyner's, Bricklayer's, Mason's, Plumber's, Plasterer's, Glazier's and Painter's work.   The costs under these headings are as follows:

		£.	s.	d.
Carpenter		401	0	0
Joyner		462	12	6
Bricklayer		384	15	0
Mason		46	10	0
Plumber		67	10	0
Plasterer		47	10	0
Glazier		40	0	0
Painter		53	10	0
	£	1503	7	6

The costs were partly offset by old materials in the Green House (£66.1s.7d.) and vault and in 'the House' (£320.7s.5½d.).   The Green House, or orangery, was on or just in front of the site chosen for the new mansion and, accordingly, had to be demolished, although the new work for the plumber included 11½ tons of lead for covering 'the old vault under the terrace', which rather suggests that the greenhouse had a vault (probably for heating stoves) which was subsequently to be used for storage in conjunction with the new building.   The old materials from 'the House' consisted mainly of old brickwork (42¼ rods) and much boarding of different kinds - rough whole deal, naked floor, straight joint, dowelled joint etc - but also 370 yards of bead and raised panels and 182 yards of 'plain square work' and 10 steps of stairs.   The exact source of these materials is debatable.   The old mansion is still shown on Jenner's plan of c.1721 on which the completed new mansion appears, although the service quarters on the east side of the former have been removed, and this may account for at least some of the material, such as the old brickwork and the 10 steps of stairs, which might have led to a servants' garret.   However, 224 yards of old deal wainscot bead work was stated in later accounts as having come from the Library and the Yellow Room.   The 370 yards of old bead and raised panels were also taken down from these two rooms and additionally the Dressing Room and Bed Chamber.   The six-bay house just east of the old mansion contained, according to the inventories, 'my Lord's Bedchamber' and 'my Lord's Dressing Room' in 1716, and the earlier list of 1713 includes a Library, although this is not subsequently specified as such.   Lord Tankerville may have wished to have the familiar surroundings from his favourite rooms put in his new mansion, and this would account for the panelling being stripped from the six-bay house in which it had been installed only some seven years before.   Removal of panelling would not, of course, have affected the main structure and the house appears to be intact as shown in Jenner's sketch, although probably demoted to servants' quarters or other purposes.

By extracting some details of the materials and quantities quoted in the estimate we can add depth to the picture of the new mansion.   First, the ground area was approximately 3100 square feet (30½ square of rough boarding was used in the flat roof - which must be approximately the same in area as the ground plan). This is confirmed by the '236 (ft) Modillion Cornice' which would surround the four sides of a building approximately 78 feet by 40 feet.   (This figure is strikingly confirmed by later evidence.)   Modillions are a series of brackets supporting a cornice and the term is, strictly, used in connection with the Corinthian or

Composite orders of architecture.   At Dawley, the cornice was just below the parapet level.   The house was of brick construction, as is attested by the item '50¼ rods of Brick Work', approximating to 4000 square feet of wall, excluding window and door openings.   The roof was flat and lead-covered, for which '11 tun of Lead New Cast and layd' was estimated at a cost of 3/- per hundred - total £33-.   This was laid on '30½ square of Naked Floor under the lead' at 46/- per square.   The structure supporting the roof was described in the estimate as '31 squares of Naked Flooring the girders [timber beams] 13 by 10 inches the Joysts 10 by 2½ inches at £2-5-0 per square'.   A quantity of '30½ square of rough boarding under the lead' at 28/- per square was presumably to form the ceiling of the upper storey, immediately below the roof joists.   The 'Ceiling Floor' (30½ square) - the floor of the upper storey, which formed the ceiling of the ground floor rooms below - cost 20 shillings per square.   The ground level flooring, which was a suspended floor over the offices at basement level, consisted of two types.   An area of about 450 square feet - representing a room of, say, 30 feet by 15 feet, was estimated for '4¼ square of Clean Deal Dowled Boarding' at £6-0-0 per square.   As this price was over three times the cost of the rest of the flooring on the ground floor, the materials must have been for one of the most important rooms, if not necessarily the largest.   The remaining flooring consisted of '26 square of Streight Joynt Boarding at £1-16-0 per square'.   The offices in the basement were floored with '220 yards of Paving with Red Tyles' at 3 shillings per yard.

'Eight hundred foot super of crown glass' was quoted for the windows, which included 28 sash windows (to be painted at 2s. 6d. each), seven on the upper floor of the south front, six larger ones on the lower floor and, presumably, a corresponding 13 windows on the north side, with the remaining two, it can be assumed, at either end on the short elevations, which must have been largely 'blind' facades.   There were also windows in the basement, which were probably casements.   Six can be discerned in the south elevation showing partly above ground level in Jenner's sketch and there was probably a similar number on the north side of the basement.   Only two exterior doors are mentioned, as follows: '2 Frontispieces to two Out Doors that out of the great Room into the Garden and as directed the value of which to be left to the Judgement of the Surveyor'.   (An amount of £12 was allowed in the estimate.)   These doors and their surrounds evidently formed an important part in the architectural composition of the principal facades of the house, particularly in that the design of the one in the south front was to be under the direct control of the architect (surveyor) and not left to the carpenter's and joiner's discretion.   This door is shown in the estate plan sketch as being (as would be expected) in the centre of the south front, from which steps lead down to ground level.   The other would have been in the centre of the north front and was the main entrance to the house.   'The Great Room' on the ground floor was at the centre of the house facing the garden.   It was fitted out with '200 yards of Right Wainscott Board and raised Pannells'.   No doubt one of the '3 Old Marble pieces New Polished and Sett' used in the ground floor ornamented the Great Room.   These renovated chimney pieces brought from elsewhere (possibly from the old house, as their total price in the estimate was only £3) were apparently of better quality than the '3 New Marble chimney Pieces in the Upper Storey' - where the lesser rooms were situated - which cost £21.   'Six Doors and Door Cases in the Lower Story' are specifically included in the estimate, whereas none are mentioned for the upper storey or other parts of the house, so the other doors presumably were of lesser quality and included with the estimate for general carpentry or joinery work.   Access to the upper floor was by means of '2 Stair Cases one Four Foot going and the other Three Foot the first well finished one with another'.   The 4 foot wide staircase was the principal one and the smaller one the second or 'back' stairs for servants which would also have continued down to the basement.   There is no indication of the location of these staircases but they would quite likely have been at the east and west ends of the house, on either side of the Great Room.   The only specific references to the basement floor of the house in the estimate are for '3 Portland Stone Chimney Pieces in the Offices' and for '220 yards of Paving'.

Building work on the new house at Dawley appears to have been commenced at least by July 1719, because the first payment to John Jenner, the master bricklayer, was made on the tenth day of that month. Before this, from November 1718 onwards, in particular, payments were made to up to 30 or more labourers for work in 'the wood' including digging, and some of the men may have been diverted for excavating the house foundations. Payments for brickwork in September and October indicate that James Jenner, who signed some receipts, was working with his father on the site. (13) Further payments in April 1720 refer to new bricks being brought by John Jenner from Brentford. These may have been high quality bricks for window surrounds, quoins etc, since it is likely that the majority of bricks for the house were made near the site from the plentiful supply of brick-earth that was available on the estate. (As mentioned earlier, a working brick kiln was shown in Kip's engraving of c.1700.) John Lock, the joiner, received his first payment for carpentry and joinery work on 23 July 1719. Later payments to Lock took account of timber brought from Brentford and London in one of Lord Tankerville's wagons and for carriage of a Mr Young's tools from Cranford (2s.0d). The first payment to the plumber, David Arnott, for 'new casting and laying of lead' was made on 13 November 1719, lead having been supplied by a Mr Finche a few days previously. This indicates that work was in hand (or perhaps completed) on the roof by the end of the year, although the final payment for plumber's work 'at the New Buildings at Dawley' (to one Robert Bourne) was not made until 15 April 1721. The final external structural work on the new house at Dawley seems to have been carried out by the stone mason, John Frank, who received his first payment on 13 February 1720 and his last one on 9 January 1722. The mason's work, in addition to installing the nine chimney pieces and 600 feet of marble paving (location uncertain) would have consisted mainly of ornamentation in the form of cornices, parapets, pilasters, etc, and also such things as the steps to the garden from the 'Great Room'. Frank's assistant was one Thomas Spencer, 'stone cutter'. The principal painter, Thomas Gregory of Richmond, was first paid on 25 April 1720 and finally on 19 August 1721, although an intermediate payment, under Gregory's account heading, of £2-8-6 for painting work was made to one Anthony Adams. The latter also received a further payment, listed separately elsewhere, of £8-7-0 on 14 August 1721 for painting work including rails and banisters and the 'oyl cloath', presumably that in the Great Parlour (see below). (14) The windows evidently had had their glass added by about 1 November 1720, when the glazier, Charles Scriven, received his one and only payment of £45-. Later in November, Joseph Hurn, smith, was paid £4-6-0 'for putting up bells in ye new Lodgings'. Hinges etc were purchased from 'Esqr Crawly' in January 1720 and Mr Piner was paid for paving tiles on 16 March 1720. John Laverick fitted the hinges - for which he was paid in October 1721. The locksmith, John Owen of London, received payment on 15 December 1720 for 'mending, cleaning and polishing of the locks at the New House of Dawley'. (Owen, although possibly unable to write, had a modern outlook, since he receipted payment with a stamped impression bearing his name !). The locks seem to have been brought from elsewhere. (There were 21 brass locks and keys in the 'new house' at Dawley recorded separately in the inventory of 1722). Payments made for upholstery in November 1720; for 'cleaning his Lordship's pictures at Dawley' in December; and for 'braziery ware' in January 1721 all seem to indicate that the house was by then nearly ready for occupation. Finally, although provision was made earlier for 'a piece of new walling on the south side of the Terras next the Lawristine [laurel] Hedge', to be built later on, the last recorded payment to John Jenner, who was responsible for the plastering as well as the brickwork, was for sweeping the chimneys. This payment was made on 20 June 1721 and demonstrates that fires had, presumably, been lit in the new mansion during the previous winter. Whilst the estimated costs of materials, totalling £1503-7-6, for building the new mansion was probably quite closely adhered to, it is almost impossible to arrive at an exact figure for the cost of labour from the details that have been recorded. (15) For instance, the value of some old materials has been included, as has some work at London in a Dawley account by Jenner. Both Jenner and Lock stated sizeable further sums ('not yet examined or allowed by his Lordship') due to them and, if paid later, the record of them does not appear to have survived. Additionally, the method of accounting is somewhat confusing, and minor arithmetical errors have been noted. This said, a total figure, probably accurate to within a few hundred pounds, can be arrived at.

The list of payments on account or for work completed are as follows. Principal Contractors (totals):

John Jenner - brickwork and plastering	£	1173- 8- 6
John Lock - carpentry and joinery		1689-19- 2
John Frank - stone mason's work		265- 0- 0
David Arnott - plumber's work		342-13- 0
Thomas Gregory of Richmond - painting		63-13- 6
Charles Scriven - glazing		45- 0- 0
		3579- 14- 2

The following are under the heading 'Incident Charges':

'Mr Piner' - paving tiles	6-15- 3
'Esq Crawly' - hinges (supply ?)	2-10- 7³/₄
Joseph Hurn (smith) - putting up bells	4- 6- 0
John Owen - locks	5- 5- 0
John Laverick - hinges (fitting?)	6- 6- 0
Thomas Boucher - braziery ware	25- 0- 0
John Bull and John Barnes - sawing	3-19-3
John Morris - upholstery	50- 0-0
Mrs Le Count - mohair	46-18-0
James Colliroe (?) - cleaning his Lordship's pictures	10-10-0
A Smith - unspecified work	14-12-6
	3755-16-9³/₄

Further amounts claimed as due and possibly paid later:

John Jenner	109- 6- 2¹/₂
John Lock	257- 0- 4¹/₂
Thomas Gregory	11-16- 6
£	4133-19-10³/₄

It would appear, from the figures available, that the Earl of Tankerville's new mansion cost him for materials and labour something approaching £6000-.

CHAPTER 16

THE NEW MANSION AT DAWLEY - THE INTERIOR

Following the first Earl of Tankerville's death, a full inventory of his possessions was made. The inventory (1) as a whole will be considered later, but the part relating to the new mansion, carried out in June 1722, will be reviewed here in order to complete the picture of the building. (The inventory references to the old mansion have been considered earlier.) The complete contents of the new mansion were itemised room by room: the same sequence has been followed here, although only the more unusual or significant furnishings are mentioned. The present writer's conclusions as to the location of rooms are put forward where applicable.

Under the heading 'In the New Buildings' the first entry - evidently in the new mansion - is for the 'Chocolate Room' in the upper storey. Although this contained '2 chocolate potts' it was apparently used by servants for the preparation of all hot beverages, because it had a fire grate, and also listed were a coffee pot and coffee mill, 2 tea kettles, 'two hand tea boards', 'a small cellar with bottles', 20 pieces of China and earthen ware, as well as tables, chairs, a draught board, a linen press and 'a small drying horse'.

The 'next room' and the 'maid's room' were both bedrooms, as was 'Mr Baysallance's room'. Daniel Baysallance was Tankerville's Valet de Chambre and his room's contents included 'two small muskettoons' - short barrelled muskets, presumably for his Lordship's defence, if required.

Lord Ossulstone's room and closet came next. His furnishings included 'a field bedstead with old silk furniture, the head board and head cloth embroidered with gold'. Field bedsteads were originally portable for use in military campaigns, but by the early 18th century the term was also applied to other types of bed that were presumably more readily portable than, say, four posters.

Next, and probably adjacent to Ossulstone's room or closet, was Lord Tankerville's room, which had 'a gold colour mohair bed complete the curtains lined with Sarcenett'. The room must have been a large one, as would be expected, because its seating furniture included 6 mohair chairs with walnuttree frames, a dressing chair and 2 square stools, 2 mohair window seats and a yellow Callimanroe easy chair. The room had a brass hearth with iron back and also contained an eight-day repeating clock and seven pairs of brass barrelled pistols and one pair of iron barrelled pistols. The dressing room adjoining seems to have been used in part, at least, for storage and it included a 'large mapp'.

The Library (listed after the 'dressing room') contained one large and two small bookcases, a reading glass and a wainscot desk, covered with green cloth, upon castors, together with other furniture. An interest in nautical science is indicated by a pair of globes, a box with a sea compass, mathematical instruments, two weather glasses, 'some small instruments with a case', a pair of compasses, a ring dial and a quadrant.

The 'Office Room' contained two large iron chests, an iron bound chest, ten packing cases and a chest for plate, together with a bed, six chairs and other furniture. It appears to have been where the valuables were kept.

The shared office of the Bailiff (John Chappell) and Thomas Robertson, Gentleman of the Horse - the senior servant - is listed next and contained only 'an old walnuttree screwtore' (a desk with drawers, or secretaire), a wainscot desk book case and two chairs.

'Mr Bennett's room' probably was used by Tankerville's surviving youngest son, Grey. (2)   It included a chess board complete, together with a bed and other furniture.

The Great Parlour, listed next in the inventory, was one of the most important rooms in the house and probably featured one of the 'three old marble chimney pieces, newly polished', mentioned in the building accounts. It contained, inter alia, 'A large wooden cistern lined with lead' (probably a wine cooler) and in addition 'twelve walnuttree India matted chairs' and 'three marble sideboards with iron scrolls'.   There were also two particularly interesting items: an eight day repeating clock by Tompion and 'a plan of Dawley'.   The latter seems very likely to have been the estate plan drawn by John Jenner about 1721, which still exists. (3) The floor was covered with a 'large painted floor cloth'.   This was presumably the one painted by Anthony Adams, for which he received payment in August 1721 (see above).   Floor cloths were sometimes used instead of imported rugs before English-made carpets became more widely available towards the end of the 18th century.

The Great Dining Room, the next entry, had in it a full length portrait of King Charles II which, valued at £50-, was the most valuable painting at Dawley.   Dining rooms in the fashionable houses of the period did not usually have one large table, but a number of smaller tables that were normally kept against the walls when not in use.   The Dawley dining room had 'two large oval card tables of walnuttree with covers' and ten chairs and two long settees made of walnuttree covered with gold brocade.   The fireplace (probably another old marble one, re-polished) had over it a 'chimney glass in a glass frame'; the hearth was of brass, with the customary 'pair of Doggs' (fire dogs - or rests, for firewood) and had an iron fire-back and was equipped with a shovel and tongs.

The Drawing Room, which followed in sequence in the inventory, was adorned with 'two pieces of fine Tapestry Hangings made by Vanderbank the Arms of the Family in the borders containing about 85 ells'.   There is good reason to believe that these two tapestries, made by John Vanderbank in his workshop in Great Queen Street, Soho, were two pieces 'Air' and 'Water' of a series called 'The Elements'.   The former ('Air') is now in the Victoria and Albert Museum (4) and is about 5 x 9$\frac{1}{2}$ ells, or approximately 11ft 3ins x 21ft 3 ins (the Flemish ell used here was a cloth measure equal to 27ins x 27 ins).   It has the coat of arms of the Lords Grey of Werke in the centre of the top border, which could reasonably be described as the 'Arms of the Family', since the late Earl's father-in-law held the title of Ford, Lord Grey of Werke (or Wark).   The second tapestry ('Water') (recorded as existing a few years ago, but present whereabouts unknown) was rather smaller, about 5 x 6 ells, but also had the lion rampant arms of the Greys of Werke in the top edge.   The two tapestries were most likely once at Uppark, seat of Lord Grey, which Mary, his daughter and heir, brought to Charles Bennet on inheritance after their marriage. It is not known if the two tapestries were first hung in the old house at Dawley before being transferred to the new house after 1720, but they could certainly have been comfortably accommodated on two unobstructed walls (without windows or fireplaces) there.   Belton House, Lincolnshire, has (or had) two Vanderbank tapestries in a room 21ft x 18ft of which two walls had clear spaces of 17ft and 15ft. (As a footnote, if, as seems likely, 'Air' and 'Water' are the two tapestries mentioned in the 1722 inventory, at 47$\frac{1}{2}$ plus 30 ells, totalling 77$\frac{1}{2}$ ells, the surveyor's estimate of 85 ells was somewhat overstated.)   The Drawing Room also contained a full length portrait of Lord Burleigh.   This was probably the Hon John, Lord Burleigh, who married Annabella Bennet at Dawley on 9 February 1696. (5)   There was a chimney glass and a panel mirror, and seating consisted of eight chairs, a settee, two stools and two window seats.   In addition, there was an Indian tea table, tea cups and saucers, and a tea kettle and stand.   The Drawing Room was the most highly valued room - at £334-2/- in the house inventory, no doubt in large measure because of the valuable tapestries.

The Red Room, next listed, was a bedroom with a 'scarlet cloth bed', seven 'matted seat' chairs, an easy chair, a 'Bason with a Slabb and a Brasse cork', and a 'red Leather Close Stool and pewter pan'. The latter was one of only three such toilet conveniences listed in the inventory for the new house (one other was in Lord Ossulstone's room and one in the basement - see below).

'The Stair Case Still Room and Closett' is listed next as a single heading. As this staircase led down to the basement floor, or 'offices', it was almost certainly the 'back stairs' of the 'three foot going'. Of the miscellaneous collection of items listed under one heading, the '37 prints and 2 mapps' (or some of them) may have been used to decorate the stairs. The 'close stool chair and pewter pan' may have been kept in the closet for use there, whereas such varied items as a pewter bed pan, three lanterns and 'some old iron' were presumably stored. A wooden mortar and pestle, 'six tin plates for bisketts', and a chafing-dish would have been among items for use in the still room, which had a hearth. Also on the basement floor was 'The Parlour next to the still room' which was almost certainly that of the housekeeper, who had charge of the still room.

Next came the servants' hall (which would have had to be large enough to accommodate at table up to about 25 servants who were not important enough to eat elsewhere). It contained 'a large table and forms about it' and must also have had one of the Portland stone chimney pieces mentioned in the estimates.

Next were the footmen's room; Nicholas' room (possibly that of Nicholas Bennet, the porter); the steward's parlour; the butler's room (Mr Thomas Davis was the butler in 1722 - he received £15- per annum); and the plate pantry.

To summarise, the new mansion, which was little more than a villa in contemporary terms, had a ground floor with high ceilings and tall windows which contained the principal rooms, including the Great Dining Room and, probably, the Great Parlour. These two rooms were most likely on the central axis of the house. One of them would have been the 'Great Room' mentioned in the building estimates having the door with elaborate doorcase leading into the garden, and fitted with 200 yards of 'right wainscott board and raised panels'. This was, perhaps, the Great Parlour, which had a painted floor cloth (see above) - one of the few rooms for which floor coverings are mentioned in the inventory, the others having plain polished boards only. The other 'great room' would, most likely, have had the other 'out door' - the one leading into the courtyard on the north side of the house. This may have been the room with the expensive '4$\frac{1}{4}$ square of clean deal dowelled boarding' (representing an area of, say, 30 feet by 14 or 15 feet). The Great Parlour and the Great Dining Room would each have had one of the three 'old marble chimney pieces new polished and set', the third was probably in the Drawing Room, or possibly the Red Room. Although some of the other rooms on both ground and upper floors also had hearths, these were (with three exceptions, mentioned below) presumably of unremarkable mason's work not specified separately in the building estimates. The rather small number of major rooms in the new house seems to be accounted for by the decision to retain, at least temporarily, the old house for accommodation as part of an overall scheme. The two staircases - the main one and the 'back', or servants' stairs - were probably at either side of the house and lighted by single windows in the east and west walls. The main staircase (of 'four foot going'), which probably led off one of the two major rooms in the centre of the house, was decorated with seventeen pictures - twelve family portraits, portraits of King Charles I and King Charles II, a view of Dunkirk, and a pair of still life paintings. The narrower ('three foot going') servants' staircase was apparently unadorned, but may have had prints on its walls. The upper storey contained several small or medium sized rooms and three larger ones - Lord Tankerville's, Lord Ossulstone's, and the Library. It is these last three that had the new marble chimney pieces listed in the building estimates and it is likely that the main bedrooms, at least, were on the side of the house with the best outlook - the south side facing the formal gardens. All the upstairs rooms had much smaller windows and lower ceilings than those in the 'piano nobile' on the ground floor. The basement 'office' rooms contained the three Portland stone chimney pieces mentioned in the estimates, and these were probably located in the Servants' Hall, the parlour next to it, and the Steward's Parlour, all of which had hearths, according to the 1722 inventory.

CHAPTER 17

THE 1722 INVENTORY OF DAWLEY; SERVANTS

Charles Bennet, 1st Earl of Tankerville, of the new creation, did not live long to enjoy his new house, for he died, in his 48th year, on 21st May 1722, and was buried (on 26th May), in accordance with the wishes stated in his will, in Harlington Church. There, he joined his wife Bridget who had died almost exactly 12 years before, on 31 May 1710. The inventories taken after his death give some idea of Tankerville's considerable wealth. In addition to Dawley, he owned Chillingham Castle in Northumberland and Uppark in Sussex - both inheritances through his wife, a London house in Conduit Street and farming lands in Middlesex, Buckinghamshire, Gloucestershire, Derbyshire, Lincolnshire, Leicestershire and Worcestershire (Wigorne'). The silver plate at Dawley alone was valued at over £2000-, and there was a similar quantity at the London house.

The complete inventory of the late Earl's possessions at Dawley was carried out between June and September 1722 (1), starting with livestock, produce and farm wagons and equipment, under the heading 'In the Park'. This totalled £384-2-6 in value. The horses were listed next, valued in total at £356-. Silver kept at Dawley was itemised in July and valued at £2039-18-10. The contents of the buildings were also listed in July, to a total value of £2498-5-6. (Some of the more significant or interesting items of furnishings, together with the rooms in which they were located, have already been discussed under the buildings in which they were housed). Together with the furniture etc, the above figure also included bed linen and 'my Lord's wearing apparel'. Finally, the pictures at Dawley were listed in September 1722 and valued at £328-4-0 in total. The contents of Uppark were also listed separately in August 1722 and amounted in value to only £154-5-0, showing how little the house must have been used at this time. A quite separate list of the servants at Dawley and London, giving their names, functions and wages was also compiled about the same time, and this is considered later. A general overview of the late Earl's possessions - excluding the contents of the buildings, farm buildings aside - follows next.

The Earl of Tankerville's coaches, horses, livestock, farm vehicles, implements and produce were all listed separately. 'In the Coach Houses' were 'An old Berlin Coach' (a type of four-seater vehicle, drawn by either two or four horses, with a system of longitudinal braces that was claimed to reduce side sway of the coach body; named after the city with which it was associated); 'a Sashmarine' (a type of vehicle that research has not identified, although the name suggests that sliding windows may have been its outstanding attribute) (2); 'an old four wheel chaise' (a type of travelling chariot, drawn by two or four horses, usually controlled by a postillion riding the nearside lead horse, with provision for carrying trunks at the front and the rear and usually fitted with a sword case at the rear of the bodywork for dress or ceremonial swords); 'a Kittering and a pair of Harness' (a light two wheeled passenger cart, its name Kittering or Kittereen said to have been derived from the town of Kettering, Northants, where it may have originated); and 'a Tumbrell' (Tumbrel or tumbril was the name given to a traditional type of farm cart, but also applied to a type of low-slung ammunition cart, drawn by a single horse, used by many Continental armies throughout the 18th century. Since this vehicle was evidently kept with the Earl's coaches, rather than with the farm wagons, the latter description seems more likely to be applicable - although rather than ammunition, it may have been used to carry household goods or luggage). (3) The coach houses also contained various items of tackle, such as harness, horse collars, bridles, saddles and halters. The saddle room housed further items of horse furniture and grooming equipment, including 'seven yards of chequered yellow Kersey', and 'a velvett furniture for a horse, with silver fringe and lace'.

The list of the Earl of Tankerville's horses at Dawley comprised the following: Sixteen bay coloured coach horses, a grey mare each for Mr Robertson (Gentleman of Horse) and Mr Baysallance (Valet de Chambre), two Dutch Dunns (greyish-brown horses), a Chillingham grey mare, a little bay mare, a Farthinglington mare, a sachie, an arche, a rose, a White Stockings (descriptions of the colour or markings, presumably), a Grey filly, a Sorrel colt, a pugg (this would be a small horse of some description), a garden horse (used, no doubt, for pulling a lawn roller), and a water house mare. The existence of a water house at Dawley, in which this animal would have been employed, has been discussed earlier. The value placed on these 32 horses was £356-. The purchase prices at various times of some of the late Earl's carriages and horses (or their predecessors) are recorded elsewhere (4) and as a matter of interest these are some of the amounts involved. A new Sash Maree (otherwise sashmarine ?) and some repairs £22-, and a new Berline chariot £90-, both from Robert Grimes in 1716; a chaise, bought of Robert Edlyn, coachmaker, of Long Acre (London) £22-5/- in 1719; a set of travelling wheels for Berline coach from John Linn (?) of Windmill Street (London) £6-, also in 1719. Some individual prices of horses are: two black coach geldings £40-, 1714; four bay geldings £73-1/- in April 1718 and two more of the same in the following month for £40-19/-. In his diary, Lord Ossulstone notes the purchase of a set of brown horses for travelling (without quoting the price) on 10 May 1705. It is interesting to note that, seemingly, Charles Bennet changed from brown to black to bay over the years for his matching coach horses. Whether this was dictated by fashion and choice or merely availability is not known.

The agricultural activities at Dawley can be summarised in that the Earl had two waggons, five carts and a water cart, together with various implements such as three ploughs, four harrows, and threshing equipment. Cereal crops, beans, hay and straw were stored in the granaries over the stables and at the dog kennel (where, however, in 1722 no dogs appear to have been kept). Standing crops in early June 1722 comprised 17 acres of wheat, $17\frac{1}{2}$ acres of barley, and 5 acres of fetches. In the Park, the Earl's livestock comprised 61 sheep, 21 cattle (including 'one white bull with spots' and three white cows, which it is tempting to think might just possibly have been wild white cattle from Chillingham) (5), and 14 pigs. All these were valued at a total of £384-2s.6d. (Strangely, although deer as well as cattle are shown in the Park at Dawley in Jenner's plan of c.1721, no deer are mentioned in the inventory of 1722 - had they been sold, or was this artistic licence by Jenner or an omission by the compilers of the inventory ?) Listed under the heading 'The Poultry' are 87 cocks and hens, eight old geese, 31 young geese, 22 old turkeys, 44 young turkeys, six bantam cocks and hens, 33 pheasants, 27 chickens, four Spanish geese, and five peacocks and hens. The latter, it may be assumed, paraded around the gardens.

A footnote to this catalogue of the first Earl of Tankerville's wealth is the record of property taxes settled later in 1722. Window Tax, paid on 3 September amounted to 15/6d. Land Tax on Dawley House, paid on 13 November for the 3rd and 4th quarters of the year, was £29-12-9$\frac{1}{2}$d, and on 'Doiley's farm' for the same period £2-12-10$\frac{1}{2}$d. These payments should have given a reasonably accurate assessment of the size and value of the house and estate, but the odd amounts paid cannot, apparently, be reconciled with the flat rates of 30 shillings for Window Tax (30 or more windows) and a nominal 2 shillings in the £ for Land Tax. (6)

Servants at Dawley (to 1725). In his last will and testament, dated 22 July 1721, Charles Earl of Tankerville, made provision for only one servant, Daniel Baysallance, valet de chambre. However, in a codicil dated 16 April 1722, he increased Baysallance's annuity from £10- per annum to £20- and added bequests to most of his other servants. To Thomas Robertson, gentleman of horse, £50-, to Mary Ann Godin (status unspecified) £20-, and Mary Dodd, chambermaid, £10-. To all his other servants who had lived with him one whole year at the time of his decease, he gave a year's wages each.

A list of the Earl's servants (7) was compiled on 21 May 1722, together with their salaries. This was obviously important for all those concerned, in view of the

61

provisions in the will.   The list is given below.   As the date is that of the Earl's death, it may be assumed that it excludes servants who had been with the Earl for less than one year.

Mr John Barton, Chaplain	£	30.0.0
Mr Thomas Robertson, Gentleman of Horse		50.0.0
Mr Jn. Bayley, Secretary		30.0.0
Mr Daniel Baysallance, Valet de Chambre		26.0.0
Mr Alex Brown, Valet de Chambre		15.0.0
Mr Thomas Davis, Butler		15.0.0
Mr Robert Blinkham, Cook		35.0.0
Mr Jn. Chappell, Bayley (bailiff)		20.0.0
Mr Stephen Whitehead, Kitchen Gardener		20.0.0
Mr Andrew Mollet, Principal or Head Gardener		30.0.0
Mr Jn. Gotobed, Wood Gardener		30.0.0
Jn. Sharpe and his wife, Birdman		40.0.0
Richard Colley, Keeper		15.0.0
Jn. Russell, Carter		10.0.0
Mr Beldham, Charity Schoolmaster		20.0.0
Livery Servants		
George Wilkinson, Coachman		11.0.0
Curtis King, Postillion		6.0.0
Thomas Birch, Footman		8.0.0
Thomas Kirby, Footman		8.0.0
Richard Bates		8.0.0
Jn. Noble		8.0.0
Randal Catheral, Porter, London		16.0.0
Nicholas Bennet, Porter, Dawley		4.0.0
Thomas Floyd, My Lord's Boy		0.0.0
Women Servants		
Mrs Scholfield, Housekeeper		15.0.0
Mrs Jemby, Housekeeper, London		12.0.0
Mary Dodd, Chambermaid		7.0.0
Margaret Jenkins, Laundry Maid		6.0.0
Mary Druid, Housemaid		5.0.0
Elizabeth Bish, Housemaid		5.0.0
Mary Edwards, Housemaid		5.0.0
Eliz. Norman, Housemaid		5.0.0
Mary Stafford, Dairymaid		5.0.0
Mary Drapport, Kitchen Maid		6.0.0

The range of salaries presumably represents importance in the household together with, perhaps, length of service taken into account.   The Gentleman of Horse is the highest paid servant with the Porter at Dawley at the bottom, below even the female servants.   The Cook (male, as was customary at the time) ranks second, with such varied posts as Chaplain, Secretary, Head Gardener and Wood Gardener equal third, followed closely by the senior Valet de Chambre, Daniel Baysallance, who was highly regarded by the Earl.   Poor Thomas Floyd, 'My Lord's Boy', who was apparently paid nothing at all, must have been more or less a slave, although this is not to say that he was ill-treated.   Was he the one to whom the following enigmatic entry in Thomas Robertson's account book (8)   for 19 March 1718 refers ?   'Gave to Little Tom when he went into the Bagnio and for a Coach Here to him £1-1-0'.   Thomas Floyd may have been a negro.   It was fashionable to include at least one such in noble households of the time, and one of the Earl's paintings was described in the probate inventory as 'The late Earl of Tankerville and Lady with a black'.   'Robert a Black more of my Lord Ossulstone' was baptised at Harlington Church in 1708, and a predecessor, also probably at Dawley, 'Charles a Black more age about 17 years' was baptised in 1701 (9).   Two members of the skeleton staff of the Earl's London house, the Housekeeper and the Porter, are included in the list with the Dawley staff, although some of the latter would have accompanied the Earl when he went to stay in Town. (10)

The names of two further servants at Dawley are mentioned in the main inventory of 1722 - John Weedon and John Glanville. Both were housed in accommodation at the stables. Another document (of 1719) refers to Robert Peel, blacksmith, and Henry Hays, gardener. (11) No list of the servants at Dawley at a given time prior to 1722 is known to exist, although Thomas Robertson, Gentleman of Horse, compiled a chronological account of the names of over a hundred servants engaged between November 1716 and November 1720. Of these, only about a score were still at Dawley on 21 May 1722 when the Earl died and the list given above was drawn up. This seemingly high rate of turnover in employment would need a detailed investigation to be accounted for, death (see below) representing only a small proportion of the total. Earlier, the descriptions of some rooms in the inventories of 1713 and 1716 name some servants. Mrs Hobborn, 'Sr James' (possibly the chaplain?), Gander, Oliver, Mr Byslon, Mr Gordon and Will Whitehead (probably related to the kitchen gardener of 1722) are all mentioned in 1716. Mr Chappell and Mr Bayley, still serving in 1722, were also there in 1716; the latter also in 1713. The 1713 inventory includes the names of Mr Challoner and Mr Levett as well as Major Parsons who, as has been suggested, was probably a member of the Earl's family, or an old friend, and not a servant. Finally, the names of some of the Bennets' servants at Dawley between 1690 and 1723 have been recorded in the Parish registers because they were married or had their children baptised in Harlington Church, or were buried in the churchyard. These are: Alexander Green, butler (buried 1690); Margaret Fairchild, housekeeper (buried 1700); John Short, 'a huntsman' (presumably at Dawley - buried 1702); Nicholas Thorn, servant (son buried 1704) and in 1708 referred to as 'late gamekeeper of Ld Ossulston's' when his daughter was buried; also, a Nicholas Thorn, huntsman (at Dawley?) had daughters buried in 1714 and 1716; John Taylor, groom (buried 1705); Richard Holloway, servant (buried 1706); Mary and John Jambe, servants (twin sons and a daughter buried 1710); Elisabeth Ironside, housekeeper (buried 1711); Joan Hedges, servant (buried 1712); James Hatchett, footman (presumed at Dawley, buried 1713); Henry Brown, described as 'Ld. keeper' (presumed at Dawley, daughter baptised 1715); John Slayter, 'My Lords Keeper' (presumed at Dawley, daughter baptised 1717); Adam Stokel, servant (buried 1716); Richard Peel, 'smith at Dawley' (doubtless related to Robert Peel mentioned above, daughter baptised 1717); Thomas Roaf, servant (buried 1718); Richard and Hannah Day, servants (married 1720); Edward Wilson, groom, and Peter Booth, porter (both buried 1723).

As a footnote, the following report from a newspaper of 1725 may serve to highlight the Earls of Tankerville's concern for their servants, and their successor's apparent lack of it: 'When the late Viscount Bolingbroke took possession of Dawley, late the earl of Tankerville's, a gardener who had wrought 83 years in the grounds was, amongst others, discharged, being about 100 years of age. The Earl of Tankerville has ordered for him to be provided for'. (12)

CHAPTER 18

SALE TO HENRY ST JOHN, VISCOUNT BOLINGBROKE
(1678-1751)

The Earl of Tankerville's son and heir, Charles, who became the second Earl, did not inherit the full financial resources of his father, who had made separate provision in his Last Will and Testament for his younger children Bridget (Lady Lymington), Henry, Grey, Annabella (wife of William Pawlett Esq) and Mary (wife of William Willmer Esq) each to receive £8000 from the fee farms rents. Although Henry pre-deceased his father, the reduced income available to the second Earl may have influenced his decision to put Dawley up for sale. (1) (One cannot discount the possibility also that the Earl had a greater interest in his other estates at Uppark and Chillingham). In any event, Dawley was purchased by Henry St John, Viscount Bolingbroke, in 1725 for the sum of £22,200, the sale Indenture being dated 14 September. This transaction followed immediately after a nominal lease of Dawley for one year by the Earl of Tankerville to Rene Baudowin, merchant of London. (2) Although Rene Baudowin (also spelt Badouin, Baudouin, Bodewin, or Baudovin) was only involved with Dawley through this property deal, he deserves brief mention. A merchant of Lombard Street in the City, of French Protestant descent, he is described as being of high standing in the silk and wool trade. In 1698, however, he was impeached for having taken part in a silk smuggling combine and was fined £3000-: a considerable sum, apparently based on what he was judged able to pay. He married shortly after the trial, and died in 1728. He was buried in the City church of St Mary Aldermanbury, where a stone recorded his virtues. This church, badly damaged in World War II, was removed to Fulton, Missouri, USA (3) where Winston Churchill made a memorable speech in 1946.

Henry St John, Viscount Bolingbroke, was an important national figure, and although it is unnecessary here to describe his earlier life in detail (full accounts exist in the many published biographies) (4) any account of Dawley would be incomplete without at least an outline of his background, particularly because it was his political intrigues that led him to choose the rural retreat of Dawley as his home when he returned from exile in France.

Henry St John was born on 16 September 1678, according to Dickinson, one of his more recent biographers. (5) Dickinson also thinks it likely that he was born at Lydiard Tregoze, the family seat in Wiltshire, where his mother was buried on 2 October 1678, although he was later Christened at Battersea, the home of his paternal Grandparents.

Although it is usually claimed that he was educated at Eton and Oxford, Dickinson points out that there is little evidence to support this and his name is not recorded on any lists or registers of either place. Information about St John's early life does not become substantial until 1698 when he toured Europe, in the course of which he visited France, Switzerland and Italy before 1700. On his return to England he succeeded his father as the Member for the family parliamentary seat at Wootton Bassett, Wiltshire, for which he was elected in February 1701.

The aspect of his character that attracted most contemporary comment at that time was his flagrant debauchery, and he appeared to take a positive delight in displaying that he could live a life of pleasure while also excelling in public affairs. In May 1701 he married his first wife, Frances Winchcombe. Though it was a marriage of convenience, she was an attractive personality who remained faithful to him, even although he showed her little, if any, consideration. This aspect of his conduct invited the criticism, among others, of Queen Anne, with whom St John was anxious to curry favour.

Upon entering Parliament, St John's eloquence soon brought him to the front. He acted with the Tories, and after three busy years was made Secretary at

War in 1704. In 1708 he and his close colleague, Harley, left office, but in 1710 the two returned to power, St John being Secretary of State for Foreign Affairs. In 1712 he was created Viscount Bolingbroke, and in 1713 concluded the treaty of Utrecht, which was directly advantageous to England, although at the expense of her former allies.

Peace being restored, the succession to the British throne became a question of first importance. Bolingbroke was in communication with James, the Old Pretender, but his exact aims are still a matter of controversy. The evidence suggests that, although by no means a fervid Jacobite, he was prepared to see James crowned on Anne's death. Harley (now Earl of Oxford), from whom he was now parted, left office in July 1714 and Bolingbroke became chief minister. However, Bolingbroke's triumph was shortlived. On 1 August Queen Anne died and Bolingbroke's power was broken. In his own words 'The Earl of Oxford was removed on Tuesday; the Queen died on Sunday. What a world is this and how does Fortune banter us'. A negotiation with the Whigs proved futile and he was dismissed from office. The Tories' hopes that George I might employ them in a mixed ministry were wrecked upon the Hanoverians' exclusive associations with the Whigs and Oxford's determination to seek his own security at Bolingbroke's expense. For himself, Bolingbroke expected nothing, and even in Autumn 1714 was planning, after Parliament adjourned, to go abroad for treatment of a neglected disease. By March 1715 the ministry clearly intended Bolingbroke's impeachment and execution and, on the advice of the Duke of Marlborough, he fled to France. He did not at first join the Old Pretender and his claim may be true that he did so only when urged by his friends in England, who had become exasperated with the new government. By July 1715, however, the Old Pretender had appointed him his Secretary of State, and in the following month an act of attainder was passed against Bolingbroke in England.

In 1717, Bolingbroke, who had always neglected his wife, formed a liaison with the widow of the Marquis de Villette and, following his wife's death in November 1718, he resolved to marry her. In this marriage (in 1722) Bolingbroke proved happy, though perhaps not completely fulfilled. At the same time he bought La Source, a small estate near Orleans, and began biblical, philosophical and mathematical studies. In 1722, he complained to Lord Polworth that his pardon was delayed and was encouraged to apply to the English Ministers. In May 1723 he received his pardon, but the restoration of his peerage and estates still required the intervention of Parliament. He now worked secretly for the government, in both domestic and foreign affairs, but to the end Walpole resisted any concession to him. Finally, on a private mission to London, Lady Bolingbroke secured the King's approval by a gift of £11,000 to his (the King's) mistress, the Duchess of Kendal, and in 1725 an Act was passed to enable Bolingbroke to hold real estate but leaving him excluded from the House of Lords.

Bolingbroke was deeply upset by his exclusion from politics, which he believed was solely due to the influence of his bitter political enemy Sir Robert Walpole. In his usual way he tried to hide his disappointment by affecting to disdain political life and to renew his genuine interests in country life. Dawley, which he purchased in 1725, fitted well into his plans, it being a rural retreat but sufficiently close to the Capital for him to dabble in politics by visiting London 'to divert myself now and then with annoying fools and knaves for a month or two'. The choice of Dawley may have been influenced by, among others, his friend the Earl of Essex, lessee of Bolingbroke's London house in Golden Square, who was familiar with the estate through having rented part of it from the Earl of Tankerville. (6)

CHAPTER 19

DAWLEY - 'NEW MODELLD' FOR BOLINGBROKE

Bolingbroke decided, apparently with little delay, to enlarge the new mansion at Dawley completed only 4-5 years before, and engaged James Gibbs as his architect. Gibbs (1682 - 1754) was one of the leading architects of his day, with many public buildings, churches and houses to his credit. His most celebrated work is the church of St Martin in the Fields, then nearing completion. Because of its central location in London, this fine building became widely known and copied all over the world. The University Senate House in Cambridge by Gibbs was also in the course of construction in 1725, but the building with the greatest significance for Dawley was, with little doubt, Ditchley in Oxfordshire. This mansion designed by James Gibbs was started in about 1720 and was structurally completed, probably, in 1722, although the interior decoration was not finished until 1725.

The choice of James Gibbs by Bolingbroke as his architect may well have been through a recommendation by his friend Alexander Pope, who had himself consulted Gibbs (probably in 1719), and also possibly by Lord Bathurst. (1) Bolingbroke was also most likely influenced by the architect's Tory sympathies and his patronage by leading members of the Tory nobility (although Gibbs' high degree of professional skill also led to his employment by Whigs). In any event, the new and splendid mansion of Ditchley would have provided a tangible sample of the sort of house that Dawley might be turned into.

Ditchley, in 1725, would have been the best example of a country house built entirely to his own design for Gibbs to show to a prospective client. James Gibbs may well have shown the drawings to Bolingbroke, but the house itself, north of Oxford and not far from the Duke of Marlborough's palace at Blenheim, was only 60 miles from London and about 45 from Dawley. There is no direct evidence that Bolingbroke visited Ditchley, but he was, in fact, a distant kinsman of George Henry Lee, 2nd Earl of Lichfield (1691-1742) for whom Ditchley was built. This was through Sir John St John, 1st Baronet of Lydiard Tregoze, whose daughter, Anne - Bolingbroke's aunt, married Sir Francis Lee, 2nd Baronet. They were the 2nd Earl of Lichfield's grandparents. (2) Lichfield was, like Bolingbroke, a Tory (also a Catholic) and, like his father, the 1st Earl, who died in 1716, a firm Jacobite. Bolingbroke would have had more than one reason, therefore, for visiting Ditchley.

A minor point of interest linking James Gibbs with an architect probably involved earlier with Dawley is that Nicholas Dubois was a subscriber to Gibbs' 'Book of Architecture', published in 1728. (3) (John Jenner, the master bricklayer, and John Lock, the joiner, who both worked at Dawley in 1719 were, incidentally, also subscribers.)

The architectural evidence for Gibbs' work at Dawley is discussed below, but the only known written evidence is 'A short account of Mr James Gibbs' architecture', a manuscript volume now held by Sir John Soane's Museum. Additional notes were added to this volume, after it was first compiled in 1707, covering later works by the architect. An entry relating to Dawley is one of these additions and reads, in full, as follows:

'Lord Bolingbroke's seat called Dawley. He new modelld Dawley for
Lord Bolingbroke and made large additions to it. He made it a most
delightfull place, and laid out a great deal of money upon it. He used
to call it his Farm and indeed it was one of ye finest Farm-houses in
England, but his Lordship being obliged to go to France, sold it for a
great deal less money than it cost the building.'

Apart from this important passage in the manuscript account of Gibbs' works, and occasional written references by Bolingbroke's contemporaries, all the strongest evidence - both pictorial and written - for the layout and appearance of the house enlarged and embellished by James Gibbs for Bolingbroke dates from 1753 onwards. Therefore, the description that follows is a composite of all the available information on the house, and it has not been possible to say what, if any, material changes were made to it between its completion about 1728 and the time it was demolished.

There is no doubt whatsoever that Gibbs' design for the 'new modelling' of Dawley was carried out. The appearance and layout of the house can be traced through several sources, from which it is evident that the Earl of Tankerville's house, built between 1719 and 1721, had cross wings added to it at either end, thus creating an H-shaped plan. Considerable changes would have been made to the interior of the 'core' house, and it may have been refaced to match the new wings, but this cannot be inferred from the only known views of Bolingbroke's house, two rather indifferent engravings by F. Cary which appeared in the 'Gentleman's Magazine', August 1802 - some 20-30 years after the place had been demolished. (4) The accompanying letter was from a contributor whose initials were 'H.R.', wrote from Nottinghamshire, and claimed intimate acquaintance with the late Earl of Uxbridge, having 'spent many pleasant days at Dawley' but, unfortunately, is not further identified. The letter begins 'If you think the inclosed sketches of Dawley, (Plate II), built by the famous Lord Bolingbroke, of political memory, of which there is not now a vestige left, are worth a place in your entertaining Miscellany, they are very much at your service'. After quoting from the famous letter written by Pope which begins 'I now hold my pen for my Lord Bolingbroke ...' (this is given in full and discussed elsewhere in the present account), the writer continues later '.... the apartments were large and elegantly fitted up. It was built with brick, and the tops of the windows arched, which had not a good effect with the flat roof'. The letter ends 'Fig 1 is the west front, Fig 2 the south; they both looked into the garden'. What the engravings show is a two-storey house with a seven-bay centre block and a two-bay wing at either end. The ground floor windows are larger than those above. The points about brick construction (which is not apparent from the engravings) and the orientation of the house and garden are useful. The original sketches, from which the engravings were made, must have been drawn many years earlier. This was perhaps when the house was derelict before being demolished, apparently around the late 1770s (see below). The window openings certainly appear to be empty or boarded up, although no firm conclusion in this respect can be drawn from the rather crude engravings.

The second important piece of evidence for the layout of Gibbs' Dawley is the description, with dimensions, drawn up for the insurance policy issued by the Hand in Hand Fire Office and dated June 19, 1753. (5) This was 25 years after the house was completed, but it is not unreasonable to assume that the block plan was substantially unaltered during this time and also that the main internal layout remained the same, although the use of some rooms may well have changed. The owners of Dawley after Bolingbroke and up to 1753 are discussed later. The 1753 insurance policy describes the house in three parts - east front, centre and west front - each insured for £2000. The centre block was noted as being 78 ft x 41 ft, amounting to 3198 sq ft - remarkably close to the 1719 building estimate for Tankerville's house of approximately 3100 sq ft encompassed by 236 ft of modillion cornice. The east and west parts, or wings - those added by Gibbs - were each 95 ft x 28 ft 6in (2707½ sq ft), with smaller projections, which will be referred to later. The 1753 insurance policy describes, therefore, what must be a building with an H-shaped plan having a main frontage totalling 135 ft, with east and west facades of 95 ft. This layout fully agrees with that shown in the 1802 engravings.

The south front had an 11-bay arrangement of two windows wide in the south projection of the west wing; seven in the centre block (with its centre part, of 3 windows, brought forward slightly from the main wall face); and two windows wide in the south projection of the east wing. This layout is identical to that of Ditchley, built by James Gibbs just before Dawley, which has a frontage (measured from the ground floor plan in Gibbs' 'Book of Architecture') (6) of 139 feet, with east

67

and west facades each 92 feet wide. Ditchley has, of course, also an attic storey and was originally designed with a pitched roof although, as built, it has a flat roof. The contributor to the Gentleman's Magazine in 1802 said that the roof of Dawley was flat, but the accompanying illustrations show that the east wing, at any rate, had a pitched roof behind the parapet, although nothing can be seen of the roof in the centre block, so no very firm conclusions can be drawn from this somewhat unreliable source. The centre block of Ditchley is deeper than Dawley's was, and the projection of the end wings is less than that of Dawley. (The Ditchley wings project only one bay, compared with two at Dawley). Dawley may not have had the proportions that Gibbs would have adopted had he had a free hand, but the architect was obliged to provide the accommodation his client, Bolingbroke, required while under the constraint of incorporating an existing building. This evidently accounted for another important difference from Ditchley in that the main entrance was via the existing courtyard on the east side. The hall was, therefore, in the east wing. Dawley was very unusual in having its main entrance through one of the shorter frontages: very few other large houses of this period are known to share this feature. (Calke Abbey, Derbyshire, is one of the exceptions - only just - although this was a mediaeval house remodelled in the 18th century, work in which Gibbs was involved, incidentally). The windows on the south front at Dawley are shown in the 1802 engraving as segmental-headed (a shallow curved arch) unlike those at Ditchley. This, however, would not be a departure from Gibbs' known works - his Sudbrooke Park at Petersham, Surrey (c1728), referred to later, has segmental windows, and Senate House, Cambridge (built 1722-1730) has semi-circular arched heads to the windows on the upper storey. The west end of Dawley, shown in the other 1802 engraving of Gibbs' house, appears to have rectangular windows with the rusticated keystones featured at Ditchley and in many other designs by this architect. The centre of this (west) front is composed of a deep arched portico in antis (recessed instead of projecting) with twin clasped (Ionic ?) pilasters either side and surmounted by a plain triangular pediment. The arch as engraved appears to be a pointed (Gothic) one instead of the classical round Roman arch, but this may be an artist's or engraver's error. It seems unlikely that an architect of Gibbs' calibre who, moreover, had studied classical prototypes in Italy, would have used a Gothic arch in this way. (7) There appear to be few parallels in 18th century British architecture with a portico like this. Gibbs did, of course, feature a portico in antis at Sudbrooke Park, Petersham, although this had a flat architrave on four Corinthian columns. The nearest comparison with a high arch anything like that at Dawley that has been discovered is in The House of Dun, near Montrose in Scotland. Beyond the fact that the architect, William Adam (1689-1748) was, like Gibbs, a Scot and the patron, David Erskine, 13th Laird of Dun, shared Bolingbroke's Jacobite loyalties, no connection between the two houses has come to light. The guide book for The House of Dun (National Trust for Scotland, 1992) describes the portico in antis as a 'monumental niche'; 'an implied triumphal arch'. A possible, more accessible, source of inspiration for Gibbs might have been the east range of the King William building at Greenwich Royal Hospital, built by Vanburgh about 1720, which has an uneasy combination of a triangular pediment in a massive round arch. A somewhat similar feature is shown in some of Vanburgh's drawings for Eastbury Park, Dorset. This portico is discussed further in connection with Edward Stephenson's ownership.

No views survive of the east front of Dawley, which contained the main entrance, but it was probably generally similar to the west front. There is a later clue in a mason's account for repair work in 1770 (8) which refers to 'Portland Stone to arch and cornice over' for the forefront (east face) of the house. Over this entrance was the Latin motto, discussed below. Both the east and west entrances were approached by steps - the 1802 engraving shows a flight of five at the west end. The flight of steps at the 'forefront' (east) of the house was described as a 'Grand Flight' by the mason who repaired them in 1770 (9).

A simple cornice appears, from the 1802 engravings, to be carried round the whole building immediately above the upper windows, and the parapet of the walls has a brick or stone coping, although the two engravings are not consistent with each other on these points, so, again, no firm conclusion can be reached. Sudbrooke Park, however, which also has windows with segmental arches, has a fairly simple cornice above them and the parapet has flat coping stones, so it is not unlikely that the contemporary (but much larger) house at Dawley was given similar treatment. This question will be referred to again when discussing the Gibbs kitchen and dairy building at Dawley, which survived long enough to be recorded in reliable external detail.

There seems to have been no basement in the house as rebuilt by Gibbs. The 1753 insurance survey makes no mention of one and the 1802 engravings show no sign of basement windows, although both the east and west entrances, as mentioned, were approached by flights of steps. It seems, therefore, that although the original ground floor level was maintained, the basement of Tankerville's house had been filled in. Adequate provision was made for external service quarters near the house, connected to it in the case of the kitchen, by a covered passage, so basement rooms were apparently considered unnecessary in Gibbs' design. A plinth shown in the 1802 engravings is perhaps the last trace of the former basement.

Internally, according to the 1753 insurance survey, the 'grand stairs' were in the east wing and the 'back stairs' were in the west wing, so it would seem that the staircases must have been moved by Gibbs out of the existing house to leave more room in the centre block. Separate and unexplained dimensions of 27 ft x 14 ft 6 in (391½ sq ft) are quoted in conjunction with both east and west wings in the insurance survey, and these may possibly represent small projecting staircase blocks. If so, these would have been on the north side, as there is no sign of them in the 1802 engravings which show only the south and west fronts. For comparison, the staircases at Ditchley, which are in the centre block of the house, each occupy approximately 25 ft x 13 ft on the plan.

It is not possible to tell, as Bolingbroke's building accounts have not survived, how far the other internal arrangements of the Earl of Tankerville's new building were changed by Gibbs. However, in 1753 the centre block contained the ballroom, which may well have been an adaptation of the 'Great Parlour' and/or the 'Great Dining Room' of 1722. The door in the centre of the south front leading into the garden was, it appears, replaced with a window by Gibbs, according to the 1802 engraving. The other principal rooms on the ground floor of the central block were listed in 1753 as the drawing room, small parlour and a winter parlour. All, together with the ballroom, had marble chimney-pieces - a 'grand marble chimney-piece' in the case of the winter parlour. The latter was most probably in the north-east corner of the block, because winter parlours were frequently placed as near as possible to the kitchens, so that food served in them should be as hot as possible: the kitchens at Dawley in the 1753 description were somewhere on the north side of the courtyard. (On the other hand winter parlours were also, where possible, placed on the south side of the house to catch what sun there was). The winter parlour and the ballroom only are described as having 'clean deal floors' - softwood. The former is 'right wainscott' - panelled, for warmth, probably to the ceiling, in contrast to the ballroom which is only 'wainscott ½ way'. It is impossible to say how many of these features of 1753 remained from the Earl of Tankerville's house (although the marble chimney-pieces were most likely those referred to in the 1719 estimates) or even from Bolingbroke's time. The '6 chambers over' the ground floor of the central block are not described in further detail in the 1753 survey, but with a total area of 3198 square feet they might have comprised, say, two principal rooms of about 30 ft x 20 ft and several others of up to about 20 ft x 20 ft, although some may have been much smaller rooms for servants. The number of upper rooms in 1719 was apparently greater (and included two staircase heads), which suggests that Gibbs may have created fewer, but larger, chambers for Lord Bolingbroke.

Turning now to the west wing of Dawley, this is described in the 1753 insurance policy as containing the 'Venetian Room, wainscott and richly painted, fretwork ceiling and right wainscott floor, grand marble chimney-piece', and three other rooms downstairs, all of which had right wainscott floors. The walls of one of these rooms were fully panelled 'right wainscott', the other two simply described as 'wainscott'. The term 'right wainscott' probably distinguished oak from deal panelling or flooring.

The so-called Venetian Room with its 'fretwork' (decorated plaster) ceiling was highly likely to have been created by members of the group of 'Italian' plasterers ('stuccatores') who carried out many important commissions in both country and town houses in England during this period. They are known to have worked on other houses by Gibbs at about this time, including Ditchley and No 11 Henrietta Place, St Marylebone, London, a house forming part of a terrace designed by James Gibbs and built between about 1722 - 1725. This house was let to Gibbs himself, although he did not occupy it: the fireplace and ceiling from it are now in the Victoria and Albert Museum, London. The plasterwork of the ceiling of No 11 Henrietta Place is considered to be the work of Guiseppe Artari (1697 - 1769) and Giovanni Bagutti (active between 1685 and c1735), two of the 'Italian' stuccatores (the members of this group were, in fact, Swiss from the Italian-speaking part of their country). Artari, together with two other countrymen of his, Francesco Vassalli (c1700 - after 1763) and Francesca Leone Serena (1700 - after 1729) were brought by Gibbs to Ditchley, where the saloon they decorated still remains much as they completed it.

No direct evidence for the identity of the plasterers who worked at Dawley survives, or any pictures of their work there, but it is very likely indeed that Gibbs would have recommended to Bolingbroke Artari and/or other members of his group to carry out the plaster work on a 'Venetian' room in particular and elsewhere at Dawley. It is much more difficult to guess at the identity of the painter of the Venetian Room, although the ceiling paintings at No 11 Henrietta Place are attributed to Antonio Belluci of Treviso, who was working in England around 1725. The Venetian room may have been entered direct from the garden on the west side of the house through the arched portico referred to above.

The upper storey of the west wing contained, in 1753, three bed chambers and the Library. This was where Bolingbroke was likely often to have entertained Alexander Pope and his other literary friends. Sadly, no information on these rooms survives, except in the general description, from which it seems that they had marble chimney-pieces and were wainscotted.

Now looking at the east wing of Gibbs' Dawley, this contained the hall - probably centrally placed behind the main doorway, which, as suggested above, may be supposed to have been entered through a high portico in antis similar to that of the west end; dining parlour and summer parlour. Over the entrance, according to Oliver Goldsmith in his biography of Bolingbroke (10) was a motto in Latin embodying Bolingbroke's overt philosophy (and perhaps, to some, foreshadowing what was to be encountered inside) 'Satis beatus ruris honoribus', which can be roughly translated as 'Happy is he who is satisfied with the honours of the countryside'. Such inscriptions were not uncommon - witness Buckingham House, London (c1705 - now altered) and Easton Neston, Northants (1702 - 1711).

The hall is famous for Alexander Pope's account of it: '.... I overheard him [Bolingbroke] yesterday agree with a Painter for £200 to paint his country-hall with Trophies of Rakes, spades, prongs, &c and other ornaments merely to countenance his calling this place a Farm'. This was in a letter to Jonathan Swift dated 28 June 1728, and so provides evidence that the work at Dawley must then have been at an advanced stage. Goldsmith (11) states that the decoration of the hall was painted in black crayons only, so that at first view it brought to mind the figures often seen scratched with charcoal, or the smoke of a candle, upon the kitchen walls of farm houses. It, however, produced a most striking effect. Bolingbroke's choice of decoration is eulogised in some lines of a poem printed in 1731 -

'No gaudy colours deck the rural hall
Blank light and shade descriminate the wall .....',

and   'Here the proud trophies, and the spoils of war
Yield to the scythe, the harrow and the car .....' (12)

(This poem is quoted in full in the discussion of Bolingbroke at Dawley.)

    The form of decoration is also mentioned by Lady Luxborough (Bolingbroke's sister) in a letter dated 28 April 1748 to William Shenstone: 'When my brother Bolingbroke built Dawley, which he chose to call a 'Farm', he had his hall painted in Stone-colours, with all the implements of husbandry placed in the manner one sees or might see arms and trophies in some General's hall; and it had an effect that pleased everybody'. (Henrietta Luxborough, incidentally, did not like James Gibbs' architecture: she wrote to Shenstone (on 8 November 1749) 'I thank you for sending me Gibbs' book; which I will take care of, but never yet could admire his taste in Architecture. The monument for the late Duke of Newcastle gives a specimen of it; and even his genteelest things he disgraces commonly with some awkward ornament. His building at Cambridge I have seen, but never could like'). (13)

    This 'rustic' decoration of the hall was completed by 7 November 1728, when Pope mentions it again in a letter to Lord Bathurst. (14) It had not been changed in 1753, for the insurance survey carried out then prosaically confirms what Pope, Lady Luxborough and others wrote, as follows: 'Hall painted with implements of husbandry'. Examples of this chiaroscuro or grisaille work can be seen in the ceiling from Gibbs' No 11 Henrietta Place in the Victoria and Albert Museum, and at Blenheim Palace, where, however, the Duke of Marlborough's painted trophies are not rural but warlike, as was indeed appropriate for 'some General's hall'. A rough idea of the extent in relation to the cost of the painting at Dawley can perhaps be gained from the fact that Sir James Thornhill, who painted the great hall at Greenwich Hospital (1708-1727) received £6685 -, having asked £5- a yard for the ceiling and been paid £3- a yard, and £1- a yard for the walls. (15)

    The hall at Dawley had two 'grand Portland chimney-pieces' - these, perhaps, being felt somewhat more compatible with rustic simplicity than marble. The wall was of 'stuchoe' (stucco or, in this context, imitation stone) and it had a fretwork ceiling - decorated plaster. The hall was apparently the full height of the house, since a plasterer's account for repair work in 1770 refers to the '2-storey hall'. The plasterers also worked in the 'Long Room', the 'four post hall' (associated with the portico in the bill) and the 'two post hall', none of which have been identified with certainty, but will be discussed under Lord Paget's occupancy of Dawley. The absence of further details makes it impossible to decide what, if any, new decorative or structural features had been introduced between 1728 and the 1770's, when these repairs were carried out.

    The summer parlour and dining parlour had, like the hall, 'stucco' floors, and both had 'fretwork' ceilings. One or both of them (the 1753 survey is not clear on this point) had similar decoration on the walls. Also, one of the two parlours had a 'grand marble chimney-piece'. The dining room is described as 'white-panelled' by Hopkinson, on what authority is not given. (16)

    The staircase hall, containing the 'grand stairs Portland stone Iron rails and balusters' is described in the 1753 survey with the east wing but, as suggested earlier, the stairs may possibly have been in an annexe to it, perhaps at its north-west corner. It had a 'fretwork ceiling and sides'. 'Stucco ornaments to the grand staircase' feature in a plasterer's repair bill for 1770. (17)

    There were six chambers upstairs in the east wing: these were wainscotted, with marble chimney-pieces and had 'clean deal floors'.

    Some of the more important of the rooms described above were, possibly, ornamented as further described in the 1731 poem entitled 'Dawley Farm' -

> 'Young winged Cupids smiling guide the plough
> And peasants elegantly reap and sow' (18)

since rural decorative themes were not necessarily confined to the hall.

Before turning to the service buildings at Dawley, it is interesting to consider the general effect of the house. It must have had much of the appearance of Gibbs' Ditchley, but with the warmer feeling of brick instead of stone and lacking the attic storey. The rather austere lines of the south front may have recalled for Bolingbroke his house in France while in exile, the Chateau de la Source at Loiret, near Orleans (which is still in existence) (19) although no closer comparison can, it seems, be made. The porticos were grand features of Dawley lacking at Ditchley where, however, Gibbs had originally intended at least to provide a pediment on the entrance front.

The exact dates of the 'new modelling' of Dawley are not known. However, Bolingbroke's ownership of Dawley dated from 14 September 1725, and many of his letters are headed 'Dawley' from 1725 onwards, implying residence there, but in September 1726 Lord and Lady Bolingbroke were staying at Lord Berkeley's newly rebuilt house at Cranford, which Sherburn (editor of Pope's correspondence) suggests had been lent or briefly leased to Bolingbroke. (20) This would lead one to suppose that Dawley was then temporarily uninhabitable, presumably because the new building operations had been commenced. It would seem that building work was still in progress on 31 October 1727, judging from the following letter that Bolingbroke wrote to his half-sister '..... Lord Berkshire intends, I find to dine at my farm tomorrow with my brother. I am still at Cranford, but will receive them at Dawley the best I can .....'. (21) The 'rustic' paintings in the hall were completed by early November 1728, (22) so it can be assumed that most of the work in the house was also finished by that time.

CHAPTER 20

BOLINGBROKE'S DAWLEY -
THE COURTYARD AND SERVICE BUILDINGS

In his scheme for the 'new modelling' of Dawley, Gibbs included the service buildings in the courtyard. This would have been an important part of the overall plan, since the new entrance front of the house faced the Harlington-Hillingdon road, overlooking the courtyard. (The main approach to the house may, in fact, already have been intended to be from this direction, since gates on the road and an avenue leading to Tankerville's new house are shown on the estate plan of c1721).

First, the courtyard itself was modified from the rectangle shown on the 1721 plan into an octagon. This arrangement is first shown in Rocque's map of 1754, (1) but there is no reason to suppose that the change was not one of those carried out for Bolingbroke.

The 1753 insurance survey values the courtyard buildings separately from the house at a total of £2000-.

The two principal buildings on the north side of the courtyard listed in the survey are the 'house' containing laundry, pantry and dairy, which was 63 ft x 45 ft; and the combined bakehouse and slaughterhouse, a single-storey building which measured 47 ft x 24 ft.

On the south side of the courtyard was a stable block, 63 ft x 45 ft and a single-storey coach house with stable, 47 ft x 24 ft. There is reason to believe that the laundry cum pantry cum dairy building had a wind dial on its front (south) wall (one certainly existed there later), and the stable block had a turret clock which probably faced it in a corresponding position. (2)

It is a fair assumption that these four buildings of matching dimensions faced each other across the courtyard in a balanced arrangement. It is also tempting to believe that these buildings were a remodelling of the two large and two small buildings shown north and south of the courtyard in Jenner's estate plan of c1721. However, the 1753 survey describes both the stables on the one hand and the laundry, pantry and dairy building on the other as of '2 storeys and garretts', so if the pre-1721 buildings were used in this way they must, at the very least, have been reduced in height. A key to what Gibbs did do, in fact, lies in the building in the centre of the north side of the courtyard that still existed, converted into a dwelling house, up to the Spring of 1951 (3) when it was demolished. This building was shown in a watercolour in the early part of the 19th century and was photographed externally in the 20th. (4) A local man, Mr H O Meyers, writing in 1857 (5) said of Dawley 'The large house has been pulled down, but the laundry is still standing, and is a nice commodious house'. The identification of this recently surviving building with the laundry can be confirmed because the size, measured from the 25in Ordnance Survey plan, corresponded almost exactly with the 63 ft x 45 ft quoted for the laundry cum pantry and dairy in the 1753 insurance survey. There is, therefore, practically no reason to doubt that this house (described by the Director of the National Buildings Record in 1942 as 'a particularly interesting example of an early 18th century type, the detail has great distinction ....') (6) was built by James Gibbs as one of the service buildings. Some of its external features are found in other buildings by Gibbs, although the more elaborate forms of decoration should not be sought for, as this was, after all, designed originally only as a service building and not a nobleman's house. Sudbrooke Park (already mentioned) has similar rusticated brick corner quoins and recessed panels in the brick parapet which also has a stone coping. In addition the brick 'aprons' under the windows at Sudbrooke have a parallel in a similar feature under the wind dial of the Dawley laundry building. The main doorway in the Dawley house is similar to drawings in Gibbs' 'Book of Architecture', although doorways like this of classical design with Doric pilasters were common enough throughout the 18th century. More will be said of this building later.

Of the other service buildings in the courtyard area listed in 1753, not so much can be said, since none of them has survived into recent times and if any of them were shown in the estate plan of c1721, they cannot be identified. However, the 'Kitchen 1 storey', 53 ft x 29 ft, was to the north side of the courtyard and was most likely placed near the north-east corner of the house. There was, in fact, a passage 82 ft long and 11 ft wide which led from the kitchen to the house, presumably as a means of preventing the food from becoming too cold on its journey to the table, and a plasterer's account of 1770 mentions 'the long passage leading to servants hall and kitchen'. A servants hall is not mentioned in the 1753 survey and may have been located in the laundry, pantry and dairy building. This passage quite likely formed a link between the right hand side of the entrance front of the mansion and the north range of service buildings. If so, Gibbs would almost certainly have balanced the prospect of the buildings when approached from the courtyard by a passage or a wall of similar appearance on the left side. (This was a feature of Gibbs' design for Kelmarsh Hall, Northants.) (7) This may account for a structure of 37 ft x 1 ft 3 in listed in 1753 with the east block, for which no other explanation can be offered. There is no means of knowing the location of a staircase 15 ft x 11 ft (presumably an external stair distinct enough to be listed separately from the building it served); a 'cellar and rooms over and staircase' (40 ft x 17 ft and 15 ft x 11 ft respectively) and a brewhouse 34 ft square, all listed in the insurance survey. There were also five lean-to buildings, varying in area from 144 sq ft to 351 sq ft.

There is a contrast between the principal service buildings at Dawley and those at Ditchley, in that in the latter Gibbs concentrated on two large pavilions each about 82 ft x 55 ft rather than four main smaller buildings as at Dawley.

Other buildings at Dawley known to exist in Bolingbroke's time (although not mentioned in the 1753 insurance survey) are the menagerie, the lodge, the dovecote, and kennels.

Bolingbroke evidently owned a menagerie, because his letters reveal that he had an arrangement with the Earl of Essex (who was then away on the Continent) whereby he employed the Earl's stud groom, Harry Wankford, to look after it and to improve it. Wankford was apparently very capable, but Bolingbroke wrote to Essex in a letter dated April 26th 1733 that he considered getting rid of him because, although 'he can do that business better than any servant I ever had in the same post', without strict supervision he had 'fallen off in his diligence, or has learned to play ye Rogue this last year'. (8) In the 18th century, a menagerie was not necessarily a collection of wild animals, but might consist only of birds, such as Indian pheasants. Unfortunately no other evidence about Bolingbroke's collection has survived, so nothing can be said about what building, if any, housed it. The pond north of the kitchen garden shown in the c1721 plan has been discussed above. A field at Pinkwell in the Dawley estate was named 'The Menagerie' in the 1821 Harlington Inclosure Award (9) so Bolingbroke's beasts or birds may once have been located there.

A building described as 'The Lodge' is on Rocque's map of 1754, in the same position as a small irregular-shaped gabled building depicted on the Tankerville estate plan of c1721. This site was at the south-east corner of the estate, roughly where Bourne's Bridge is now. This was where the roads from Southall and Botwell to the east and from Harlington village in the south met at Dawley Park.

The dovecote with a pyramid roof, shown in Kyp's engraving and the c1721 estate plan, was still in existence in 1753, although not mentioned by the insurance surveyor. It survived, in fact, as late as about 1932 and will be referred to later. Finally Hassall (10) mentions, without quoting a source, that Bolingbroke built stables and kennels at Dawley. The stables referred to may be those on the

74

courtyard, but the location of the kennels is not known.   The Earl of Tankerville had dog kennels, apparently near 'Harlington Lane', that were used for storage of farm vehicles and implements, fodder, rat traps, bird baskets etc.   As there are two separate references to kennels in the 1722 inventory it is not clear if there was one or more buildings for them: either or both may well have been replaced by Bolingbroke, who was known to be an enthusiastic huntsman.   (In the Autumn of 1725, he was reported in several newspapers to be badly hurt by a fall while hunting, but Pope wrote to Swift soon afterwards that he 'had not the least harm by his fall'.) (11)

Very little evidence for the appearance of the Dawley estate during Bolingbroke's tenure is available, and it is felt more appropriate to discuss this question more fully in a later chapter in the context of the information given in Rocque's map of 1754.

CHAPTER 21

BOLINGBROKE'S LIFE AT DAWLEY

During his 10 years at Dawley, Bolingbroke, who was a man of many parts, engaged himself in country, literary and philosophical activities to counteract his exclusion from the political scene. Not that he had lost interest in politics - far from it - and although he could take no overt part he continued to exert a considerable political influence behind the scenes.

Nevertheless, his enforced political exile meant that he could devote more time to other matters and as part of the pretence of his disdain of politics he insisted that he was a country gentleman pursuing his interests from what he was pleased to call his farm at Dawley. To use his own allegory he lived at Dawley, 'in a hermitage where no man came but for the sake of the hermit, for here he found the insects which used to hum and buzz about him in the sunshine fled to men of more prosperous fortune and forsook him in the shade'. (1)   Bolingbroke adorned the house with mural paintings of rustic subjects, and over the entrance he placed the Latin inscription 'Satis beatus ruris honoribus' (2)   (Happy is he who is satisfied with the honours of the countryside). The decoration of Dawley has been discussed more fully in the description of the house as rebuilt for Bolingbroke.

A poem entitled 'Dawley Farm' in the first volume of the Gentleman's Magazine (3) gives us some glimpses of the place as it appeared in 1731 and also touches on Bolingbroke's banishment from politics:

> 'See emblem of himself his villa stand
> Politely finished elegantly grand
> Frugal of ornament but that the best
> And with all curious negligence expressed
> No gaudy colours deck the rural hall
>
> Blank light and shade discriminate the wall
> Where through the whole we see his loved design
> To please with mildness, without glaring shine
> Himself neglects what must all others charm
> And what he built a palace calls a farm
>
> Here the proud trophies and the spoils of war
> Yield to the scythe, the harrow and the car
> To whate'er implement the rustic wields
> Whate'er manures the gardens or the fields
>
> Here noble St John in his sweet recess
> Sees on the figured wall the stacks of corn
> With beauty more than theirs the room adorn
> Young winged Cupids smiling guide the plow
> And peasants elegantly reap and sow.
>
> O Britain! but 'tis past. O lost to fame
> The wondrous man, thy glory and thy shame
> Conversing with the mighty minds of old
> Names like his own in time's bright lists enrolled
> Here splendidly obscure, delighted lives
> And only for his wretched country grieves.'

Stephen Switzer, a leading writer on gardening, as well as being a practical commercial gardener, referred to Dawley, in a publication of about 1730, as a 'ferme ornee'. (4)   This may have been merely to support his theories, rather than recording reality, because there is evidence from several contemporary comments that Bolingbroke was genuinely concerned with the running of his estate, farming as well as improvement of the gardens, although politics were always his chief underlying interest. He often discussed gardening at length with Alexander Pope (who had not the slightest care for farming but whose garden at Twickenham was an absorbing interest) and is known to have invited a mutual friend, Charles Bridgeman (1680-1738), the garden designer, to Dawley. Pope wrote to Bridgeman (from Dawley) 'My Lord Bolingbroke received yours, and shall be glad to see you at your conveniency'. This letter, although undated, seems to have been written in the Autumn of 1725, the year in which Bolingbroke bought Dawley. (5) Bridgeman had worked in conjunction with James Gibbs at other houses, so it would be logical to assume that he might be employed to work with the architect at Dawley. (He was one of many subscribers to Gibbs' 'A Book of Architecture' published in 1728). This said, although Bridgeman was one of those who began to move away from the strict formality of 17th and early 18th century gardens, there is little evidence, as late as 1754 from Rocque's map, of the landscape type of garden, characterised by the work of Lancelot ('Capability') Brown (1716-1783). Some indication that the gardens were changed by stages lies in the fact that in the Spring of 1729 Bolingbroke had some yew hedges removed and a mount, that he considered an eyesore, levelled. (6) The location of this mount is not known. The one in the Lanthorn Garden would, seemingly, have been too far from the house to be regarded as an obvious eyesore, whereas a feature shown in Jenner's plan directly in line with the centre of the south front of Bolingbroke's house, if it was a mount would certainly have obstructed the view. On 1 October (O.S.) 1732 Bolingbroke wrote from Dawley to the Earl of Essex in Turin asking the Earl to remind Monsieur Villette (a kinsman of Bolingbroke's wife, also in Turin) of the seeds that had been promised him, and could he have them by the end of January ? Finally, some further evidence of his interest in garden features is that there exists a design by James Gibbs of a 'Bridge for Lord Bolingbroke'. (7) The drawing is undated, but the bridge, of brickwork and stone, was presumably intended to embellish the grounds at Dawley. It does not appear to be shown on Rocque's map and it is not known if the bridge was ever built or, if it was, where. There is only one insignificant stream (the Frogsditch) at Dawley, so the bridge in question was almost certainly intended for an ornamental pond or canal. It was apparently designed for a site near the house, though, since the drawing is endorsed 'Level of ye Bridge 14 ft above the door of ye house'. Was it intended to replace the mount ?

Bolingbroke's hunting has already been mentioned in connection with the dog kennels at Dawley.

Apart from his activities as a country gentleman, Bolingbroke was a cultivated man with an active interest in literature and philosophy. He had met the French philosopher Voltaire while in France and when the latter came to England in 1726 he was a guest at Dawley during that Summer and almost certainly on other occasions in the two years he remained here. (8) In the field of literature, Alexander Pope was closely attached to Bolingbroke, who he called 'my Guide, Philosopher, and Friend' (9), and was his most staunch supporter. Living only seven miles away at Twickenham, Pope was often at Dawley and his correspondence abounds with references to it. On one occasion the poet sustained an accident that was almost fatal when returning to Twickenham from Dawley early in September 1726. Dr John Arbuthnot, a member of the circle, wrote to Swift on 20 September, as follows, 'Mr Pope has been in hazard of life by drowning. Coming late, two weeks ago, from Lord Bolingbroke's, in his coach and six, a bridge on a little river being broke down, they were obliged to go through the water, which was not too high, but the coach was overturned in it; and the glass being up, which he could not break nor get down, he was very near drowned; for the footman was stuck in the mud, and could hardly come in time to his assistance'. (The coach was Bolingbroke's; the servant (one of Bolingbroke's) who pulled Pope out was one Phil Hanaus.) (10) Fortunately, Pope had only a cut on the hand and, although he lost a lot of blood, suffered no more serious harm. (11) Voltaire was staying with Bolingbroke at this time, and sent a letter of sympathy to Pope. (12)

Bolingbroke also kept up a lifelong correspondence with Jonathan Swift; Maxwell in 'Highwayman's Heath' (13) states that the manuscript of 'Gulliver's Travels' was read aloud before its publication by Swift to an audience at Dawley which included Bolingbroke, Pope and Gay (the composer of 'The Beggar's Opera'). Although Maxwell does not give the source for his statement, Swift was at Dawley and at Twickenham (with Pope) in the Spring and Summer of 1726 and had with him the manuscript of 'Gulliver's Travels', which was first published anonymously. (14) A reading from the manuscript at Dawley, and discussion of it, seems, therefore, by no means unlikely.

Through the influence of Dean Swift, Bolingbroke appointed Dr Joseph Trapp (1679 - 1747) as his chaplain and as Rector of Harlington in 1732. (Since 1670 or earlier the owner of Dawley House had had a pew in Harlington Church.) (15) This clergyman (whom Swift referred to once as 'your parson, Slap, Scrap, Flap (what d'ye call him), Trap') was the first Professor of Poetry at Oxford and the author of several religious tracts. His eldest son, who died as an infant, was named Henry after Bolingbroke, who was his godfather. Joseph Trapp died at Harlington on 22 November 1747 and is buried in the church there. (16)

Bolingbroke was often a visitor to the Earl of Essex' house at Cassiobury near Watford, and to his near neighbour at Cranford, Lord Berkeley, whose house had only recently been rebuilt (c1722). (17) As mentioned earlier it seems that Bolingbroke stayed at Cranford at times during the rebuilding of Dawley, probably to avoid the worst of the disruption caused by the workmen, but at the same time to be near at hand to keep an eye on the progress of the work.

Among former politicians, one of Bolingbroke's closest friends was Sir William Wyndham, once Secretary at War and Chancellor of the Exchequer. St John not infrequently visited Wyndham at his home at Orchard Wyndham in Somerset and Wyndham, in turn, was entertained at Dawley. Indeed, Wyndham married his second wife, Maria Catharina, widow of the Marquess of Blandford, at Harlington church by 'licence extraordinary' on 1 June 1734. (18)

Other well known people to visit Dawley included Oliver Goldsmith and John Dryden. Thus during Bolingbroke's ownership of Dawley it became one of the most celebrated houses in England, both on account of its owner and of the many famous visitors he entertained there.

A brief account of Bolingbroke after he left Dawley follows later.

CHAPTER 22

BOLINGBROKE'S SALE OF DAWLEY
AND HIS LAST YEARS

Lady Bolingbroke went for a long visit to France in the Spring of 1734.   By 1735, Bolingbroke had seriously compromised himself by accepting money from the French authorities to finance his attacks on the British Government.   He had been completely outmanoeuvred by Walpole and decided to join his wife in France.   He let Dawley to the Duke of Norfolk (1) early in 1735 and departed for France on 5 June of that year. (2)

The Duke's tenancy appears to have extended to at least 1738, because Lady Bolingbroke, writing from France to Isabella, Countess of Denbigh, on 15 May 1738, (3) mentioned that the Duchess of Norfolk had left Dawley a year ago, although she (the Duchess) had evidently returned there recently.

As early as the beginning of 1736, however, Bolingbroke had already made up his mind to sell Dawley for, writing to Sir William Wyndham from Chantelou on 5 January, he says (4) 'Let me depend on you and Bathurst for enabling me to live like a Cosmopolite for the rest of my days.   For this purpose you must dispose of Dawley for me.   Were my father likely to dye, this measure would be prudent, and since he is likely to live it is necessary.   To what purpose should I keep an expensive retreat where in all probability I should never retire'.

Wyndham and Bathurst were soon in negotiation with Judge Denton for the sale of Dawley (5) but nothing came of this.   Likely purchasers evidently were few - despite Bolingbroke, through increasing desperation, reducing his price from £26,000 to £25,000, and then to £23,000, or £20,000 down and £1000 per annum until his own death, or the death of his father. (6)   Lady Bolingbroke wrote to Lady Denbigh on 22 March 1738 saying that no buyers had presented themselves.

Because of the lack of success of his friends and his agents, Bolingbroke decided to return to England to promote the sale of Dawley himself.   He evidently arrived about the end of June 1738, as Pope was expecting him soon when he wrote to Hill on 20 June. (7)   Bolingbroke stayed with various friends, including five months (8) with Pope at Twickenham, from where the latter wrote on 31 July to Hugh Bethel (9) suggesting that the sale of Dawley should not take more than a month and that three 'treaties' had been on foot for some time.   One prospective purchaser, of whom Pope formed a low opinion, was Joshua Vanneck, a rich London merchant.   Pope wrote to the Earl of Orrery on 19 October 1738 (10) as follows:

'It [Dawley] cost him not twelve years ago near £25,000 and will be
sold for £5000; The Furniture, (perhaps the compleatest any where in a
private house) for which an Upholsterer in my hearing offrd 3000, to
take down & make money of, he will part with at that price where it is
ready put up; And the Land by measurement, at the Rent it is
now let at & Tenanted.   There is an Advowson of 300 a year & a
Royalty, which last is not to be valued nor the Timber.   I am thus
particular to your Lordship because after I mention'd the Thing in
general at your house, I heard you had some thoughts of buying a
large one, & had even your eye on this.   I wish I had known as much
then, & I think verily I could have brought You to agree, had it been my
good fortune to have seen you together.   I knew then & do now, that
Such a Successor to his Labors would have been in some degree a
Pleasure to Him, at least it would be more a Comfort to see any English
Nobleman of any worth there, than some Child of Dirt, or
Corruption; at best, some Money-headed & Mony-hearted Citizen:
Such an one as Van Eck has prov'd himself to be, who has gone off,
(after the most open & Gentlemanly Usage in the world on my Lords

side,) in the most paltry manner imaginable. He suffered his Wife & him to live a fortnight in the place, to Examine the Wholsomness & Dryness of the House, take opinions of the Soil, & converse with the Farmers, &c. The Upshot proves 'twas a mere Contest between Vanity & Avarice, & the Mean hope my Lord was so prest as to sell for little or nothing.'

Pope again expressed his feelings when writing to Lord Bathurst (11) on 23 November 1738 (12):

'Another reason [for writing then] was, my desire to satisfy your question about the affair of Dawley, which after many offers, is at last quite broke off, I think rather on the part of my Lord than of Vanneck, for he has been piqued so much at their dirty way of dabbling, rather than dealing, about it, that though the last offer came within £2000 he will hear no more of them. The total was, that Vanneck expected the lands for 4s. per acre less than the tenants actually pay, the house for as little as the materials pulled down will bring, the furniture for £1000 less than is offered by an upholsterer, the gardens and timber for nothing. My Lord has sent for Burward (13) to set the rents of what is yet unlet, and I believe will find a difference of near £2000 value in the whole, above what he himself first computed, provided he will have patience to sell part of the lands separately, and improve the rest, and let the house stand awhile the chance of a separate bargain'. (14)

Again, Pope writing about Bolingbroke and Dawley, this time to the Earl of Burlington, on 19 December 1738 (15):

'He has found, that a Great House in this Nation is like a Great Genius, too good for the Folks about it; They are as little worthy of the one, as the other. You will therefore find him still here ....'.

However, Bolingbroke was either lucky, or had pressed his own interests harder than had his friends and agents. Pope wrote to Ralph Allen on 17 April 1739 (16) 'I am now alone and left to myself. My Lord Bolingbroke executed his Deeds for the Sale of Dawley on Friday [13 April 1739] and set sail the next day for France from Greenwich'; and Pope to Swift (on 17 May 1739) 'He has sold Dawley for £26,000, much to his own Satisfaction'. (17)

Finally, the last years of the most outstanding owner of Dawley. Henry St John, Viscount Bolingbroke, then had no further connection with Dawley and decided to live, once again, permanently in France. He paid several visits to England, however, mainly to settle his financial affairs and to keep in contact with his friends. Then his father died in 1742 and Bolingbroke inherited the family's manor of Battersea, although the family seat at Lydiard Tregoze and his father's title passed to his younger half-brother. Returning to England in 1744, Bolingbroke lived at Battersea until his death on 12 December 1751 at the age of 73. He was interred with his wife in Battersea church. The present church was built after his death, but the monument to Lord and Lady Bolingbroke in the old church was re-erected in the new building. (18)

CHAPTER 23

GOVERNOR STEPHENSON & ABRAHAM HUME

The new owner of Dawley was Edward Stephenson, recently retired from the Honourable East India Company. He was a complete contrast with his predecessor, although he may have shared some of Bolingbroke's political beliefs.

Stephenson was born in Keswick, Cumberland in 1691. In November 1708 he was elected as a Writer in the service of the East India Company (1). This was probably due to the influence of his uncle, Jonathan Winder, who had not long before retired as Chairman of the Company's united council. He arrived in Calcutta early in 1710 and soon rose steadily in the Company's service, so that in 1715 he was chosen to accompany John Surnam, a senior Company official, on an embassy to the court of the Mogul (or Mughal) emperor in Delhi to try and obtain territorial and commercial privileges for the English traders. With patience and tact, Surnam and Stephenson eventually succeeded in obtaining valuable concessions, which were an important landmark in English fortunes in India. The Mughal empire was already in a state of decline, following the death of Aurangzeb's son, Bahadur Shah, in 1712, to be succeeded by a series of weak rulers, but this does not diminish the importance of the mission in which Stephenson took part. He returned to Calcutta at the end of 1717 and was then made chief of the Company's trading post at Balasore, near the coast of the Bay of Bengal south-west of Calcutta, and in 1718 was put in charge of the post at Patna. By 1728 he was described as the Honourable Edward Stephenson Esq, Chief of Council at Cossimbazar (now known as Kazimbazar, a place on the river Bhagirathi, about 110 miles north of Calcutta) which was the chief English agency in Bengal. This was a great centre of the silk trade in the 17th and 18th centuries, and the seat of French and Dutch, as well as English, factories, or trading posts. Among Stephenson's duties was the responsibility for sending bales of raw silk down to Fort William (Calcutta) under the armed guard of European soldiers and peons (native soldiers) of the East India Company.

On 23 August 1728, Henry Frankland, President and Governor of Bengal, died. Frankland's appointment had dated from 2 February 1725, and his successor, John Deane, had already been appointed, on 14 February 1728, but had not yet arrived in Calcutta from England to take over. Deane was expected to arrive at any time, but the voyage normally took anything from six to nine months. (2) Accordingly, Edward Stephenson, who was then next in succession on the Council, was asked to act as Governor, and arrived at Fort William (Calcutta) from Cossimbazar at 9 o'clock on the morning of Tuesday, 17 September 1728. The Commission (as Governor) and the keys of Fort William were handed to him. Stephenson's time of glory was very short-lived, however, because the ship carrying John Deane arrived at Fort William at 8 pm on 18 September. Deane produced the Honourable East India Company's Commission appointing him President and Governor of all their affairs in Bengal. The Commission was read out in the Consultation Room in Fort William in the presence of all the Company's covenanted servants, and the keys of the Fort were then delivered to John Deane by Edward Stephenson. This very short tenure of the highest office in Bengal did not prevent Stephenson commonly being referred to in later life as 'Governor Stephenson'. (3) Little else is known about Stephenson's career in India (4). He continued as the head of the Company's affairs at Cossimbazar until the end of 1729, when he resigned and returned to England in the following year.

Edward Stephenson had become a very wealthy man as the result of his twenty years in India - an experience he was fortunate to survive, since very few of his countrymen managed to avoid the diseases and other dangers that caused the deaths of so many Europeans. The East India Company's ledgers record that between 1730 and 1741 he sold his stocks in the Company, the proceeds of which he invested widely in property in England. He had a house built in his birthplace of

Keswick which was, it has been claimed, the largest in that town (5); Bardfield Lodge, Great Bardfield, Essex, together with several adjacent properties, was acquired by 1732 (6), the year in which he bought the manor and Abbey of Holme Cultram in Cumberland (7). In (or before) 1734 and up to 1738 his London address was in Bedford Row; later, he lived in Queen Square, where he owned several houses, including that occupied by the girls' boarding school run by his sister-in-law and nieces, known informally as 'the ladies Eton'. (8) The purchase of Dawley came next. Then (jumping ahead in the story for the moment) in 1741 Stonegarthside Hall, in the very north of Cumberland, near the Scottish border, was conveyed to Edward Stephenson (which he sold in 1761) (9); and in about 1748 he obtained through a law suit Scaleby Castle, (10) also in Cumberland, from Richard Gilpin, who owed him £7000.

In 1734 Edward Stephenson contested the Parliamentary constituency of Sudbury, Suffolk (about 20 miles from his estate at Great Bardfield, Essex), voting against the Administration. He held this seat until 1741 and did not stand again, but was appointed sheriff of Essex, 1742-1744. (11)

Stephenson signed the purchase documents for Dawley in April 1739 and presumably moved in soon afterwards. In any event, it was as the owner of Dawley that Stephenson married, in the parish church of Harlington, Anne Jennings (of the parish of St George's, Bloomsbury) on 30 April 1741. (12) She was the daughter of William Jennings, an East India Company servant, of Fort St George, Madras. (13) In the following year, one Edward Stevenson Esq, was appointed an additional trustee of the Tyburn Turnpike Trust, covering the Oxford road between Tyburn and Uxbridge. This post he occupied with members of local land-owning families, such as Iremonger, Blencowe and Mills, so despite the different spelling it may be assumed that this trustee was the owner of Dawley. The Minute books of the Trust's Board and Committee reports give no indication that Edward Stevenson or Stephenson attended any of their meetings, however. (14) Anne Stephenson died on 24 February 1744 and was buried at Harlington on 7 March. (15) She was simply described as 'Mrs Stevenson, wife of Edward, the Governor' in the Gentleman's Magazine obituary.

During the early part of his tenure of Dawley, Stephenson extended the area of the estate by various land purchases, but the death of his wife after less than three years there may have caused him to lose interest in the house. In 1748 he sold the advowson of Harlington Rectory (16) and leased some of his land to a local farmer. The terms of agreement between him ('Edward Stephenson of Queen Square') and the farmer, John Dorrell of Gould's Green, dated 17 May 1748, refers to 'those closes or parcels of ground situate and lying in the parish of Harlington in the said County of Middlesex being parcel of Dawley Park (that is to say) one close called the Long Walk another field called 12 acres, another field called the 7 acres, another field called the old apple orchard and cherry orchard, another field called the paddock, one other field called the 12 acres another field called the 9 acres'. (17) This land totalled 81½ acres, according to a later Tithe computation. (18) The fact that Stephenson was leasing out all or part of the Long Walk, one of the principal avenues leading from the house, for agricultural use is rather surprising and seems to be indicative of his decreasing interest in Dawley as a residence by that time. However, on 13 May 1752, one Catherine Stephenson was interred at Harlington church. (19) The fact that she was buried in linen, on payment of the appropriate fine, shows that she was a woman of means and indicates that, from her name, she was probably related to Edward Stephenson and was presumably staying with him at Dawley at the time of her death. Although Stephenson bought 12 acres of land in Harlington on 25 June 1753 (20), in the same year he let Dawley House to Abraham Hume, who belonged to a branch of the Berwickshire family of that name settled in England. Hume soon afterwards started negotiations, ultimately unsuccessful, for the purchase of the estate.

It is not known what Abraham Hume's intentions were at the time he took on the lease of Dawley house and estate from Edward Stephenson in 1753, but he actually lived there, so it was more than a financial investment, and it may well be that his aim, right from the start, was to negotiate the outright purchase of the property. On 19 June 1753, Hume took out a fire insurance policy with the Hand-in-Hand Fire Office, in his own name, on Dawley house and outbuildings for a total cover of £8000- (this was split as to £2000- for the east block of the house, £2000- for the centre, and £2000- for the west part, with a further £2000- for the outbuildings). The fire policy, the four parts of which are numbered 74224, 74225, 74226 and 74227, gives descriptions of the rooms of the house (still described as 'Dawley Farm') and the outbuildings, together with dimensions. It was renewed periodically and both the ledger entry and copies of the policy have survived. (21) As a vital piece of written evidence for the appearance and layout of Dawley, it has already been referred to here, and will be quoted subsequently. Hume also laid out several 'considerable' sums of money, later estimated at a total of £1000-, in repairs to the house, outbuildings, and other premises on the estate, and in 1754 purchased a parcel of land adjoining the estate, which he subsequently valued at £1035-. (22) At some stage, Edward Stephenson had evidently agreed to sell Abraham Hume the Dawley estate for £25000-, but subsequently changed his mind, it seems, since Hume commenced a suit in the Court of Chancery against Stephenson for performance of his contract. Whether or not the Earl of Uxbridge persuaded Stephenson to renege on the contract has not been established. The fact is, however, that Hume withdrew voluntarily from the contract to purchase Dawley in 1755 in favour of the Earl of Uxbridge after acceptance by the Earl of an agreement imposing rigorous financial conditions to Hume's advantage. (23)

After this, Abraham Hume ceased to be concerned directly with Dawley, although the fire insurance policy was not rendered by him until 12 June 1760, (24) and he made a loan to the Earl's successor at Dawley, Lord Paget, around 1770, possibly to pay for repairs. (25) For the record, Hume was left the manor of Wormley Bury, Hertfordshire, by his elder brother in 1765. He was created a baronet in 1769 and died in 1772. (26)

As for Edward Stephenson, after he sold Dawley (which probably meant little to him by then) he continued to live on his other estates, such as Bardfield Lodge in Essex (he is on record as still being there in 1765); probably also at times in his house in Keswick or his other Cumberland properties; and in his house at 29 Queen Square, where he died on 7 September 1768. (27) He was buried at his birthplace of Keswick, in Crosthwaite parish church, where there is a memorial slab to his memory set in the floor in front of the altar. (28) It appears that his considerable fortune may have been left to his nephew, another Edward Stephenson, who also lived in Queen Square and who died insane in 1782. (29)

The fact that 'nabobs' - rich, retired servants of the East India Company - sometimes used Indian architectural features in building or rebuilding their country seats towards the end of the 18th century inevitably raises the question as to whether Governor Stephenson did so at Dawley in the 1740's. The only surviving piece of evidence that might - just might - suggest an exotic alteration to Dawley is the high arched portico at the west end of the house, shown in the poorly drawn engraving reproduced in The Gentleman's Magazine of August 1802. (30) This drawing appears to depict a pointed arch, sprung from twin engaged columns either side and surmounted by a triangular pediment. High, arched entrances to 18th century country houses are rare, and this example (even if the arch is wrongly drawn as pointed, rather than classic Roman) cannot convincingly be related to work elsewhere by James Gibbs, the architect responsible for the alterations to Dawley, including the addition of both east and west wings. (31) On the other hand, the Mughal architecture of India has many examples of high pointed arches in gateways to forts, mosque enclosures and entrances to prayer halls or tombs. These arches do not normally spring from columns. However, there is at least one instance, in the Alai Darwaza gate in the Qutb mosque in Delhi, where the Muslim architects imitated the columns used in Hindu architecture. (32) During the journey between Calcutta and the Mughal court at Delhi in 1715-1717, Edward Stephenson's party would have followed the Ganges and its upper tributary, the

Jumna, and Stephenson must have seen many of the outstanding buildings of the Mughal dynasty in Agra and in Delhi itself. He can hardly have failed to see such superlative edifices as the Jami Masjid mosque in Delhi and the Taj Mahal at Agra, which was completed little over fifty years earlier, and on his retirement in England may well have wished to be reminded of Indian architecture through alterations to his house at Dawley. If Stephenson did endeavour to imitate a Mughal arch there, any anomalies, such as the triangular pediment, might well be accounted for in a local builder attempting to carry out instructions for work well outside his knowledge or understanding. The absence of any distinctive Indian decoration on the arch at the west end of Dawley in the 1802 engraving could be accounted for by changes made by subsequent owners, or decay. Prominent houses with Indian architectural features are, for example, Daylesford and Sezincote - both in Gloucestershire. The first was built in 1787 for Warren Hastings and has an onion-shaped dome. Sezincote, built about 1805 for Sir Charles Cockerell, who had made a fortune in the East India Company's service, is a full-blooded affair in which all the external features were inspired by Mughal architecture, including the high arched entrance. It was designed by Sir Charles' architect brother, who had also done the drawings for Daylesford. (33) The truth may never be known, but it is an interesting thought that Edward Stephenson might just possibly have anticipated features of these Gloucestershire houses by upwards of forty years.

84

CHAPTER 24

EVOLUTION OF THE DAWLEY ESTATE TO 1754 -
ROCQUE'S MAP

Rocque's map of Middlesex is our best source of information on the development of the Dawley estate from the time it was shown in Jenner's plan of c1721 through the thirty years or so when it was owned, successively, by Lord Bolingbroke and Edward Stephenson. Published in 1754, Rocque probably carried out his survey in the last years of Stephenson's tenure. The map, although only drawn to a scale of 2 inches to one mile, is surprisingly detailed in the information it gives on Dawley and, as far as can be ascertained from other sources, is reasonably accurate.

To start with, the mansion rebuilt by James Gibbs for Bolingbroke is shown simplified as a rectangle at the west side of an octagonal courtyard (with a circular feature in the centre - perhaps the original ornamental pond) and is linked by walls to service buildings on its north and south sides. Only one service building is shown at each side, although we know from the insurance description of 1753 that there were two major buildings on the north of the courtyard and two on the south - but the small scale of the map excuses this simplification. The old (17th century) mansion is not shown and, as suggested above, this had probably been demolished some time after about 1728. Also missing are the extensive formal gardens shown by Jenner south of the house, and these have been largely replaced by a square plantation of trees, although from the shape shown on Rocque's map it seems possible that the old kitchen garden may have been retained.

A new wall (rectangular in plan) is shown running north from the west end of the house and enclosing the service building north of the courtyard, to create a new enclosure north of the house. This wall will be referred to later.

A rectangular grassed area appears to have been created between the courtyard and the public road, from which a carriage way bisecting it leads to the east front of the house. (On the Tithe map of 1839 this area is named 'Bowling Green Close' - a name which, by a somewhat illogical back formation from the French ('boulingrin') had come to mean any sunken grassed area in a garden). The tree avenue running north from the house with single lines of trees (1) is unaltered but is now matched by a similar avenue to the south, terminating at the estate boundary, although the canal that used to be in this area and the radiating avenues are not shown by Rocque. The elaborate formal gardens with a mount and various water features that ran west from the house no longer exist and appear to have been replaced by a simple avenue. A vista to the west has therefore been created in direct line with the west front of the mansion. This new wide avenue of two lines of four trees each is connected by an angular plantation (step-shaped in plan) with the south-west end of the north tree avenue and by a similar plantation to the north-west end of the south tree avenue. West of the house, and nearer to it, is a new (since c1721, that is) layout of rectangular parterres, ponds and/or lawns - ten in all - in line with the avenues running north and south with, at their centre, an apsidal-shaped wall or possibly line of bushes. This might represent the edge of a raised terrace overlooking the east-west avenue.

The new layout of gardens and avenues as shown by Rocque relates logically to the house remodelled for Lord Bolingbroke by James Gibbs, just as the old formal gardens had been orientated on the old mansion of c1672. How the house and service buildings reached the state shown in 1754 can be confirmed from other sources, but exactly when, and by whom, the gardens had been altered, quite drastically, is a matter for conjecture.

Bolingbroke's interest in gardens, and his mutual friendship with Alexander Pope and Charles Bridgeman, the garden designer who had worked with James

Gibbs on other house and garden projects, has been discussed earlier, so it is sufficient to say here that it is more than likely that Bolingbroke was, in large measure, responsible for bringing the gardens at Dawley to the state shown in Rocque's map of 1754. Bridgeman was, almost certainly, consulted by Bolingbroke and, although no evidence has been uncovered, it seems likely that Bridgeman was the designer of the Dawley gardens.

Edward Stephenson, with his immense wealth, had adequate resources to change the gardens at Dawley, although he may have been disinclined to alter the works of his noble predecessor. He could, however, have undertaken extensive tree-planting, for example. There are some unanswered questions about the apparent rise and disappearance of woodland areas at Dawley.

The farming activities of both Bolingbroke and Stephenson (mostly through tenant farmers) show up in Rocque's map. The Dawley estate outside the gardens adjacent to the house and the main north, south and west avenues is shown conventionally by Rocque as mainly pasture land to the north and mainly 'plowed land' in the south - the latter, by the time of the Harlington Tithe Award of 1839, at least, being divided between Pinkwell Farm and Woolpack Farm. The northern area, still tenanted by John Dorrell of Gould's Green at least as late as 1762, seems to have been known as Dawley Park Farm. (2)

The formal 'wilderness' or Wood Garden at Pinkwell that existed in c1721, is shown simply as a field by Rocque, although the two-tree avenue (known from later evidence as probably lime trees) (3) leading to the Pinkwell garden is still there. A single reverse L-shaped building is shown outside this field's north-west corner, together with a long rectangular pond, both apparently surviving from c 1721. The only other identifiable building on the Dawley estate shown by Rocque is The Lodge, named as such on the map, and in the same position as a lodge shown in Jenner's plan.

Finally, it cannot entirely be discounted that Abraham Hume, who claimed to have spent considerable sums of money during his brief tenure before handing over to the Earl of Uxbridge, may possibly have created some new garden features just before Rocque's survey for his map.

CHAPTER 25

HENRY PAGET, 2nd EARL OF UXBRIDGE

Henry Paget (1719 - 1769), who succeeded his grandfather in 1743 as 8th Baron Paget and 2nd Earl of Uxbridge, is described in the Dictionary of National Biography as 'chiefly remarkable for an inordinate love of money'. He was bequeathed in 1746 by Peter Walter, his former steward, the principal part of Walter's immense wealth. The Earl apparently allowed the Paget ancestral home at West Drayton to fall into ruin, and the Manor House is believed to have been demolished about 1750. (1) On the other hand, whatever may be claimed about his parsimony, he continued to pay a large annuity throughout her life to Peter Walter's daughter, Mrs Bullock, without taking advantage to the full of the letter of her father's will. (2)

By 1755 the Earl, it seems, felt the need to establish fresh roots in Middlesex, and he must have wanted the Dawley estate strongly enough to be prepared to pay a substantial premium to induce Abraham Hume to withdraw from his contract with Edward Stephenson. The Dawley mansion was less than two miles from the Drayton Manor House site: the Earl of Uxbridge continued to hold the Manor of West Drayton throughout his life and maintained active interests there (see below).

An agreement under which Abraham Hume undertook to give up the Dawley estate that he was in the process of purchasing was signed by the Earl of Uxbridge on 8 March 1755 and by Hume on 11 March. This document can be summarised as follows :

The purchaser (the Earl of Uxbridge) to pay Mr Stephenson the purchase price of £25000-, together with the interest due up to the time of payment.

The purchaser to pay Mr Brown's commission on the purchase already agreed by Hume. (This would presumably have been Thomas Browne, probably a lawyer, who was one of the witnesses to Hume's signature on the agreement).

The purchaser to pay Mr Cooper's bill relating to the title to the estate and the conveyance thereof. (This would presumably have been Francis Cooper, Hume's other witness to the agreement).

The purchaser to pay the costs and charges of the suit commenced in the Court of Chancery by Hume against Stephenson for the performance of the contract.

Hume expected to receive from the purchaser an amount to cover the costs of repairs to the house and other premises and the cost of fire insurance, totalling £1000-.

Hume also required payment for a parcel of land he had purchased adjoining Dawley (which would then go with the estate), £1035-.

The purchaser to pay Mr Hume in consideration of his giving up the estate to him a further sum of £1500-.

The purchaser to pay Mr Hume for all the live and dead stock with the horses and utensils of farming and tools in the garden that Hume may choose to leave of an appraisement.

The purchaser to pay all manner of rates, taxes and other outgoings to which Mr Hume would have been subject to.

On the credit side, the purchaser was not required to pay for corn in the ground or any expense in ploughing or sowing.

Mr Hume would leave behind any furniture or pictures that were in the house when Stephenson delivered possession of it to Hume - to be ascertained by inventory or otherwise. (Hume reserved the right to take away all the other furniture, pictures and other goods which, presumably, he had introduced into the house).

The purchaser to have all the rents from the several tenants at Dawley from Ladyday 1753 (25 March) and from the tenant of the estate (name left blank in the copy of the agreement in the Greater London Record Office (3) but presumed to refer to Hume himself) from Michaelmas 1753 (29 September).

Hume to abate from the sums to be paid to him £500- for the rent of the lands he had occupied and for having lived in the house.

Following this agreement, an indenture for the sale between the Right Honble Henry Earl of Uxbridge and Abraham Hume Esquire of Hill Street near Berkeley Square was made on 17 April 1755. (4) Despite the fact that the earlier agreement specified that the payment of the original purchase price should go direct to Edward Stephenson, the indenture stipulates that the Earl is to pay all to Hume (who presumably settled with Stephenson), namely a total of £27300-, by £650- on 18 October next, and the £26650- residue on 18 April next following (1756).

The document mentions the manors in Harlington and Dawley, and itemises 'that Capital Messuage or Mansion or Manor House commonly called or known by the name of Dawley House and all that Park commonly called Dawley Park' - amounting to 700 acres. Also mentioned are the farms of Burbank's, Bird's and the Red Mead; the close of meadow and wood ground called Long Mead (9 acres meadow, 3 acres wood ground); and properties in Harmondsworth, Irken (5), Ickenham, Cranford and Iver (Manor and Farm of Mansfield).

The full financial implications of the indenture are not entirely clear because, for example, the Hand-in-Hand fire insurance policy (6) was assigned from Hume to the Earl of Uxbridge on 23 April and assigned back to Hume by the Earl on 24 April. (It was not rendered and discharged by Hume finally until 12 June 1760). (7)

As Abraham Hume had apparently put the house in a good state of repair, there is no reason to doubt that the Earl of Uxbridge did not move into Dawley in 1755, but few records of his life there seem to have survived. That he maintained a close interest in his horses, some kept at West Drayton as well as Dawley, is shown by a series of reports sent to the Earl (who was apparently staying at Crowsley Park, near Henley, for at least part of the time) by William Eldridge, his agent, between April and May 1766. (8) For example - 'The Stone horses [stallions] and Geldins and the Mares and Stone colts and fileys (9) are in health at Dawley and the Stone horses and Geldins and the two year old Mares are in health at Drayton'. In one report, Eldridge mentions that the horses are in the field by the wood near Pinkwell, and in another he asks how many horses are to go to the Park (Dawley, it is assumed) and 20 to 25 geldings and ten fillies seem to be suggested by him. Thirty or forty cows, steers and yearling calves are there already, it seems. A little later - 'The Bay stone horses as was at Drayton are put into the Long Walks for the grass growes at a great pase at Dawley at this time'. On 4 May, Eldridge reported the bad news that the larger of the two Dun colts had dropped dead in its manger at Dawley.

John Dorrell, who had leased land at Dawley from Edward Stephenson, was still there (or a relative with the same name) in 1762 at 'Dawley Park Farm'. (10)

The Earl of Uxbridge appears to have had reopened a direct link with West Drayton. A plan, dated 1767, of an adjoining farm estate (11) shows a gate on the west boundary of Dawley in a direct line with Porter Lane, which leads to West

Drayton.   Although a gate at or near this point almost certainly existed earlier ('Pinkwell Gate' is referred to in documents as early as 1586) (12), one is not shown on Jenner's plan of Dawley drawn for the Earl of Tankerville in about 1721. Although Bolingbroke or Edward Stephenson might have been responsible, the Earl of Uxbridge certainly had the most cause to restore the gate, as a means of direct access to his Drayton properties.   Incidentally, the 1767 estate plan, referred to above, also shows a hedge, or possibly palings, but not a wall, separating the two estates, thus giving some support to the belief that the Dawley wall, discussed below, only ran along the east boundary.

The Earl of Uxbridge's earliest Dawley manorial court baron was held in 1755, when his steward, who officiated, was Francis Parry Esq. (13)   Full records have not survived, but by 1768 (14) the steward was John Gwatkin, Gentleman. The names of some of the Earl's other, lesser, servants have only survived because they got married in Harlington Parish Church, and are recorded in the parish registers. (15)   These are John Vaux (married in 1756) and John Elmes (1761), both coachmen;   William Worthington, groom (1756);   Charles Elliot, cook (1757); Thomas Barnes, gardener (1756);   John Stroud, servant - unspecified (1756) and Richard Cripps, labourer (1757).

The Earl's two actions, from the historical point of view, having the greatest effect on the Dawley estate were to have what was then known as Pinkwell House demolished about 1760 and to have built the brick estate wall along the boundary by the Harlington-Hillingdon road.   'Pinkwell House' and its predecessors on the same or nearby sites are discussed separately in the next chapter.   The 'Dawley Wall', as it has become known, is for much of its length still in existence today and is the major piece of tangible evidence for the historic Dawley estate and its interesting and illustrious owners.   No precise documentary evidence has been traced for the date of construction of the estate wall or its builder.   However, a paling fence surrounded the estate about 1721 when John Jenner drew the plan of Dawley for the Earl of Tankerville, and Rocque's map of 1754 also shows a wooden paling fence. (16)   The opinion of architectural historians (17) is that the wall is of 18th century construction, although incorporating late 16th or early 17th century bricks - presumably re-used from an earlier building or buildings.   Local legend attributes the building of the wall to the Earl of Uxbridge, and there seems no reason to disbelieve this.   For example, H O Meyers in his 'Lecture of the Village of Harlington' given in 1857 (18) says of the Dawley wall it 'is said to have been built to keep out the small pox, - the owner of that property (Lord Uxbridge) being greatly alarmed at the dreadful scourge'.   Elizabeth Hunt (1832-1916), the historian of Hayes, who had strong local family connections, said of Dawley in her reminiscences (19) 'The garden [sic] wall there was a mile in length and was built by the father of our Great Uncle Smith.   It was said to have been built to keep out the plague'. Later, she says of a man named Blanchard who once owned Court Farm, Hayes, 'One of his sons had so come down in the world that he worked as a labourer in the building of Dawley Wall'.   A similar tradition was also passed down in the De Salis family, who subsequently owned Dawley - that the wall was built to keep out smallpox, in the form of beggars who might have brought infection to the house. An interesting addition to the story from this source (20) is that the Earl of Uxbridge is said to have died from smallpox which he caught in a hackney carriage.   Such stories, handed down locally and, in some cases, repeated less than a hundred years after the alleged event, must have an element of fact in them.   The Earl might, of course, have had an obsession about diseases, although it is hard to believe that he would have imagined that a wall would have provided an effective barrier against them.   The wall (as far as is known) ran only along the public road, but he might have considered it a deterrent against vagrants or others infected with disease from casually trespassing on his estate.   There do not seem to have been any really notable outbreaks of disease in this country in the mid-to-late 18th century (21). However, a serious cattle plague, or murrain, ravaged England at this time and ranged all over the country between 1745 and 1757.   It had subsided in Middlesex by 1747, but even after the main outbreak in England was over, by 1757, various parts of the country suffered mildly from it for a further twelve years after that.   It was raging again on the Continent in the late 1760's, when in Holland, for example, in 1769 nearly half the cattle were attacked by it, and there was fear that there would be a fresh outbreak of this contagious disease in England. At least half a million cattle died at the peak period: the total over the whole time is unknown. (22) It is at least possible, therefore, that the Dawley Wall was built to prevent infected animals that might be driven along the public road from coming into contact with the Earl's beasts on the estate. This said, many large estates, such as Petworth and Blenheim, have brick walls along their boundaries with public roads which are known to have been built to keep out human trespassers.

Estate walls of this kind, substantially built, were an expensive undertaking. For example, James I built a 12 foot high brick wall round Greenwich Park (23), 2 miles in circumference, which cost £2000- in 1625, and Dr Johnson told Boswell in 1783 'We compute, in England, a park wall at a thousand pounds a mile .....'. (24)

The wall at Dawley was built strongly, if somewhat crudely, with no regular brick bond being used consistently. It varied somewhat in height but was, on average, about 9 feet high, including the brick plinth at its base and the coping bricks (shaped and sloping on the inside) at its summit. It was about 14 inches ($1^{1}/_{2}$ bricks) thick, and had buttresses at intervals of between 18 feet and 18 feet 6 inches. The buttresses were about $22^{1}/_{2}$ inches wide and projected about 2 inches from both inner and outer faces of the wall which was at these points about 17 inches to 18 inches thick, overall. The only decoration (or the only decoration to survive, because several sections of the wall have been demolished at different times) is a diamond-shaped feature, formed from headers of light grey bricks. This consists of a solid diamond, composed of nine bricks, surrounded by two outer, outline, diamond shapes and is located in the section of the wall where the old Dawley road is called Bolingbroke Way and has been by-passed by a new length of road. The brickwork in this area is of a higher standard than elsewhere and may possibly represent a later rebuilding of the wall. (25)

If the legend is correct and, as seems likely, the Earl of Uxbridge had the estate wall built, it must date from between 1755 and 1769. If, by chance, the threat of cattle contagion was his reason for building it, then its construction is perhaps most likely to date from the early days of his arrival at Dawley, say 1755-1757. It is interesting to speculate that bricks from demolished buildings at Pinkwell may have been used for the wall: the materials from Pinkwell sold by the Earl in 1760 and 1761 did not include bricks, although it has to be said that the full lists of the items sold may not have survived. This topic is discussed more fully in the next chapter.

The 2nd Earl might also have been responsible for a further, less spectacular, change at Dawley. The 'implements of husbandry' that Bolingbroke had had painted in the hall were specified, as mentioned above, in the insurance policy of 1753. In the renewal document for the policy in 1767, (26) however, the wording for the description of the hall is changed to 'elegantly painted'. Does this mean that the Earl had tired of seeing the rakes and prongs etc and had them painted over ?

Henry Paget, 2nd Earl of Uxbridge and 8th Baron Paget of Beaudesert, died on 16 November 1769 at the age of 50. There is a brass plate memorial to him in West Drayton Church. The Earldom then became extinct, as he was unmarried and had no children. The Barony of Paget, however, devolved on his cousin, Henry Bayly, whose father had married Caroline Paget, a descendant of the 5th Baron. Bayly assumed the surname and arms of Paget and was summoned to Parliament on 13 January 1770 as the 9th Baron Paget. He also succeeded to the Dawley estate.

CHAPTER 26

THE HOUSES AT PINKWELL

This seems an appropriate point for a discussion of the rather difficult question of the various houses at Pinkwell, since the Earl of Uxbridge was responsible for disposing of the last 18th century house on the site and whatever then may have remained of its predecessors.

To start with, Pinkwell is an area in the south west and south part of the Dawley estate that apparently took its name from a well or spring which feeds the small stream known as the Frogsditch. No evidence has been found of the name being applied to a building there earlier than 1760 when 'Materials sold from Pinkwell House' were recorded by William Eldridge for the Earl of Uxbridge. (1) Elizabeth Hunt's reference (2) to Pinkwell (and by implication the house there) was, of course, written in 1861 - a hundred years after the sale of materials mentioned above and probably nearly 200 years after the old manor house had ceased to exist.

'Dawley Courte', discussed earlier, the original manor house at Pinkwell, must have been large to enable Ambrose Coppinger to entertain Queen Elizabeth and her entourage there in 1603. Very little else can be said about this house, since no pictures of it are known to exist and there are no documentary records to give any idea of its layout (with one doubtful exception, considered below) or appearance. Although there was presumably a mediaeval manor house within the manor of Dawley, the house assessed in 1664 at 22 hearths - the same as Hayes Park Hall and more than Hayes Manor House (20 hearths) - may well have been one of the many country houses newly built or enlarged in the so-called 'Great Rebuilding' in England in the late 16th and early 17th century.

The last time that Dawley Court was occupied was probably not much later than 1670, when Dame Mary Selby, widow of Sir George Selby, sold it to Sir John Bennet. Bennet might have used the house occasionally, but certainly not after about 1672 when the new Dawley manor house on the east side of the estate was completed. Dame Mary evidently had had difficulty in meeting the cost of repairs to the house, and it probably had become dilapidated. (3) As suggested earlier, Sir John may have followed a not uncommon practice and used materials from the old house in building his new one. In any event, the 1674 Hearth Tax return for Harlington gives no indication of the existence of the 22 hearth house occupied by George Selby ten years earlier. Sir John Bennet's splendid newly-built house was assessed as 27 hearths. In Jenner's plan of Dawley, drawn about 1721, only farm or service buildings are shown near the probable site of the old manor house in the north-west corner of the rectangle of gardens at Pinkwell that had been re-fashioned by Lord Ossulstone. It was quite usual for large houses in the 16th and early 17th century to occupy a corner of a formal garden layout - Penshurst and Knole, both in Kent, Brympton d'Evercy, Somerset, and Didmarton Manor, Gloucestershire, all shown in Kip engravings, are examples. Another building - single storey and like a reversed L in plan - is also shown in Jenner's plan a little way north-west of the Pinkwell gardens site. As suggested earlier, this is probably the stables built by the Earl of Tankerville in 1715, although there is the very slight possibility it was originally one of the outlying service buildings of 'Dawley Courte'. This building is also shown on Rocque's map of 1754, but does not appear on the Harlington Inclosure map of 1821. The sale of materials on 21 and 22 November 1760 and again on 23 May 1761 (4) from what was then called 'Pinkwell House' poses some problems. Apart from the sale item '40 yards of wainscotting in the long room', which could possibly refer to an Elizabethan long gallery, the other items (although the sale details surviving may not be complete) seem to suggest only a fairly modest house and, furthermore, from some of the objects mentioned, one unlikely to date back to Elizabethan times. The south front, according to the sale record, had six windows, which were presumably contained in sash frames from among the nine sash frames and equipment listed separately. Since sash windows did not come into use in England until, at the earliest, the 1670's, the house at Pinkwell from which these sashes came could not have been Elizabethan. (Although sash windows could be and, later, often were, quite easily substituted for mullions, Sir John Bennet is highly unlikely to have carried out this form of modernisation in an oldish and possibly decaying house. This type of window conversion was, in any case, uncommon before about 1700). The sale item 'West front quartering and wall plates 3 square' (300 square feet) might suggest part of a timber-framed house, although this may more likely be internal partitioning. A large timber-framed house would be very unlikely to have survived as such in Middlesex in late Elizabethan times, and Ambrose Coppinger's house was almost certainly a brick one. The four parlours (one of which may have had the cove ceiling, listed separately) from which floor boards and joists came, and the four marble chimneypieces, suggest a comfortable, but not necessarily very large, building. The tiles sold (quaintly called 'tilning') are in two categories. First, plain tilning, totalling 16 squares (1600 square feet) which could be either floor or roof tiling - if the former, this could represent a ground area (if completely tiled) of, say, 50 feet x 32 feet - not a large building, by any means. The second category is 'pantilning', of which an indeterminate quantity was sold as Lot 2 at £5-2-6, plus up to fourteen other lots, seemingly suggesting rather a large roof area if for the house only, although there was also a brew house and a kitchen, which may have been separate buildings. However, the pantiles cannot possibly have dated to earlier than the 17th century, when they were first imported from the Netherlands, and it is believed that they were not made in England before 1701.

All in all, it seems most likely that the materials from Pinkwell sold by the Earl of Uxbridge in 1760-1761 came from a not very large house that had been built after about 1721, although two other possibilities exist. First, some materials from the old 'Dawley Courte' may have been stored for future use or sale, excluding, presumably, the timber, unless it were kept dry and under cover. This could not refer to either the pantiles or the sash windows, for the reasons explained above. The '3 old marble chimney pieces new polished and set' used for the Earl of Tankerville's house built in 1719-1721 may have come from among items saved from Dawley Courte, whether or not they were re-used in another house at Pinkwell. Second, some materials may have come also from West Drayton, from the manor house there that it is said the 2nd Earl of Uxbridge had had demolished about 1750. It was a large house, assessed at 45 hearths in 1674. (5) Some marble and stone from this house had been stored, and in 1766 William Eldridge reported to the Earl that a stone mason from Brentford had made an offer for it. The possibility that some of the items purporting to have come from Pinkwell may, in fact, have originated from West Drayton is raised by the fact that a surveyor, Samuel Stretch, was paid £3-3-0 on 5 September 1760 'for his trouble in estimating the materials of Pinkwell House and offices and house at Drayton'. (6)

Lord Uxbridge was credited by the 'Lady of the Manor' with being the former owner of the staircase at Poyle Manor House, Stanwell, Middlesex. Gordon S Maxwell, who recounts the story (7) says that the lady understood (this was in the 1930's) that the staircase had been at Poyle about a hundred years. Maxwell concluded (without evidence) that it had, in fact, come from Dawley about 200 years ago. The staircase in question rises from the hall floor of Poyle Manor through two flights, at right angles, to the first floor, and the balustrade continues round the other sides of the hall as a gallery. From photographs (8), the staircase appears to be early to mid 18th century and the balusters, downward-tapering and fluted, are very similar to those at Moor Park, Hertfordshire. If the staircase was indeed disposed of by the 2nd Earl of Uxbridge, it seems more likely to have come from Drayton Manor House rather than Dawley.

A round-headed open-fronted niche cupboard at Church Farm, Harlington (now demolished) was said to have come from Dawley house. It had carved wooden Doric pilasters and a painting was once inside the half-spherical top. It was of early to mid-18th century appearance, but there was no way of confirming its provenance. (9)

The 19th century farm buildings at Pinkwell, shown on the 1825 Harlington Inclosure Award map, are discussed later.

CHAPTER 27

HENRY BAYLY, 9th BARON PAGET OF BEAUDESERT   (1744-1812)

Henry Bayly, 9th Baron Paget of Beaudesert, the 2nd Earl of Uxbridge's heir, was evidently an ugly looking man, whose face was described by Peter Pinder as 'And he who lours as if he meant to bite / Is Earl of Uxbridge with his face of night'. He was also said to be indolent, pleasure-loving and negative. (1)   Perhaps these characteristics applied more to his later life (he was not given the revived title of Earl of Uxbridge until 1784) because Lord Paget almost immediately on inheriting Dawley made arrangements for the house to be cleaned and repaired and have alterations made.   He evidently intended to make use of Dawley for, at least, an occasional residence.   Although Beaudesert in Staffordshire was the main seat of the Pagets it was, no doubt, convenient to have another country seat, like Dawley, so much nearer to London.   The extensive nature of the work done at Dawley is testified by builders accounts dated between early 1770 and the middle of 1771. (2)   The whole exterior of the house, including its steps and pavements, was cleaned, and stonework reset where necessary.   New solid Portland stone astragal steps (3) were provided for the front of the house and Portland stone was also used for the arch and cornice over the entrance.   Internal work included a 'New Portland chimney piece, and slab in chamber' and a 'New purple Marble soffett [underside of arch] to chimney piece in Nursery'.   The change of accommodation to a nursery was certainly made by Lord Paget, who already had two young sons by 1770 - Henry William, born in 1768, and William, 1769, followed by Arthur in January 1771, just before work on the nursery was completed.   (Perhaps Paget suffered from tardy workmen, like so many people since !)   Lord Paget, in due course, had another nine children - four more sons and five daughters.   Lady Paget was to be confined no less than five times between 1769 and 1775, either in London or Kingston on Thames. (4)

Other work included stucco (plasterwork) repaired on the grand staircase (which had an 'Enricht cornice'), 'the Little Room', the back staircase, the 'Long Room', the 'four post hall', 'the 2 post hall', and 'the long passage leading to servants hall and kitchen'.   The 'Ovens mouth' (presumably in the kitchen) was repaired with new Reigate stone, and the Laundry was re-paved.   Thomas Hardwick was the master mason employed at Dawley and John Pritchard of Twickenham was the master plasterer.   The bills of various craftsmen employed at Dawley mention the names of further rooms, such as the Yellow Room (which was near the top of the back staircase, and for which a servants' call bell system was installed), the Picture Room, 'my Lady's dressing room', and 'his Lordship's Library' (for which books, including Bundy's Roman History (4 volumes), Smith's Xenophon, and the Annual Register were ordered and catalogued in 1770).

Other rooms mentioned in connection with Dawley and the Pagets' London house in Savile Row in 1770-1771 (and unfortunately it is not always clear from the bills which refer to which) are as follows: Drawing Room, Back Parlour, Front Parlour, Bed chambers (3?), My Lady's Dressing Room, My Lord's Dressing Room, and Dining Room.   An interesting fact is that water closets had been installed at Dawley by April 1770, since there is an account for three repair jobs on them at this time.   'Coal' was used for heating, and 50 chauldrons of coal and 5 tons of Scotch coal were delivered in February 1770 at a total cost of £114. 10s. (5)

Of the staff quarters and service buildings at Dawley there was also mention of the kitchen (which had an eight-day clock in it), the Beer Cellar, the House Cook's room (where a hatch door was installed), the Brew house (which had a water pump), Servants' Hall, and house-keeper's room.   A 'mangle and engine' (for which a beam was supplied) was presumably housed in the laundry.

William Gatford cleaned and repaired the turret clock and the wind dial at Dawley in April and May, respectively, of 1770. (6)   The wind dial was almost certainly that shown in the early 19th century painting (7) on the laundry cum dairy building on the north side of the courtyard, and it is likely that the turret clock was on the stables building facing it on the south side. There was a pump in the stable yard, and other out-buildings mentioned include six dog kennels at Round Copps (a site not identified, but possibly the old kennels at Pinkwell) and a 'green house with Sash Windows', which presumably, had the '38 orange tubbs painted green' standing in or near it. (This greenhouse must not be confused with the one shown in the Kyp engraving, which was demolished about 1719 when Lord Tankerville's new mansion was built). There are also references to 'a large lanthorn' and '12 garden lights' - the latter, perhaps, lighting the way to Drayton, through Lord Ossulstone's Lanthorn Garden, or what may have remained of it. The 'marble water stools' and a marble fountain in the gardens were cleaned, and re-set where necessary, and 'the summer house in the wood' was repaired inside and out. It appears to have had a plaster ceiling and cornice, and the exterior was roughcast. (This was presumably one of the old buildings located in Lord Tankerville's Wood Garden.) On the estate, the pales (wooden fence) in the park were mended in 1771, and there were two mills - a malt mill, worked by means of a horse wheel, and a corn bolting mill. Messrs Nuttall & Hadley were the contractors for work on the mills in 1770. (8)

Beside the repair work on existing buildings carried out at Dawley, Lord Paget appears to have undertaken some fresh building at Dawley and Goulds Green towards the end of 1770. Two thousand plain tiles were invoiced in November and December, 50 ridge tiles, 200 'Fier' bricks, 200 rubbing bricks, and several loads of lime. It is not known what these materials were used for, but the quantities seem too large just for repair work. (9)

To guard against fire, Lord Paget purchased in April 1770 a 'horse engine with brass barrels', 'a new third size fire engine' complete with 36 buckets painted with his crest and coronet, and six lengths of leather pipe. This equipment supplemented an existing '2nd size fire engine by Newsham'. (10) Paget kept a full establishment of carriages at Dawley, and these included a 'Rushia rooft crane neck post chariot', two Phaetons, a post chaise, a post coach and a town chariot (costing £350 and, no doubt, normally kept at the Savile Row house). The post chaise and post chariot were painted in Naples yellow with a black frame, with Paget's crest or cypher and coronet on the panels; the post coach had a 'fine glazed green' body with gilt frame. William Howse was the supplier of these vehicles; John Foster provided a Phaeton, another coach and a town chariot. (11)

There are few clues to leisure activities of the Paget household at Dawley but, apart from the books purchased for the library and reference to a card table, a 'large billiard table' and a harpsichord are mentioned in the Dawley accounts. Twelve bowls and three jacks were among the contents of Dawley sold in 1772. (12)

Lord Paget appears to have inherited the burden of repaying the interest on the loan with which the Earl of Uxbridge had purchased Dawley from Abraham Hume (or Edward Stephenson - see above), unless the property had been re-mortgaged. A document dated 25 April 1772 records receipt by Hume of £440 for half a year's interest 'on £22000 lent his Lordship on Dawley and estates at rate of £4 per centum per anumm'. The burden of debt on a second country seat perhaps became too much for Paget and this may well have been the last payment of its kind, because another document dated a few days earlier than the above - 21 April 1772 - promises to a Mr Curzon and a Mr Pastington that the money arising from the sale of Dawley shall be paid to them towards lessening the debt owed them. (13)

The contents of Dawley were sold by auction by 'Mr Christie' over eight days in July 1772. The catalogue states that 'The Mansion, with Gardens, Plantations and Land - all Freehold, will be sold at one o'clock in the 1st Day's Sale' (viz 23 July 1772). However, although the catalogue is interleaved with the results of the sale of furniture etc, the outcome of the sale of the house and land is not noted. According to Lysons (14) the site of Dawley house was purchased by Thomas Flight Esq, who sold it to Mr John Thistlewood. This suggests, although uncertain, that the house had been demolished before the site was sold.

The full list of rooms itemised in Christie's sale catalogue, and some of their contents, is included in the following chapter.

With the sale of Dawley, the Pagets finally severed their long connection with the area. As a footnote, however, it should be mentioned how they later made the name of Uxbridge famous. The 9th Baron Paget was, after he sold Dawley, granted the re-created title of Earl of Uxbridge. This was in 1784. His eldest son, Henry William Paget, who almost certainly spent some of his childhood at Dawley, succeeded to this title on his father's death in 1812. Already a distinguished soldier, the 2nd Earl of Uxbridge (of the second creation) achieved ever-lasting fame as second-in-command to Wellington and leader of the Allied cavalry at the Battle of Waterloo in 1815. During the engagement he lost a leg: this limb was buried near the field of battle and commemorated by a monument. Lord Uxbridge was elevated by the Prince Regent to the title Marquess of Anglesey in recognition of his bravery and achievements. (15)

CHAPTER 28

DAWLEY - THE CONTENTS, 1772

'A Catalogue of all the entire Household Furniture, Pictures, Hangings, Brewing, Garden and Farming Utensils, Hay &c of that Spacious Mansion called DAWLEY .....', 'Which will be Sold by Auction by Mr Christie on the Premises on Thursday, July 23, 1772, and the seven following Days, (Sunday excepted).'

In this printed catalogue (1) the rooms in the house and outbuildings and certain lots (e.g. garden furniture) are listed and numbered (in Roman figures) from 1 to 82, divided up into the eight days of the sale. For each room the contents are itemised and given lot numbers. The sale seems to have been organised so that on most days some rooms with valuable furniture were paired with rooms containing furniture for servants or household items. For example, on the sixth day's sale, the contents of the coachman's and grooms' rooms were linked with those of the State Bedchamber. Also, the kitchen, with its numerous contents, was featured in the 3rd, 4th and 5th days sales. The list of rooms, therefore, does not follow a logical sequence (as in the Dawley inventories of 1713, 1716 and 1722) and it is very difficult to deduce, in most cases, the relationship of one room to another. It is felt preferable, therefore, to simply list the rooms in the order in which they appear in the catalogue, with an added commentary where appropriate. Some of the more important, unusual or significant items are noted, although it must be borne in mind that certain pieces may not have been put into the sale. In only a very few cases has it been found possible to identify rooms mentioned in the 1753 insurance survey, or those refurbished by Lord Paget in 1770-1771, with the Christie's catalogue. The function of some of the rooms may well have changed over the years, and there is also the possibility that the Earl of Uxbridge or Lord Paget may have added extra accommodation, particularly on the north side of the house, for which no pictorial or other evidence exists.

Messrs Christie's archive copy of the catalogue is interleaved with details of the price earned for each item or lot, and the purchasers' names. These include some prominent local gentry, such as Blencow, Barnardiston and Newman.

In the list that follows, the room description has been reproduced exactly and in full, including the puzzling notation 'two pair of stairs' or simply 'two pair' (or 'one pair') where it occurs in the original. In brackets, I have in all cases noted where beds are listed, and also, with the symbol 'H', where a hearth or stove is listed or implied (e.g. chimney glass, fender or fire dogs), although in only some instances selected items of the contents.

1.   The Lumber Room

2.   The Laundry-Maid's Bedchamber   (1 Bed)

3.   The Red Bedroom   (1 Bed - four-post bedstead, serge furniture)

4.   Lumber Garret

5.   The Maids Bedroom   (4 Beds)

6.   The Upper Laundry   (H. 'a large wainscot mangle, with a jack compleat'; 24 pictures, including 4 for door pieces)

7.   The Gardener's Room   (1 Bed)

| 8. | The Footmens Room | (4 Beds, H) |

8. The Footmens Room (4 Beds, H)

9. The Waiting Hall (H - 'a brazier')
(This is where the footmen would
have been on call to serve meals,
or for other duties)

10. The Valet's Room (1 Bed, H)

11. Passage Room, two pair of (H. Various tables, chairs,
stairs sofa, surveying stands and
maps)

12. The Uxbridge Bedchamber, (1 Bed - 'a whole tester
two pair bedstead, yellow sattin
furniture'; 6 armchairs;
yellow silk damask hangings; H.)

13. Dressing Room adjoining, (1 Bed)
two pair

14. Best Stair-case ('A very fine stair-case lanthorn,
plate glass, silk in and balance
weight' (sic))

('The Grand Stairs' were in the east block in 1753 (insurance survey) and there is no reason to suppose that these, at any rate, had changed their location. What was, presumably, the late Earl of Uxbridge's bedchamber by association was also in the east block).

End of the First Day's Sale.

15. The Cook's Bed Room (2 Beds, H)

16. The Salting L... (Larder ? -
original obscured)

17. The Dairy

18. The Laundry (H)

(The Laundry and Dairy (also Pantry) were included in the largest building on the north side of the courtyard in 1753.)

19. Still Room

20. Servants Hall (H. A Large table and benches,
a fender, a table and 1 chair)

(The servants hall was almost certainly among the buildings on the north side of the courtyard.)

21. The inner Nursery two Pair (H)
of Stairs

22. Nursery Dining Room two Pair (H)
of Stairs

23. Bedroom to the Nursery, two (H, but no bed listed !)
Pair of Stairs

24.	Bedchamber to the Nursery, two Pair of Stairs	(1 Bed, H. Yellow silk mohair bedfurnishings, hangings and curtains)
25.	Dressing Room to the Nursery, two Pair of Stairs	
26.	Barrack Room two Pair of Stairs (This, by definition, would have been a communal dormitory for bachelor guests or visiting menservants)	(H)
27.	French Bedchamber, two Pair of Stairs	(1 Bed, H. Bedstead yellow damask with serge curtains. The furniture included 'A French commode marble top and 4 French armchairs')
28.	Dressing Room adjoining, two Pair of Stairs	

End of the Second Day's Sale.

29.	The Kitchen (see also Nos 38 and 45) (This was a separate building 53' x 29' on the north side of the courtyard listed in 1753)	(Twenty lots, including 'a large jack with multiplying wheel and 4 spits', an 8 day clock by Rainsford, and numerous copper utensils)
30.	The Bread Room	
31.	Housekeeper's Room	(H. Three armchairs and 3 small chairs; a barometer; 10 pictures including 'a view of Harlington church yard')
32.	The Passage (This was, almost certainly, the passage 82 feet long leading from the house to the kitchen)	(A candle box, 2 lamps and a mahogany corner table)
33.	The two Post Hall	(H (possibly two?) Wainscot dining table, another small table, one chair, etc - possibly stored ?)
34.	The four Post Hall	(A Fire-engine, an armchair, 2 lamps, a coal tub and a lanthorn)

(The two Post and four Post Halls are not readily identifiable with rooms or buildings listed in the 1753 insurance survey, unless they are among the five 'Leantos' of various sizes. They must, however, have been service buildings at ground level, presumably - certainly the one containing the fire engine.)

35.	The Library, two Pair of Stairs (The Library in 1753 was in the west wing, but here it seems more closely associated with rooms in the east block)	(H. Six mahogany bookcases, six assorted tables, a bureau, steps and 3 armchairs)

36.	Cupola Room (This room is not identifiable with the 1753 insurance survey, but its name implies that it had overhead lighting from a cupola in the roof: it may have been a centrally-placed chamber over the ball room)	(H. Two armchairs and smaller chairs; a strong chest; an ebony cabinet; 'a large historical picture' and nine others, including Herodias' daughter and Joseph with Potepher's wife)
37.	The Dining Parlour	(H. This had a painted floor cloth 18' x 14'; a sofa and ten French armed chairs; two side tables; 'a very fine marble cistern')

End of the Third Day's Sale

38.	Kitchen continued	(More copper utensils were up for sale)
39.	The Stewards Room	(2 Beds, H. The 22 lots in what appears to have been a large room included a fowling piece by Newton of Grantham)
40.	The Ball Room, one pair (This was in the centre block of the house in 1753 and it may be assumed was in the same location in 1772)	(2 H. A sofa and 12 arm-chairs; 2 card tables; a model of a yatch (sic); 2 Venetian window- blinds and 19 yards of matting. The pictures included 4 door pieces)
41.	Crimson Bedchamber, two pair	(2 Beds, H. Crimson silk damask bed furnishings, window curtains and some chair covers)
42.	Dressing Room, two pair	(H. 47 prints and drawings, fram'd and glaz'd)
43.	Closet adjoining, two pair	
44.	The Great Hall (This would have been in the east wing: the hall once, but possibly no longer (see above) painted with 'implements of husbandry')	(2 H. Four folding chairs, six stools; rose wood dining table; a side lanthorn; 10 yards of matting and a mat; a wainscot door, with 4 plates of glass, each 37" x 23")

End of the Fourth Day's Sale

45.	Kitchen continued	(The remaining copper (and pewter) items were offered for sale)
46.	Housekeeper's Room (This is a different room from No 31 - perhaps the housekeeper's dining room for senior servants)	(H. Four armchairs and six small chairs; table; two pictures and about 30 dozen of home- made wines)
47.	Steward's Bed-Chamber	(1 Bed, H)

48.	Bottle Room	(H. Probably used for general storage, since contents included a bird cage and 19 candlesticks, but no bottles !)
49.	Pantry	(1 Bed. Several knife boxes; a pewter crane (= a bent pipe for drawing liquor out of a cask ?)
50.	The white Sattin Needle-work Bed-chamber, one Pair	(1 Bed - the room's name describes the furnishings; H)
51.	The Bath	('Two arm'd chairs leather seats, and 2 models of bridges')
52.	Dressing Room, one Pair	(H. Picture of Charles II)
53.	Drawing Room, one Pair	(H. A silver tea table; sofa and 11 arm chairs; chimney glass, under plate 57" x 47"; pier glass 64" x 40"; tapestry hangings of room)

End of the Fifth Day's Sale.

54.	Rooms over the Stables	(The contents included an old bedstead and a fender, apparently stored)
55.	The Grooms Rooms	(2 Beds, H)
56.	The Helpers Bed-room	(3 Beds, H (stove))
57.	The Coachman's Room	(2 Beds, H (range))

(The stables and coach house were on the south side of the courtyard)

58.	The Payne Dressing Room, one pair	(H. The pictures included a portrait of King William)
59.	The Payne Bedchamber, one pair	(1 Bed, H. Sofa and 7 armchairs. The bed furniture and room hangings were yellow silk mohair)
60.	The Venetian Room, one pair	(H. Six back-stool chairs; 'a Turky carpet 14' x 12' '; 3 Venetian window-blinds)

(In 1753 the Venetian Room was in the west wing, as, presumably, in 1772.)

| 61. | The State Bedchamber, one pair

(The bed was sold to Sir Robert Lawley for £41-) | (1 Bed - 'a most noble and elegant four-post bedstead, with three-coloured silk damask furniture, with 4 elegant vases compleat' - the window curtains and hangings matched the bed furniture; 8 arm chairs and six other chairs) |
| 62. | Dressing Room to the State Bedchamber, one pair | (H) |

| 63. | The Chapel Room, one pair | (H - this was unfurnished except for the hearth implements and a chimney glass, plate 40" x 26") |

End of the Sixth Day's Sale

64.	The Bed-room adjoining the Chapel-room	(1 Bed, H)
65.	Passage-room adjoining	(Three tables; silk damask hangings)
66.	Drawing Room, One Pair	(H. Sofa and 9 elbow chairs; small table; Turky carpet 17' x 11'; 3 green Venetian window blinds; three crimson silk festoon window curtains; 2 paintings door pieces; a pair of pier glasses in 3 plates, under plates 38" x 28"; tapestry hangings)
67.	The Breakfast parlour, One Pair	(H. Four small tables; 8 chairs; an eight-leaf leather screen; 'a barometer and regulator of time'; whole length portrait of Queen Ann; 2 Venetian blinds)
68.	Wines	(These were the contents, presumably, of the Small Cellar, listed next. Nine dozen Malmsey, 4 doz Sherry, 3 doz Madeira)
69.	Small Cellar	(Equipment only listed)
70.	Strong Beer Cellar	(Five beer pipes, 16 ale hogsheads, various items of equipment)
71.	(No room heading) ('Cellar & Rooms over & stair-case' 40' x17' and 15' x11' was listed in the 1753 insurance survey)	(Equipment from one or both cellars presumably, including butts etc)
72.	Passage over the Stables	(Used for storage of miscellaneous items)
73.	The Four Stall Stable	
74.	Coach-house ('Coach house and Stable 1 story' 47' x 24' was listed separately from the main 2 storey stables in the 1753 survey)	(A chaise marine (2), a tilted cart; 2 small carts; a solid timber roller, and equipment)

End of the Seventh Day's Sale

| 75. | The Harness Room | (Horse and coach equipment; two leather postillion jackets) |

76. The Coach Stable
('Stables 2 storeys & Garrets'
63' x 45' was listed in 1753)

(Horse and coach equipment,
including lanthorns)

77. Brewhouse
(A square building 34' x 34', per
1753 survey)

78. Back Yard

('A very large wire safe on wheels';
90 stave and 50 stave ladders;
large iron boiler; 3 peacocks and
2 hens, 6 wild turkeys, etc)

79. Slaughter House

80. Bakehouse

(The Bakehouse and Slaughter house were combined in one building 47' x 24', per
1753 survey.)

81. Out Houses
(Some of these may have been
the five 'Leantos' of various sizes
listed in 1753)

(Bricks and tiles; bottles;
'a boat and a load of Scotch
coal; 2 chicken coops and 2 dog
houses; four stone figures')

82. (No room heading)

(This collection of 38 lots is
mostly garden or outdoor
equipment and includes urns,
garden chairs, tools, 12 bowls
and 3 jacks, rollers, growing
frames, earthen (drain ?) pipes,
over a dozen bee hives, 37 orange
trees in green tubs, and 40 green
house plants in pots)

Finis. (This was the end of the Eighth Day's Sale, on Friday, July 31, 1772.)

CHAPTER 29

DAWLEY - THE LAST OF BOLINGBROKE'S HOUSE
AND THE NEW 'DAWLEY HOUSE'
THE DE SALIS OWNERSHIP

It has not been established exactly when Bolingbroke's mansion house was demolished, although it is very likely that it was not occupied after being sold by Lord Paget in 1772. (1)   Thomas Flight Esquire, the purchaser, was probably only a speculator, and Mr John Thistlewood, into whose hands it passed not long after, whether he was just another speculator or perhaps a farmer, probably had no use for a large house divorced from its estate, except for the building materials to be obtained from it.

Dawley House is not likely to have existed after about 1780, at the latest. The following brief account by J Norris Brewer in 'The Beauties of England and Wales', published in 1816, is probably fairly accurate - 'It [Dawley] was taken down as we are informed by those who remember the structure about 40 years back. From a portion of the out offices is formed a commodious farmhouse which is now the only building on the estate'.   This would put the date of demolition at around 1776.   Hassall, writing in 1889, says categorically 'The Manor House was taken down in 1780'. (2)   A house in Hayes known as 'Little Dawley' was said to have a brick dated 1787 built into a wall, and was reputed to be built of materials from Dawley House. (3)   J Cary's map, printed in 1800, shows a house at Dawley only in conventional form (a square box with windows, identical to that shown for Cranford House) but it is interesting to note that although the main east-west tree avenue and the south avenue appear to be the same as depicted by Rocque (1754), the north avenue is truncated and stops well short of Goulds Green.   The reverse-L-shaped building at Pinkwell is still there.   Cary's accuracy cannot be relied on, however.

Jerome, 2nd Count De Salis was the purchaser of the Manor of Dawley in 1772, although the house and its immediate environs was excluded from the sale. It was his son, Peter, the 3rd Count, who in 1797 bought the site of Dawley House - which had, as discussed above, almost certainly been demolished by then.   The De Salis family would have had no incentive to live on the Dawley estate, since they had existing seats elsewhere in the area.   Count Jerome lived in London (he had a house in Harley Street) throughout his life in England, although his wife stayed occasionally, between about 1775 and 1780, in a specially built annexe to a farmhouse on their Harlington property.   The house still exists in the High Street, known today as Dower House. (4)   Countess De Salis also had a family vault built in Harlington churchyard, where she and several of her descendants are buried. Her son, Peter, 3rd Count De Salis, built a new house, known as Hillingdon Park at Little London, Hillingdon, and his son, Jerome, the 4th Count, lived after his marriage at his wife's inherited home, Hillingdon Place, and later (before 1825) purchased Goulds Green House, which was confusingly renamed Dawley Court, despite the fact that it was in Hillingdon, not in Dawley. (5)   Although they obviously had a sentimental attachment to Harlington Parish, the De Salis family never had a seat there.   They may have been responsible, however, for creating what was to become known as the last 'Dawley House' - the 'commodious farmhouse' referred to by J Norris Brewer.

The part of the 'out offices' kept for conversion into a farmhouse was the building in the centre of the north side of the courtyard.   This is shown on the 1865 edition of the 25 inch Ordnance Survey map, from which its dimensions can, as mentioned earlier, be equated with those of the laundry, pantry and dairy building described in the 1753 insurance details, thus confirming the tradition (6) that the house had once been a laundry.   Walford, in 'Greater London', published first in 1883, says that the surviving wing of Dawley was made into a steward's residence, and this is confirmed by Mrs J Wadsworth (nee De Salis). (7)   The 1841 Census records the occupier of 'Dawley Farm' as Thomas Pool, bailiff: he might have been deputy to the De Salis' steward. Important evidence for the early appearance of this remnant of 18th century Dawley is a rather charming watercolour in the Guildhall Library collection (8) which shows what was finally known as 'Dawley House'. This is believed to have been painted in the early 19th century (9) and although the angled walls that formed the north side of the octagonal courtyard are shown, there is no trace of any other building nearby. There are several characteristics of James Gibbs' style to be seen, as has been discussed earlier, and it seems that the alterations to convert it from the laundry, pantry and dairy building were chiefly internal. Eighteenth century service buildings (such as those at Ditchley, for example) were often given good facades with house-like fenestration when they formed part of one of the main approaches to a mansion house, so it is unlikely that much conversion of the front would have been needed. Even the classical doorway with Doric pilasters almost certainly formed part of the original Gibbs building. The painting shows that different coloured bricks were used to emphasise the quoins, parapet and window openings. An attractive little white-painted cupola with a weather vane is on the roof above the centre of the parapet and below this, above the doorway, is a wind direction dial, operated by the weather vane through a simple system of pulleys or gearing. West is shown at the right instead of the left-hand side of the dial: although probably an error by the artist, if this is accurately depicted it appears that the linkage between the vane and the indicator spindle was wrongly located. Wind direction dials are not uncommon on public buildings, such as on the dome of the King William Block of Greenwich Hospital (1698 - 1728) and outside the Model Room, Royal Arsenal, Woolwich (built 1719), but are rare - or known examples are - on private houses. The upswept design of the parapet seems to indicate that a dial was originally intended to occupy this position, but one can only speculate why Bolingbroke or one of his successors wanted a wind dial. The cupola and the wind dial do not appear in 20th century photographs. (10)

The early 19th century watercolour shows a sundial in front of the house, north of the centre of the courtyard, and just west of the path crossing it. The circular pond that stood there in the Earl of Tankerville's time, and still appears to be represented in Rocque's map of 1754, had, by this time, presumably been removed.

There is the interesting possibility that a smaller building to the east may, at first, also have been retained and connected to the laundry etc building by means of a short passage, because a plan of 1853 (11) appears to show that this was so. This smaller building might have been the bakehouse-cum-slaughterhouse. The plan in question does not appear to be very accurate in other respects, however, and if there were two old buildings when it was drawn, the smaller one had been removed early in the second half of the 19th century.

The occupiers of this final building to be called 'Dawley House', some discussion of its internal layout, and its eventual demolition, will be covered in a later chapter.

CHAPTER 30

THE GRAND JUNCTION CANAL; TATTERSALL'S

The end of the 18th century was to see the first of the great changes - physical, social and commercial - that were to lead to the dismemberment and virtual disappearance of the Dawley estate.

The Grand Junction Canal was intended to link the Thames at Brentford with the Midlands, and in its planning a line was chosen through the Thames Valley running first north-west, then west as far as West Drayton, thence turning north through Uxbridge on a route to Braunston in Northamptonshire. The route ran through the Dawley estate, entering it a short way north of the dovecote, avoiding all buildings, and leaving the western boundary on a line a little to the south of the point of entry. The enabling Act of Parliament for the Grand Junction Canal was passed in April 1793, and the acquisition of all the land needed, including 4 acres 3 roods 26 poles at Dawley from the Hon Jerome De Salis, was achieved. Construction was soon under way, both in the Midlands and on the southern section of the canal from Brentford. The work in the west part of Middlesex was relatively straightforward (there are no locks on the canal for over 3 miles in each direction from Dawley) although a deep cutting was necessary at this point. William Jessop, the engineer in charge of the construction, in a report dated 24 May 1794, said that 'The Canal from Uxbridge to Brentford is all cut, except about 2 miles of the deep part at Dawley, of this deep part about two thirds is done, but as the number of labourers will be less and less during the summer, it is hardly probable that it will be completed before Michaelmas' (29 September). (1) The delay at the 'Dawley Deep', as it was called, probably led to willingness to try out a digging device invented by Ralph Dodd (c1756 - 1822). It was 'a machine to be worked by men, by the means of levers, for excavating canals, which was tried in the year 1794, in the deep cutting at Dawley on the Grand Junction Canal'. It was claimed that the machine could dig a cart-load at a time, and that two men could do the work of seven. (2) The canal between Brentford and Uxbridge via Dawley was opened on 3 November 1794, although nearly six years elapsed before the line to Braunston in Northamptonshire was completed. (3)

Three bridges over the canal were provided at Dawley: one (numbered 198 by the Grand Junction Canal authority) carried the Harlington-Hillingdon road at the east boundary of the estate; another (No 197) was in line with the centre of the Long Walk, and served what later became known as Rigby Lane; and the third (No 196) was not on a road but was probably placed to meet the needs of a tenant farmer whose field had been bisected by the canal. The last named bridge was removed in 1820 (4), no doubt because it had been made redundant by changes in the tenancy of the fields north and south of the canal.

The whole of the Dawley estate, including the park lands, was broken up during the 19th century, and this will be discussed later in connection with the Harlington Inclosure Award, for which detailed information is available. An early use of part of the estate during this period, of which the old Earl of Uxbridge would certainly have approved, was in connection with race horses. Tattersall's, the well-known racing bloodstock agency, had a stud farm at Dawley for forty years or so up to about 1838. (5)

It is one of those minor curiosities of history that the establishment of the fortunes of the firm should have been the sale of the famous racehorse 'Highflyer' to Richard Tattersall (1724 - 1795) by Frederick St John, Viscount Bolingbroke, a descendant of the famous owner of Dawley some forty years earlier.

The price paid for Highflyer, who it was claimed had never lost a race, was what was then considered the enormous sum of £2500. This stallion was the foundation of the financial success of Richard Tattersall, and repaid its purchase price many times over in stake money, stud fees of between £12000 to £15000 a year, and the sale of its progeny.

Richard Tattersall's son Edmund (1758 - 1810) came of age in the year Highflyer was purchased, and in Richard's later years it was Edmund who looked after Tattersall's breeding interests. Edmund married Elizabeth Wilshin, who came of a family that farmed extensively in West Middlesex, including Harlington. It may therefore, have been the Wilshin connection that caused Tattersall's to take a lease on land at Dawley for a stud farm. Richard Tattersall had offices and stables at Hyde Park Corner in London, that were founded about 1773, and a 60 acre stud farm at Red Barn Farm, Ely, in Cambridgeshire, that was in existence by 1785, where Highflyer was kept. It appears that the Dawley establishment may have been intended only to be subsidiary to the Ely stud farm. It was probably convenient to have somewhere nearer to London where, apart from accommodating brood mares and young stock as well as a few stallions owned by the firm or its clients, other stock for which Tattersall's were temporarily responsible could be kept.

The Dictionary of National Biography's entry for Richard Tattersall implies that the stud farm at Dawley was started soon after the purchase in 1779 of Highflyer, and the Tattersall's historian (6) merely states that the Dawley stud farm was acquired in Richard Tattersall's day (namely before 1795). No evidence has been found for dates as early as these although Tattersall's may well have been at Dawley before 1800. The historian of Tattersall's recounts how Edmund Tattersall (1789 - 1851) (grandson of the founder of the firm and son of Edmund, who died in 1810) induced his younger brother George, who was farming in Norfolk, to take over the management of the Dawley stud farm. The earliest specific reference to Tattersalls at Dawley so far discovered is, in fact, to 'George Tattersall, farmer, Harlington', in Pigot's directory for 1827-1828. (7)

The plans for the Great Western Railway, deposited in 1834 (8), show George Tattersall to be the occupier at Dawley of three fields of pasture and two of arable land (one of the latter including as well the final 'Dawley House') owned by Count and Countess De Salis.

Among the celebrated racehorses bred or at stud at Dawley were Sir Hercules (1826), Recovery (1827), Glencoe (1831), Harkaway (1834), Charles XII (1836), and The Colonel, winner of the St Leger in 1828, bought at the sale of the Royal Stud at Hampton Court in 1837.

George Tattersall appears in the Register of Electors for Harlington, published in 1838 (9), qualifying (at 'Dawley Farm') as a tenant paying a rental in excess of £50 per annum, but he cannot have had much interest in Dawley for very much longer after this time.

There is a tomb memorial in the churchyard at Northolt, Middlesex (10) to Edmund Tattersall (1758 - 1810), his wife Elizabeth (Wilshin) (1770 - 1848) and their sons Edmund (1789 - 1851) and George (1791 - 1852).

The Great Western Railway's plans for the line through Dawley were approved and the tracks were laid by 1838. The railway cut through the middle of the land leased by Tattersall's and was the cause of their decision to move away. They transferred their livestock in stages to a new stud farm at Willesden.

THE INCLOSURE, THE G.W.R.,
THE TITHE AWARD AND 1841 CENSUS

The Inclosure Act for the remaining open fields and commons in Harlington took effect in 1821. This resulted in little change in Dawley, beyond some minor additions to the west boundary of the estate. The Inclosure Award and the map that went with it is of considerable value to historians, however, because, for the first time, it accurately delineates all the fields and records the names of their owners, enabling a comparison to be made with the Dawley estate of a hundred years earlier, when it was owned by the Earl of Tankerville.

The Inclosure Map and the details in the Award show that the De Salis family in 1821 owned about 65% of the land at Dawley within the bounds of the estate as shown in the plan of c1721 drawn by Jenner for the Earl of Tankerville. Practically the whole of the estate boundary in the earlier map can accurately be related to field boundaries shown in 1821. The Honourable Jerome De Salis, as he is described in the Award, owned all the northern part of the old estate but his property terminated in the south with what was then called the Lantern Ground - two arable fields where the avenues and formal gardens running west from the old mansion used to be. His property also comprised the site of the formal gardens, including the patte d'oie, south of the house, together with the old courtyard and the final 'Dawley House' on its north side. In addition, De Salis had been awarded some 13 acres in Hyde Field ('Hyde Piece'), formerly in Hillingdon Parish, which was added to the western extremity of the estate. He also retained (now separated from the main part of his estate) some 24 acres in two fields (the Farther Beech Wood and First Beech Wood) at the south- west corner of Dawley. In all, De Salis owned 267 acres 1 rood 28 poles at Dawley, compared with the approximately 400 acres of Tankerville's estate.

The remaining 35% of Dawley was held by four other owners. The Dowager Countess of Berkeley had, by 1821, acquired just over 52 acres at Dawley, in the Pinkwell area, no doubt managed with the main Berkeley properties in Harlington proper; John Sprang had 74 acres in the south and south-east of the old estate, including the site of the old Pinkwell formal gardens; and James Griffiths owned just over 6 acres - a field known as Frog Ditch, which adjoined his further, much larger, holdings outside the old Dawley estate, in Harlington proper. Finally, the Grand Junction Canal Company held a strip of land totalling 4 acres 3 roods 26 poles, being the canal and its towpath.

All the land at Dawley was held Freehold by its five owners and all of it, with the exception of 'Hyde Piece', was described in the Inclosure Award as 'Old Inclosures' - namely, piecemeal changes that had already taken place by mutual agreement between individual landowners.

Once the canal had been completed, the passage of barges (or 'narrow boats') caused little disturbance to the rural scene. The railway, that was also to cut across Dawley some 40 years after the canal, was another matter.

The plans for the Great Western Railway that was proposed to connect London with Bristol were deposited in 1834. (1) These showed I K Brunel's projected line running through the north side of the Thames Valley out of London and crossing the Dawley estate, entering it near where a lodge was shown on Jenner's plan of c1721 and leaving it a short way south of the Grand Junction Canal, from whence the two transport systems ran parallel for about a mile. The line at Dawley mostly cut across fields owned, as stated in the Book of Reference accompanying the plans, by Count and Countess De Salis (and occupied by George Tattersall), but also traversed one field owned by the Dowager Countess of Berkeley, and two of John Sprang's.

After some difficulties, the Great Western Railway Act of Parliament was passed in August 1835, and the gangs of 'navvies' started work. The line had no gradients to speak of in the Dawley area, the main problems in the section out of London being the crossing of the Brent valley at Hanwell and the Thames crossing at Maidenhead. The first two locomotives to be tried out on the line, the 'Premier' and the 'Vulcan', passed through Dawley in barges on the canal from Brentford in November 1837, having been shipped to London from Liverpool by sea. At West Drayton the engines were lifted from the barges with sheer legs anchored to an elm tree. 'Vulcan' was tried out on a length of track during the following weeks. The whole route from Paddington to Taplow was completed with track within the next few months, and this section of the line was opened to passengers on 4 June 1838, the 8 o'clock train from Paddington being the first scheduled service to run through Dawley. There were at first eight down and eight up services each weekday. A year later, there were 14 trains each way through Dawley to and from Maidenhead or West Drayton. The line was opened as far as Reading in 1840, although it was not fully completed to Bristol until 30 June 1841. (2)

There was originally a bridge crossing the railway line at Dawley. This connected fields, bisected by the track, farmed (in 1839) by Matthew Newman. The need for this bridge had evidently gone by the beginning of the 20th century, and it was removed. (3) It should perhaps be mentioned that the bridge carrying the Harlington-Hillingdon road over the railway, Bourne's Bridge, is just outside the old 1721 Dawley estate boundary.

As mentioned earlier, the coming of the railway meant the departure of Tattersall's establishment from Dawley, highly-strung racehorses and noisy smoke-belching trains being incompatible !

The Harlington Tithe Award map was published in 1839 in connection with the commutation of tithes in the parish for fixed rents based on the price of corn. The information given on the map and in the Award itself is particularly valuable in that it has the names of tenants as well as owners, and also the names of fields and their use. The first detailed Census, that of 1841, supplements this information.

In Dawley, the ownership of the land had changed little since the Inclosure Award, but Warrick Bagley was now shown as the tenant of both Dawley House (the converted laundry cum pantry cum dairy building on the north side of the courtyard) and Dawley Farm (at the south-east corner of the courtyard) and the fields directly north of them. Bagley must, presumably, have sub-let one or the other of the dwellings to Tattersall's up to the time of their departure from the area a year or so before. (In the 1841 Census, the occupier of what is described as 'Dawley Farm' (Dawley House is not mentioned as such) was Thomas Pool, Bailiff - who was presumably in the employ of Count De Salis.) The other principal farmer in Dawley was Matthew Newman, who rented Pinkwell Farm and most of the adjacent land. He appears to have sub-let the farmhouse to one or other of his labourers, as he lived at Church Farm in Harlington High Street and in the Census return for 1841 (and subsequent returns to 1871) agricultural labourers are recorded as being the occupants of the Pinkwell farm house, which must have been a 19th century building or reconstruction. It was located just west of where two barns or cattle shelters are shown on the Jenner plan. One of Newman's fields was called 'The Ruins', presumably for the remains of a building there: if so, this would have been the stables (reverse-L-shaped in plan) that once occupied the site. Woolpack Farm, the only other farm house in Dawley on the Tithe Award map, was rented by James Bourne. The farm house and barns etc were just north of the railway, and the three fields in Dawley belonging to the farm were south of the line, with access via what is now (and probably was then) known as Bourne's Bridge.

It is interesting to note that in the 1841 Census, the residence of James Bourne, Farmer, is described as 'Woolpack Lodge', suggesting the possibility that a former lodge of Dawley House was then in use as the farmhouse. Richard Wickliff Philp, Daniel Gregory and Joseph Jessop also rented fields in Dawley - in the south, north-west and south-east parts, respectively, of the former estate.   Philp and Jessop both lived in Harlington proper, the latter at Dawley Manor Farm: he farmed a large acreage in Harlington outside Dawley.   Finally, Thomas Curnock had an isolated holding of an arable field and adjoining close in the centre of the former estate north of the canal.

The information on land use in Dawley in 1839 (and largely confirmed by later maps and other details) derived from the Tithe Award indicates that Warrick Bagley was primarily concerned with fruit farming, having a series of orchards along the Harlington-Hillingdon road inside the estate wall, although The Long Walk he rented was meadow land north of the canal and arable (part of land called 'The Garden Ground') south of it.   The north- west part of the former Dawley estate farmed by Daniel Gregory was all arable, except for one large orchard west of The Long Walk.   Another large orchard, part of Philp's holding, was on the site of the old formal gardens at Pinkwell.   The south part of the former estate consisted mainly of meadows, but with some arable lands, principally in the south-west, including the field still in 1839 called Beech Wood.   Much of the produce of Dawley, whether hay, cereal crops, fruit or vegetables, must have been destined for the London markets.

The past history of the Dawley estate is also reflected in the names of fields in the Tithe Award.   Most of these have already been cited in discussing the previous 200 years of history, so they will simply be recalled here briefly: The Long Walk (the field so-called closely following the shape of the old north avenue leading from the house); The Lantern Ground (two fields and another called Hither Sixteen Acres on the site of the old formal gardens leading west from the house); The Lime Walk (a field that once contained a tree avenue leading south from the formal gardens west of the house towards Pinkwell); The Great Park (a meadow at the south part of the former estate; probably the remaining part of the much greater area so named);   The Ruins (a meadow believed to include the site of stables or outbuildings of the first Dawley house ('Dawley Courte') or a successor at Pinkwell). Two more names, not so readily accounted for, are Bowling Green Close and Hospital Close, the former fronting on to the Harlington-Hillingdon road east of the courtyard of Dawley House, and the latter adjoining it on the south.   No records have been discovered referring to a bowling green here (the name was also once applied to any sunken lawn) although some such feature may have been introduced here after the sale of Dawley by the 2nd Earl of Tankerville, since nothing of this nature is shown on Jenner's plan of c1721.   However, Rocque's map does show two rectangular areas on either side of the entrance from the public road to the courtyard and it is reasonable to assume that one or both of these were once bowling greens.   (A bowling green in use is shown in Kip's engraving of c1700, but this is incorporated in the formal gardens south of the house).   No refuge for sick or elderly human beings has ever been recorded at Dawley and the name Hospital Close may possibly have originated during the Tattersall's tenure for a paddock used for sick race horses, conveniently accessible to the farm buildings.

CHAPTER 32

BRICKMAKING AND BEERHOUSES AT DAWLEY

Much of the soil in west Middlesex is brick-earth - excellent for agriculture - which overlies ancient deposits of gravel that formed early beds of the River Thames. In our immediate area, commercial brickmaking, made practicable and profitable by the arrival of the Grand Junction Canal, began in Hayes - at Botwell - about 1806, and there was a brickfield at Yeading (served by the Paddington Arm of the canal) by 1824. A few years later, there were five brickfields in both parts of Hayes, all near the main line or the branch of the Grand Junction Canal. (1)

Brickmaking at Harlington proper (outside Dawley) had evidently started on a commercial, but not extensive, scale at least by 1832, when Pigot's directory lists William Hinds as a brickmaker. At the Harlington Inclosure of 1821, Hinds owned a field of 2 acres 3 roods 32 poles at the end of a road or track leading off the east side of Harlington High Street, known now as Brickfields Lane. He had roughly quadrupled his land in this same area (part of the old East Field) by the date of the Tithe Award of 1839, when it was described as 'arable'. The quite shallow depression in the area still to be seen today suggests that by no means all the available brick earth was taken out, so that the remaining soil over the underlying gravel could still be used for agriculture. (2) It is interesting to note that this site did not have the advantages of canal transport facilities that were available at Dawley, so it seems likely that William Hinds found his market for bricks in the fairly close vicinity.

At Dawley, bricks were made at least as early as 1700 (3) for use on the estate, as noted earlier, but the commercial brickmaking industry there started about 1853. The rise and subsequent decline of brickmaking at Dawley is summarised in the Harlington Census returns between 1841 and 1891. In 1841, there were five houses, of which the principal occupation in three of them was agriculture, in the others probably so. The next Census, that of 1851, where more detailed information is given for the first time, shows six dwellings, including one unoccupied, where agriculture was still predominant, but Dawley House was now the home of Thomas Jolly, described as 'excavator' - of brick earth, it is assumed. By the 1861 Census, it is evident that many new cottages had been built at Dawley, and of the 36 dwellings listed, 18 were occupied by brickmakers, ranging from 'brick merchants' to 'labourers in the brickfields'. In 1871, 29 out of the 34 occupied houses (4 were unoccupied) were the homes of brickmakers. Ten years later, in 1881, the beginning of a decline could be detected in that of the 36 occupied (2 unoccupied) dwellings 25 were those of brickmakers. The 1891 Census shows 48 occupied houses and 1 unoccupied in Dawley, of which 22 had heads of household who were involved in brickmaking. The 8 other heads of household described as 'general labourers' may well have been part-time brickmakers. The beginnings of the Dawley brickfields can also be dated from two leases by the De Salis family (who owned most of the land adjacent to the canal) to various brickmakers. Thomas Jolly, mentioned above, may have been operating as early as 1851. (4) However, one of the two earliest surviving lease documents is dated 15 November 1853 and gives permission to John Rutty and George Verey of 108 Edgware Road, described as Timber Merchants and Brickmakers, to extract brick-making materials from specified land to the west of Dawley House. In the other lease document, of the same date, Dawley House itself and the surrounding land was leased for 21 years to Thomas and William Rhodes; it specifically states that the courtyard of the house was not to be dug for bricks. (5) Another early lease by the De Salis family of land at Dawley was of about 50 acres to Messrs J D and C Rigby on 14 March 1854. This was adjoining Dawley Road north of the canal. The Rigbys appear to have transferred the lease to Thomas Maynard about ten years later, although they left their name attached to a row of cottages and the lane leading to the canal. (6) By 1861, the lease on Dawley House had also been transferred to Thomas Maynard; both the 1861 and 1871 Census returns show him as living in the house. He is recorded as a 'brick and timber merchant' in 1861 and 'brick manufacturer' in 1871. That he was a man of some substance can be seen from the fact that, in addition to his wife and seven children, two servants are listed in his household (in 1871, the second servant was a governess).

Some sidelights on the brickmaking industry at Dawley can be gathered from the local newspaper. A forthcoming auction of about 1,000,000 bricks at the 'Dawley brickfields (opposite The Woolpack)' was advertised in April 1871. The types of bricks included stocks (standard bricks suitable for facings), rough stocks (similar, but with blemishes), grizzles (grey and/or underburnt bricks), and place bricks (underburnt, usually red). The last two categories were weaker than stocks and normally suitable only for non-load-bearing walls. (7) The kind of plant in use at this time included horse pug mills, four of which were advertised for sale on a site at Dawley for which a Mr C Dearlove's lease had expired in October 1871. Five acres of potatoes were also up for auction at the same time, indicating the parallel activity that alternated with brickmaking. (8) Labour difficulties in the Dawley brickfields were not uncommon in the 1870's. Sometimes men could not get their gangs together, and were summoned for not turning up for work as contracted. One excuse given to Thomas Maynard was the inability to employ children under the age of 10 years. (9) This problem may have been alleviated three years later when, following a strike in 1876 which was said to have affected most of the brickfields in Middlesex, the master brickmakers agreed to pay 6d extra per 1000 bricks. (10)

Thomas Maynard died as the result of an accident in August 1876 (11) (and his business as brickmaker, with head office at 2 South Wharf, Paddington, became 'Maynard Son & Co') but his widow Eliza was still living at Dawley House at least until 1881. (12) Her rent for the house in the accounts of the company was £125- per annum. (13) H Odell appears alongside Maynard's in the directories as a brick manufacturer at Dawley from about 1887, and as of 'Dawley house' by 1890. By this time, the brick earth in some parts of Dawley was becoming worked out, and gravel extraction was taking the place of brickmaking. This was being carried out by both Odell (at least from 1895) and Maynard's (by then 'Alfred Lionel Maynard'), south and north of the canal, respectively. This activity continued well into the next century, with Thomas Clayton, it seems, taking over Odell's site. One Charles Evans in 1899 also had a lease on land and premises south of the canal. At 22 acres 3 roods 29 poles (an acreage suspiciously close to that purchased by EMI in 1929) the site or its use has not been identified, but brick or gravel working seems the most likely. (14)

Brickmaking at Dawley led to the construction of a number of canal docks. The earliest of these were Maynard's, north of the canal in roughly the middle of the estate, and Odell's, south of the canal and close to the 'Pigeon House'. The so-called Dawley dock was actually well outside the Dawley boundary, in Yiewsley, north of the canal. (Maynard's dock had been, however, renamed as 'Dawley Dock' on a conveyance map in 1948.) (15) One of the longest canal docks in the whole area, Pocock's (or Broad's) was just outside the west boundary of Dawley, south of the canal. This served the Stockley Brick Works, although only a small area of brick earth for it was taken from Dawley. (16) There was also a small dock, apparently unnamed, on the south side of the canal in Dawley, facing Maynard's dock on the north side. This was there at least by 1865. (17) It was joined by another small dock, further east, at a later date. (18)

Brickmaking is thirsty work, and by 1871, if not earlier, there were two beerhouses at Dawley to cater for the labourers (also, no doubt, visiting canal boatmen). These establishments were 'The Ship', south of the canal, maintained by one E Read (probably to be identified with Edward Reid, a foreman in the brickfields) and 'The Cottage', later known as 'The Dawley Cottage', kept by James Goodhall (or Goodall). This was on a site near the north bank of the canal close to the Rigby Lane bridge. The Dawley Cottage was claimed to be about 200 years old (19) at the time it was demolished and may, therefore, even have been contemporary with the building of the canal, although beer may not have been sold there as early as that.

A small single-storey side extension was used as an office by the paymaster of the brickfields. (20) 'The Ship', taken over by James Sibley in 1874 and Henry Boddy in 1890, ceased to be a beerhouse about 1900 (21) and was converted into two cottages. The Dawley Cottage, taken over by Elizabeth George by 1896, was maintained as a beerhouse or public house by her descendants until 1958. Once also known as 'The White House', the Dawley Cottage ceased to be a public house and was purchased by the daughter of the last licensee and her husband from the De Salis family in 1959. (22) It was sold some thirty years later to Stockley Park plc and demolished by them in 1990. (It should perhaps be mentioned at this point that another public house nearby, 'The Dawley Arms', was outside the west boundary of the former Dawley estate, on the road leading to Starveall Farm. It was demolished in 1912 or 1913. (23) 'The Woolpack' in Dawley Road (still existing) is also outside the old estate boundary, being on the Hayes side of the road).

CHAPTER 33

THE DAWLEY BRICKFIELDS:
HOUSES AND THE SCHOOL: AGRICULTURE CONTINUED

As has been noted above, before commercial brickmaking arrived in Dawley, the only habitations were farmhouses where tradition was, no doubt, followed and the farm workers 'lived in'.   In the 1841 and 1851 Censuses there was only one dwelling that might have been a cottage, as opposed to a farmhouse.   By 1861, the Census lists the dwellings of many workers in the brickfields and the 1865 Ordnance Survey 25in map shows these cottages, which must have been built in the preceding ten years or so.   Not all of them can now be identified by name, and the local directory compilers did not bother to list their occupants before 1928.   Some of the rows of cottages seem to have been extended later to meet the demand for on-site accommodation for the brickfields.

The oldest cottage of all was the former dovecote, converted for human habitation.   It is not known when the conversion first took place (although extra windows appear to have been added to the dovecote between c1700 and c1721), but what is certain is that the 1865 OS 25in map indicates that by then it had been extended at the north side and converted into two two-storey dwellings, the building being about 25' by 40'-45' in plan.   These were known as the 'Pigeon Houses' in the 1881 Census, when one was occupied by a 'Working Foreman', his wife and four daughters;   the other one was empty. (1)   Rigby's Row (15 dwellings - two-storied with slated roofs) in Dawley Road, north of the canal, were the only cottages large enough to be named on the 1865 OS map.   In the 1881 Census these cottages were designated 'Maynard's Row', no doubt because they bordered Maynard's brickfields and the majority of their adult male occupiers then were employed there.   The cottages had reverted to their original name by 1890. (2)   Ship Row (7 dwellings in the 1881 Census, 10 in 1928), two-storied with pantiled roofs, was south of the canal, adjoining The Ship beerhouse (later a cottage) on their north side.   A row of single-storied (3) cottages close to the north bank of the canal, west of Maynard's dock were apparently an extension of two dwellings in 1881 (Census) to seven, known as 'Canal Side' in 1928, and, reduced to four, renamed 'Maynard's Cottages' in 1933 (4).   Maynard's Farm Cottages were a little way to the north of these, it is said.   The locations of several buildings in the 1881 Census have not been established, although it seems most likely that they were on the south side of the canal.   These include Stable Cottages (2 dwellings, occupied by both brickfield and farm workers), a 'detached cottage', housing a brickfield labourer, his wife and seven children, and the 'Private House' of William Thornicroft, a boat builder.   Bolingbroke Cottages (a terrace of ten dwellings) were added immediately to the south of Rigby's Row in 1907. (5)   This date is rather late for them to have been built specifically for brickworkers, although some were probably occupied by gravel diggers and others by workers in the new industries being established in the area.

A house larger than all the cottages around the brickfields was also erected at Dawley, probably in the early 1860's, near to the canal on its south side, close to the Dawley Road bridge.   From the appearance of its roof structure this building may have been extended at a later date.   Although it seems likely, from its location, to have been built for a brickfield owner, in the 1881 Census, known by then, at any rate, as Rockfield House, it was occupied by a gardener, Daniel Grace.   (Grace moved, or was moved, to the Pigeon House by 1891).   Renamed Rockfield Villa, a carman, Horace David Lowe, (6) was in residence there by 1905 (7), where he remained until 1916 (although there is some evidence that the Maynard family may have lived there at least around 1911, as discussed further below) or until the house was taken over by the United Kingdom Glass Company as part of the site they leased in 1916.   (Lowe moved to the early 20th century house further down Dawley Road named 'Gethceln').   Rockfield Villa seems, at times, to have been known as 'New Dawley House', a name that may have been given to it by the Maynard family after they had left the (then) Dawley House.   A postcard was addressed to Miss

Maynard at 'New Dawley House' in 1911, when, according to other evidence, Rockfield Villa was occupied by H D Lowe. (8) However, the name 'New Dawley House' surfaced again in 1928 for what there is little doubt was Rockfield Villa when occupied by A W G Dixon (possibly George Dixon, said to be the De Salis' bailiff). (9) By 1963, Rockfield Villa had acquired the even grander and entirely unjustified name of 'Manor House' (or 'New House' in a 1965 directory - possibly a mistake). The house was demolished, bearing the name 'Manor House', in the 1970's.

Some other cottages of this era - the second half of the 19th century and early 20th - solely used by or mainly intended for farm workers, as opposed to brick, gravel or industrial workers, are listed below.

The influx of workers and their families into Dawley in the latter half of the 19th century called for a school in the nearby locality for the younger children. A narrow strip of land along the Dawley Road just north of Rigby's Row was provided by the De Salis family and a Church of England infants school was erected there. Opened on 30 March 1897, with Alice J S Bull as teacher, the Dawley Infants School was a single-storey building 25ft x 20ft with accommodation for up to 53 children. Only twelve children were there on the first day, although by September the school had 15 boys and 18 girls. The school log books (10) throw some light on local life and events over the 27 years of its existence, and it is felt worth while quoting from them here, although this means running somewhat ahead in the chronology of Dawley.

In May 1900, for instance, it was recorded that some of the infants stayed at home 'to take dinners' - presumably for their families in the fields - and in July only two boys and six girls were at school, because of a measles epidemic. In October 1903, the 'very boisterous' weather made the teacher fear that some of the smaller children might be 'blown over the bridges' (of the canal, that is). In June of the following year, the untidiness of children was excused because their mothers were engaged in fruit picking in the fields; and on 15 December 1904 the school was closed at 12 for the day because part of the yard and nearby low-lying roads were under water. A 7 year-old boy at the school died on 4 December 1905 after a short illness and the school was thoroughly disinfected as a precaution. In the following year, in March, children from Rigby's Row were excluded from the school because a man in the cottages was suffering from diphtheria. On 10 January 1910, it was recorded that 47 children were present out of a roll of 48, a good number despite the fact that it had recently been decided no longer to admit under-5 year-olds. (The attendance figures over the years incidentally were intermittently increased by children from canal boats moored nearby). The school harmonium was transferred to the new Dawley Mission Hall in October 1910. It was returned early in 1912, only temporarily, it seems, because Annie Burrows, the then headmistress, loaned her own piano to the school, although it had to be given up in 1921 after her death. Nineteen children from the Upper Division of the school were taken on an outing to Southend on Sea in October 1912 - 'To most of them this was their first glimpse of the sea', the teacher noted. A dramatic reminder of the manufacturing industry that was establishing itself in Dawley occurred on 29 June 1916, when the school wall was damaged by iron girders being taken to the United Kingdom Glass Company factory. In September 1919 the school building was reported to be unsafe and was closed for repairs: the children used the Dawley Mission Hall for temporary accommodation. Another outbreak of measles in June 1920 again left only eight children in the school, and it was closed for two weeks. Emergency repairs to the school were again needed in April 1923 and this may have reinforced the School Managers' decision to close it permanently due to the decrease in the roll (there were 23 children on 13 July). From 29 August 1923, the Middlesex Education Committee took over what then became known as 'Dawley Council School'. Ten children were sent to Hayes Council School (in Clayton Road, not far away) reducing the roll at Dawley to 14. Messrs Try, the builders, came to start the 'emergency' repairs on 7 December 1923. The final entry in the school log book for 1924 was 'The School closed after afternoon session on Wed 23rd July, having been open 27$\frac{1}{2}$ years'.

115

Despite all the activities of the extractive industries in the late 19th century and the beginning of the establishment of manufacturing industry that was to follow, agriculture at Dawley, somewhat surprisingly, continued in various forms well into the 20th century.

A succession of market gardeners farmed in the area, on the east side of the former Dawley estate north of the railway and more widely south of it, prior to the building of the housing estates either side of (the present) Bourne Avenue. A resident (before about 1914) of the old dovecote, by then converted into a pair of dwellings, recalled that in the fields around or nearby, corn, peas, plums, greengages and cherries were grown. (11) Later, after the First World War, a pig farm, belonging to Whichello's, the butchers, was set up in the area between Dawley House and Dawley Road. By 1914, James Benn (described in directories between 1904 and 1908 as 'carman etc') was established as a dairy farmer at Dawley. He lived in No 1 Rigby's Row (the most northerly dwelling in this terrace of cottages) and pastured his cows in the fields in the north-east part of the former Dawley estate. He was survived by his wife, Harriet, who as late as 1937 was still running a small shop in the front room of their cottage. (12)

By 1899 a roughly triangular area of land at Gould's Green in Hillingdon, known as Barnes Farm, stretching about 400 yards north from the tip of the Dawley estate wall, had been added by the De Salis family to what was then known as the Dawley Wall Estate. This land, together with some adjacent fields in Dawley, was tenanted by H J Robinson and Cecil De Salis and comprised 52 acres and 24 poles described in 1899 as 'House and lands called Barnes'. (13) The farmhouse was in Gould's Green (Hillingdon) although Barnes Farm Cottages (a late 19th/early 20th century terrace of four dwellings for the farm workers) straddled the Hillingdon/Harlington boundary. Therefore, when the bounds were beaten, according to ancient custom, the beaters processed through the most northerly cottage ! (14)

At Woolpack Farm, near Bourne's Bridge, W H Reed was in residence in 1894, and John Ridding in 1899. (15) By 1909 it was farmed by Robert Pullin Newman (who lived in Harlington) who, in 1910, also took a lease on Dawley Farm, which adjoined it, for one year. 'Dawley House Farm' was occupied by one J M Fielder in 1915 according to the 'Gazette' of 23/4/1915. Dawley Farm had two (and later three) dwellings at the farmyard near the south-east corner of the courtyard. These were let out: in 1881 (16) only one was occupied by a farm worker; the other by a brickfield foreman. In 1921, one cottage was let at 10 shillings per week and the other two were occupied by De Salis employees as part of their wages. (17) These cottages were still there as late as 1933 but by 1935 had been removed. (18)

South of the railway at Dawley, where relatively little brick earth and gravel were worked, Pinkwell Farm was also farmed by R P Newman, who recorded in a notebook (19) that he built Pinkwell Cottages in 1909, a short distance south of the farm buildings. A semi-detached pair of dwellings, they still exist, much altered, in Pinkwell Lane.

The local directories record Edward J King in 1910 and 1914 and J E King (an error ?) in 1916 at Pinkwell Farm, E S Lendrum in 1922 and R C Wills in 1928. Between 1933 and 1937, Gilbert Rose, who had operated from 'Bedwell Villa', and then 'Werrington', in Dawley Road as a market gardener since about 1914, switched to dairy farming assisted by his son, and from this time, or a little later, took over Pinkwell Farm. (20) G Rose and Son's Dairy also sold milk retail from their premises in Dawley Road. (The Pinkwell Farm buildings were demolished in 1935: the site is now occupied by houses in Carnarvon Drive.) (21)

'Bedwell Villa' and 'Werrington', mentioned above, were among the new houses (or 'villas' to use a popular description of the time) to be built either side of Dawley Road, south of the railway, from about 1904 onwards. This, however, is outside our story, since that part of Dawley Road is not within the area of the former Dawley estate of Lord Tankerville and later owners.   Nevertheless, it is indicative of the population pressures building up in and around Dawley.

Bourne Farm, incorporating parts of Woolpack Farm immediately south-west of Bourne's Bridge (and yet another of the holdings of R P Newman in 1909) had acquired a terraced row of ten cottages in 1900, according to the date they bore, and were appropriately called Bourne's Bridge Cottages. (22)   Bourne Farm Cottages (a joined pair, probably slightly earlier in date) and some barns and other farm buildings were a little way to the west and just inside the former Dawley estate, unlike Bourne's Bridge Cottages, which appear to have been just outside it.

Some traditional practices were evidently still carried out in the area well into the 20th century, for R P Newman noted in a diary that he had had all his farm buildings, including those of Woolpack Farm, thatched in 1909, and they were tarred in the following year. (23)

CHAPTER 34

MANUFACTURING INDUSTRY AT DAWLEY;
WORLD WAR I; GRAVEL EXTRACTION

The beginning of the 20th century found Dawley in transition from a mixed economy of agriculture, brickmaking and gravel extraction, to the commencement of manufacturing industry, at first on a small scale. Farming had largely become concentrated on market gardening - as in so much of Middlesex - with peas, cherries, plums and greengages being grown, although there was also some corn. (1) By the second decade of the century, if not earlier, there was a dairy herd established in the north east part of the former estate. As early as 1874, Thomas Maynard, of Dawley House, was described as 'brick manufacturer and gravel merchant', an indication of changes to come. (2)

The brickfields at Dawley had largely been worked out by 1900, although Clayton's south of the canal with about 49 acres and Maynard's north of it with 43 acres appear still to have been making bricks before the onset of World War I. (3) Dawley House and the dovecote were each said to be standing 'high' above the surrounding area because the brickearth topsoil around them had been removed. (4) Extensive gravel deposits lay under the brickearth, and gravel had for a long time been taken for local use - such as road repairs. A small gravel pit just inside the Dawley Wall near the junction with Botwell Common Road is marked on the 1865 OS map. This was probably an easily accessible patch and, significantly, another gravel pit was close by on the Hayes side of Dawley Road. Commercial extraction of gravel at Dawley followed the removal of brickearth topsoil and continued alongside the last active brickfields. It was carried on long after the brick making ceased: former brickmakers, such as Maynard's, Odell's and Clayton's, continued in business for some years as gravel diggers. Hence, 'H Odell, brick manufacturer' of the 1890's became 'Odell & Co Ltd, gravel pit owners, Dawley' by 1910, and Maynard's were the owners of the 'Dawley Gravel Works', although they were still making bricks as late as 1914. Thomas Clayton Ltd, who started as brickmakers, were also recorded as gravel pit owners in 1914. (5) To complete the story of gravel at Dawley (although running ahead out of sequence), H Sabey & Co entered the business locally about 1926, (6) taking over some sites in the north-west part of the estate, adjoining their Stockley and Yiewsley pits. They were among the last to leave Dawley, as late as the 1970's. George C Cross & Co Ltd was another relatively late entrant into gravel extraction at Dawley, working pits right across the centre of Dawley north of the canal and south of Sabey's site.

One sad result for historians and archaeologists of all this disturbance over much of Dawley is that nearly all traces of earlier occupation sites, formal gardens and tree avenues have been removed.

At nearby Hayes, manufacturing industry on a large scale arrived following the purchase in 1898 by Thomas Clayton (who had canal and brickfield interests) of a 42 acre plot between the canal and the railway. This area of land consisted in the main of worked-out brickfields and was at Botwell, just the other side of the road from Dawley. The close availability of both canal and rail links with London and the rest of the country made the Hayes site an obvious one for industrial development. Sites nearer London were taken up earlier, but by 1908, for instance, for a factory in London rated at £4000-£5000, the equivalent in Hayes or West Drayton was only £1000-£2000. (7) A variety of firms had factories built or building in The Hayes Development Company's estate, as it was called, by 1907, and the largest of them by far, Gramophone and Typewriter Ltd, opened in that year. Inevitably, development of this kind was to spread to Dawley, which had identical transport advantages to offer.

The first factory at Dawley actually preceded the Hayes factories by twenty years or more, although it was a very small one. Called Ray and Son and established there by the 1880's, it was a mineral water bottling plant at Bourne Farm, near the railway. (8)   By 1912, what was presumably the same business, or its successor, A W Ray, was described as being at 'Woolpack Bridge'. (9)   The site was just north of the railway.   Both stoneware and glass bottles (some of them the 'Cod bottle' type) marked variously 'A W Ray', 'A W Ray, Harlington' and 'Ray & Son' have been found locally.   The last was also inscribed 'Estd 1816', although it is not known if the firm was at Harlington or Dawley at this date. (10)

Possibly the very earliest industrial enterprise at Dawley, before even Ray's mineral water plant, was boat building.   Edwin Thornicroft (born in Coventry), with his wife, four sons and three daughters, living at Dawley in 1861, gave his occupation as 'boat builder'.   In the following Census, 1871, this description is amplified as 'canal boat and barge builder'.   By 1881, the family business appears to have been taken over by one of Edwin Thornicroft's younger sons, William, who is described as 'Boat builder', occupying a 'Private House' at 'Dawley Deep'.   There is no actual evidence that the boat building was carried out at Dawley, although this seems likely.   If so, one of the small docks on the south side of the canal may have been used for this purpose.   The 1891 Census has no record of the Thornicroft family or of boat building at Dawley, although in 1899 one Edwin Thornicroft was listed in Kelly's Directory, as a boat builder at North Hyde, Southall. (11)

In 1899, one Charles James Fauvel had 3 acres of land and a factory south of the canal at Dawley.   The location of the site, leased from the De Salis', is not known, although it is perhaps most likely to have been that known to have been leased in 1906 to Vegox Ltd, manufacturers of a bottled food product akin to Marmite or Bovril.   A Conveyance between the De Salis family and Vegox Ltd and Ernest Arthur Alexander was dated 31 October 1906. (12)   The factory was on a site between the canal and the railway near the west boundary of Dawley. (13)   This marks the certain beginning of the industrial development that was to spread across the Dawley Road from Botwell.   The next enterprise at Dawley was another small one, however, when a small cork manufactory was set up in a barn at Dawley Farm by, it is believed, a member of the Bowater family, who lived in Dawley House at this time.   This business was started about 1913, and lasted only a few years. (14)

To cater for the increased population of the area, and perhaps to combat 'dirt, darkness and ignorance' of the kind attributed by the Hayes historian Elizabeth Hunt to brickworkers and their families at Botwell and Yeading, a mission church was built at Dawley in 1910.   Dedicated by the Bishop of Kensington on 29 October of that year, this building was in Dawley Road immediately south of Bolingbroke Cottages. (15)   (This little church was in the early 1930's transferred to the site planned for St Jerome's church in Judge Heath Lane, Hayes, where, after the new church was completed, it served as the church hall.   Severely damaged in an air raid in August 1940, it was finally destroyed by a fire in January, 1946.) (16) Incidentally, it is not unlikely that the Dawley Mission was originally intended to serve also the Hayes factory area, since before the first St Anselm's church in Station Road, Hayes, was built in 1913, it (the Dawley church) was as near, or nearer, for many factory workers as the Botwell Mission Hall, founded in 1896.

The Great War, or World War I as it is now generally called, broke out in August 1914, and many of the Hayes factories turned to the production of war weapons and supplies.   A new factory at Dawley was the Vulcan Iron and Metal Works, established by November 1915 in the former premises of Vegox Ltd which, it was reported, had been 'empty for some long time'.   (17)   A much more important concern was the United Kingdom Glass Company Ltd, which in 1916 commenced building a factory for making bottles on a 12 acre site adjoining the canal on its south side, near the Rigby Lane bridge.   It was opened in November 1917 and the first furnace was in operation in December. (18)   Thirteen cottages (numbered 1 to 12, and 12A) were built by the company for its workers, inside the Dawley estate wall.   Six of these dwellings, 'U' Kay Cottages' are still in existence today (19) - a brick built terrace of four and a semi-detached pair, all facing the Dawley Road. These were the best ones, probably occupied by the more senior workers: the remaining seven dwellings were single-storey buildings of a less permanent nature, and they disappeared in the 1920's or '30's. Successive managers of the company lived in Dawley House. Rockfield Villa by the canal was also occupied by senior management staff and, it is understood, the Pigeon House cottages, which were on the UK Glass Company's site, were also allocated to some of their workers. (20) Also in 1916, Watney, Combe and Reid, the brewers, leased a plot of land at Dawley south of the canal from the De Salis family. What use they made of it has not been discovered: the site was ultimately taken over by McAlpine's. (21) Another factory at Dawley in this period was that of 'Sanitas', manufacturers of disinfectants. Nothing has been discovered about it beyond the fact that 'Sanitas Disinfectants' was advertised on Hayes and Harlington station about 1913, which may suggest a date for the firm's presence locally. (22)

Among varied aspects of the war affecting Dawley were that some Belgian refugees were accommodated in part of Dawley House for a time, (23) and that an anti-aircraft gun was mounted near the canal to counter German air raids. (24) Although the factories in Hayes, in particular, would have been a likely target (and one easy to locate from the air, with the canal and the railway running parallel in the area) there is, in fact, no record of any bombs falling on Hayes or Harlington. (25) In September 1917, the Hayes Filling Factory held a carnival at Bourne Farm. Over 15000 people attended and the band of the 2nd Life Guards helped to entertain them. (26)

CHAPTER 35

DAWLEY - THE 1920's TO THE END OF WORLD WAR II

The most important feature of Dawley in the period following the First World War up to and including World War II was the growth on a significant scale of manufacturing industry and housing. This period can be summarised, from north to south in the three sections divided by the canal and the railway, as follows.

North of the canal, gravel digging was in full swing, although there was also dairy farming at the east side of the former Dawley estate. What houses there were were concentrated near the canal or along the Dawley Road. The Infants' School opened in 1897 closed in 1924 as discussed earlier (1) and the building was used in the 1930's as a woodworking workshop. (2) The Mission Hall opened in 1910 was, after 20 years or so, moved bodily to Judge Heath Lane, also as mentioned earlier. The outposts of manufacturing industry were located near the east side of the former estate behind Rigby's Row and Bolingbroke Cottages. A new firm, Horsley Smith & Co (Floors) purchased a 5.723 acres site from the De Salis family in April 1937. Later, in 1944, as Horsley Smith & Co (Hayes) Ltd, they acquired a further 14.716 acres to the west and, finally, in February 1946, bought both Rigby's Row and Bolingbroke Cottages, the existing tenancies to be protected. (3) A gasholder was erected about 1938 by the Uxbridge Gas Company on a site to the west of the north end of Maynard's Dock. (4)

In the central area of Dawley, between the canal and the railway, by the late 1920's most of the land, apart from Dawley House and its environs, had been sold or leased by the De Salis family to various industrial or commercial concerns. The functions of all these firms has not been established, or the use to which they put the land. In some cases it seems that the sites, all having access to railway sidings and/or the canal, may have been acquired for storage purposes - for immediate or future use. The occupiers in 1929 were shown on a map (5) from west to east as follows. First of all, a small site adjoining the west boundary of the estate once occupied by the Vegox and, later, Vulcan factories was shown as owned by E A Alexander. It was leased to J Nathan & Co Ltd, a New Zealand company that branched out into the manufacture of baby foods under the made-up name of 'Glaxo'. (6) In January 1930 this Dawley site was leased for five years as the Glaxo 'Field Factory, Hayes, Middlesex'. In 1933 the factory buildings and premises were assessed at a nett annual value of £240- - higher than that of the McAlpine's site. (7) Glaxo Laboratories Ltd later produced their first pharmaceuticals at Dawley, synthesising Vitamin D, Vitamin A (from fish oil) and Vitamin E (from wheat germ). The lease was renewed in 1935 and evidently again in 1940. By 1944 only two people were still working at the Dawley factory (on small jobs involving 'smelly experiments') although it had been retained by Glaxo as a 'shadow factory' to be brought into full use if other factories were destroyed by enemy action. The factory building was a single-storey one of about 10,000 square feet in area. An adjacent cottage was used as an office (8) and was also occupied by a caretaker, according to local information. (9)

Next, east, was a site leased by R H Green & Silley Weir Ltd, about which little is known except that part of the site was held in the name of K Wood by 1945. (10) Adjoining this was a larger site leased in May 1920 (11) by Chappell & Co Ltd, the sheet music and musical instrument retailers. This was for use as a playing field. (12) Chappell's site was adjoined by one to the south-east, near the railway, in the name of D Colville Stewart, function unknown, which had been vacated by 1929. The United Kingdom Glass Company's site was the farthest east, bounded by the canal on the north and Dawley Road on its east side. Watney, Combe, Reid & Co Ltd, the brewers, also had a site at Dawley at one time, leased in February 1916, although they had vacated it by 1929. It may have been in the area later occupied by Chappell & Co. Two small properties faced Dawley Road. J K Neasby (who was associated with Neasby & Son, cork manufacturers at Bedwell Villa, Harlington) held in 1929 a plot immediately south of UK Cottages. Miss Alice Stead ran a coffee stall there, later to be succeeded by T Martin with more permanent, wooden, refreshment rooms, and a garage. (13) Henry Martin (presumably his son) took over in due course and, as he was a motorcycle enthusiast, used the name Speedway Cafe. It had gone by the early 1960's. The presence of the factories close by must have encouraged these catering enterprises. Also in 1929 (if not earlier), H E Pickett and H D Lowe had a rectangular site roughly opposite the Hambrough Arms, of which Pickett was the landlord from 1913 until at least 1923, although no longer in 1928. Horace David Lowe was a carman who had transferred his business from Rockfield Villa nearby. Gethceln, the house on the site, was apparently built after 1914: it is still standing today. (14)

The UK Glass Company departed from Dawley in the late 1920's or early 1930's, it is believed, leaving behind them the row of cottages that still bears their name and unemployed glassworkers, many brought down from Scotland around 1924-25 and made redundant by new machinery a few years later. (15) Sir Robert McAlpine and Co, the building and civil engineering contractors, acquired the UK Glass Co site by means of a conveyance dated 25 June 1935 for use as a machinery depot and also (perhaps later) all or part of the site once used by Chappell & Co.

Arguably, the most important and long-lasting acquisition of land at Dawley was the purchase by The Gramophone Company of a site of 22 acres 3 roods 3½ poles (16) including Dawley House. The conveyance from 'Cecil Fane De Salis and others' was dated 19 July 1929. (17) This site was conveniently close to the Company's main buildings in Blyth Road, Hayes, the other side of Dawley Road. Dawley House itself was used for various industrial purposes, as discussed later. The Company in 1937 (by then through amalgamation with the Columbia record company, known as Electric and Musical Industries Ltd - EMI) acquired a further site at Dawley - 20 acres, close to the railway, near Bourne's Bridge. This site was used for building a modern factory for Rudge Whitworth Ltd, a subsidiary at Coventry that had been taken over in 1934. Production of bicycles was transferred to Dawley when the factory was completed in 1939. The manufacture of motorcycles was ceased on 18 December 1939, although service and repair of them at Dawley may have been continued, if only temporarily. (18) Rudge Whitworth products were highly regarded, and its bicycles were generally considered second only to those made by Raleigh.

South of the railway, manufacturing industry at Dawley was confined to a Royal Ordnance Factory adjoining the West Drayton border, the construction of which commenced not long before the outbreak of World War II. The wartime activities of the Rudge Whitworth and Royal Ordnance factories are discussed more fully later. The part of Dawley, south of the railway line, which merges with the main part of Harlington, was the most affected by housing developments from the 1930's onwards. Known as the Bourne Farm Estate, much of the area between the railway and Pinkwell Lane was built over by George Wimpey & Co Ltd. It comprised such roads as Bourne Avenue, Waltham Avenue and Elers Road, and roads and closes leading from them. (Strictly speaking, the south-eastern part of the Wimpey estate is outside the scope of this book, since the old Dawley estate boundary south of Bourne's Bridge took an irregular course, moving increasingly further to the west of Dawley Road until it reached Pinkwell Lane and turned due west.) The 1932 local directory shows that most, if not all, the houses in Pinkwell Avenue, for example, had then been completed. (19) An Anglican church to serve the area, Christ Church, Waltham Avenue, was first opened in a temporary building in 1937. (20)

There is an interesting story, relating to this period, to the effect that Richard Fairey at one time wished to acquire a tract of land at Dawley south of the railway to build an airfield for his company, the factory of which was nearby in North Hyde Road. The field in question was apparently the one known as 'Lime Walk' - No 18 in the Harlington Inclosure Award. It was also rumoured locally that Merchant Taylors' School considered the purchase of this same site. However, the Great West

Aerodrome at Heathrow was established by the Fairey Aviation Company in 1930 on land purchased the previous year. Merchant Taylors' School, then at Charterhouse Square in London was, in fact, seeking a site outside London and eventually moved to its present location at Northwood, Middlesex. (21) Fairey was an Old Boy of the school and it is just possible that the school's name was used to disguise enquiries about a potential airfield site. (22) It is a fact, though, that Wimpey's building operations were terminated in Bourne Avenue just west of Clevedon Gardens (where the remains of a hedge both sides of Bourne Avenue still mark an old field boundary) not to be resumed until some time later. (23) The Hayes and Harlington Urban District Council acquired the major part of the field of about 24½ acres, once known as the Beech Wood, from the Hayward family of farmers in July 1936. This was for use as a burial ground: it is usually known today as the Cherry Lane Cemetery. (24)

World War II broke out on 3 September 1939, with Britain's declaration of war on Germany. For over a year before, measures for the protection of members of the public against aerial attack had been given high priority by the Government, and local authorities had been given instructions regarding air raid precautions (ARP), including plans for public air raid shelters. The Hayes and Harlington Urban District Council had completed some shelters in its area as early as September 1938, and a report dated 10 October 1939 listed shelters for a total accommodation of over 8000 people. (25) Some of these air raid shelters were already completed, as mentioned above, and others were nearing completion. One at Dawley, planned for 470 people (490 as completed) was on land owned by Sir Cecil De Salis inside the Dawley Wall, just south of the pond to the north of Rigby's Row. There was also a factory shelter east of Dawley House. (26) It was reported elsewhere, incidentally, that when shelters for EMI employees were being dug, brickwork footings and a brick culvert in the Dawley House area were discovered, but were not investigated. (27) Among air raid wardens' posts planned in early 1939 were F2, F3 and F4 in Dawley Road, Bourne Avenue and Mildred Avenue, respectively, all south of the railway line. (28) Compared with central London, Hayes and Harlington suffered relatively lightly from aerial attack during the war, the main factory areas in Hayes being the principal targets. A few bombs fell on Dawley, although only one incident caused fatalities, when a husband and wife and their daughter were killed on 11 October 1940 at Stormount Drive, just south of the railway. Several people were injured in Waltham Avenue in the same incident. In the same month, high explosive bombs fell on McAlpine's site and near the public air raid shelters ('De Salis Trenches') and on Pinkwell Park, and a parachute land mine dropped on the Pinkwell allotments, none of which caused damage. Five canal boats moored in the Dawley docks were badly damaged, however, and damage was caused to Horsley Smith's factory, it was reported, and also to dwellings in Rigby's Row and Bolingbroke Cottages. The 'Dawley Cottage Inn' (sic) was reported as being demolished by two high explosive bombs. (29) The latter report turned out to be, at the least, a considerable over-statement, because if the little public house was hit, it must have been very skilfully rebuilt since it showed no signs of damage (or repair) 50 years later. All these incidents occurred between 11 and 28 October 1940, and if there were others, they do not seem to have been recorded in the ARP log books, although it is known that in 1944 a flying bomb (V-1) fell near the west end of Bourne Avenue. It was near here that one of the shops completed just before the war, but unoccupied, was used to house an ARP fire tender. (30)

To combat aerial attack, a searchlight and at least one Bofors light anti-aircraft gun were stationed at Dawley. The searchlight was located inside the Dawley Wall to the west of the pond north of Rigby's Row. The Dawley Wall has been lowered at this point by the pond, and it is believed that this may have been done in the 1940's to improve visibility in that direction for the searchlight crew. (31) The location of the Dawley LAA gun was on the McAlpine's site, just south of the canal. The 97 LAA Battery (Royal Artillery) reported fires both south and north of the GWR line on 15 October 1940 and, before this, on 5 September 1940, a LAA unit (presumably the same one) reported fires both north and south of the canal. It can be assumed that this was the Royal Artillery unit at Dawley in the Autumn of 1940, although it is unlikely that any one unit manned this gun site throughout the War. Following the successful German campaign in Belgium and France in 1940, and the withdrawal of the British Expeditionary Force from Dunkirk, there was grave concern that enemy parachutists might land in England to capture important targets, such as the war factories in the Hayes and Harlington area. Pillboxes to cover vulnerable points were hastily erected all over the country, and at Dawley the main effort was concentrated on the ground defence of the Royal Ordnance Factory. There were at least eight pillboxes surrounding the site, most of which survive today. Details are given in an appendix. (32) The Home Guard (in our area it was 'T' Sector, London District, Home Guard) defending the western approaches to London was largely entrusted with manning these inland strong points. The local unit was the 4th Middlesex Battalion, Home Guard, with headquarters at Harlington, although No 6 Platoon (Hayes GWR) of 38th County of London Battalion, Home Guard, a unit with headquarters at Paddington and specific responsibility for guarding the GWR line, would also have been involved with the area in the immediate vicinity of the railway. (33)

The major contribution to the war production effort at Dawley was by the Rudge Whitworth factory and the Royal Ordnance Factory, although the smaller factories in the area would also have been involved, either in the supply of their normal products for essential wartime use or in switching to military supplies. At Rudge Whitworth the manufacture of bicycles was ceased during the war and taken over by the Raleigh company. The cycle factory was turned over to the assembly of warlike equipment, such as aircraft cannon, fuses and radar. The larger of the two Rudge Whitworth buildings (the one nearest the railway) was renamed 'Dawley 1' and the smaller one became 'Dawley 2'. Radar equipment manufactured by EMI in the Dawley 1 factory was vital to the RAF Bomber Command's air offensive on Germany. Although the first 60 sets of navigational radar known as H2S Mark I were assembled in the EMI Research Department in Clayton Road, Hayes, full scale production of the improved model H2S Mark II (and later Marks) fitted in Lancaster, Halifax and other types of bomber, was carried out, from 1943 onwards, in the Dawley 1 factory to a total of 3600 units. In late 1943, final assembly of the Rebecca Mark IV Homing and Navigation equipment for aircraft began at Dawley 1 and continued after the War (at least until 1949) until a total of 8500 sets had been completed. The Dawley 1 factory also undertook the assembly of 20mm Oerlikon aircraft cannon and test firing of these guns took place behind the factory. (34) Full details of the wartime activities of the Royal Ordnance Factory at Dawley are still security classified at the time of writing, but it is known that manufacture of artillery took place at the beginning of the War, later to be followed by the repair and modification of tanks. An example was the substitution in new American Shermans of the standard 75mm gun by the British-designed 17pr - the only tank gun in British service capable of defeating the German Tiger tank. British cruiser tanks were also overhauled at the Dawley ROF. Tanks were taken into the factory by road on transporters as well as by rail, for which sidings were provided. (35)

CHAPTER 36

DAWLEY - GENERAL DEVELOPMENT, 1945 - 1995

The story of Dawley from the end of World War II is characterised - like the adjoining parts of Hayes - by, firstly, a gradual withdrawal of major manufacturers and their replacement by smaller undertakings of light industries and services. Secondly, at Dawley, as elsewhere, there was also a change in that industry's reliance on the canal for transport of bulk materials ceased entirely (the freeze-up in the Winter of 1962/63 was the canal's industrial death knell) and also decreasing reliance on the railway. The latter came about because of the greater load capacity and reliability of road vehicles and the development of improved road systems in the vicinity, including nearby motorway links, such as the M4, followed by the M25. The use of oil fuel instead of coal for power by EMI, for instance, inevitably meant the employment of road tankers instead of railway wagons.

It is almost impossible to envisage what might have happened had Richard Fairey really intended to build his airfield at Dawley, and done so, instead of acquiring the Heathrow site. As it is, the requisitioning of Fairey's Great West Aerodrome, overtly for war purposes but covertly for development as London's main post-war airport, is regarded as one of the main factors in the Fairey Aviation Company's demise. In 1960 it was absorbed by the Westland Helicopter Company, the North Hyde Road factory was closed in 1972 and its manufacturing capacity transferred to Yeovil in Somerset. The inevitable rise in importance of Heathrow as Britain's premier airport led to the demand for sites for warehousing and service industries in the area, and this was met by the Fairey Aviation site, among others, and the further industrial development of Dawley.

The changes at Dawley are again best described under the three segments into which the former estate had been divided by the railway and the canal. The southern part of Dawley, south of the railway, has seen the least change since 1945. There has been some addition to the housing, which since the 1930's has been predominant in this area, although there are playing fields and some remaining farming land in the south-west corner. The large hanger-like buildings of the Royal Ordnance Factory were taken over as a repository by the Public Record Office between 1951 and 1953. (1) This is where old files from various Government departments are transferred to be sorted and weeded out before being moved to Chancery Lane or Kew for permanent accession. This could be regarded as a 'growth industry'! In August 1967 it was reported that there were 160 linear miles of shelving, increasing by an estimated 4 miles a year: 350 tons of paper had left the Hayes site (as it was called) in 1966 for pulping. The shelving measured 215 miles (the planned maximum was 215¼) in 1971. By December 1979 the repository had 230 miles of shelving - an increase of over 5½ miles per annum, on average, since 1967, although the storage requirement must have slowed down in the later years. Around 500 tons of documents a year were being destroyed by 1979. (2) The Heathrow Express rail link from Paddington leaves the main line by a spur running across the north-west corner of the Public Record Office site. Work was commenced in 1990.

Dawley between the railway and the canal in the post-war years gradually changed its emphasis on manufacturing to mainly service industry. The former Rudge Whitworth factory, however, continued its wartime function of radar production as the EMI Radar and Equipment division which, after the merger in 1980, was renamed Thorn EMI Radar Division. (3) The buildings, then known as Radar House 1 and Radar House 2, were vacated when the Radar Division was moved to Crawley in Sussex and were demolished in 1992. The water tower, a local landmark, was brought down in spectacular fashion by a controlled explosion. (4) It was reported that water had been pumped into it from a well 600' deep. The earliest production by EMI of magnetic recording tapes was carried out in the former Rudge factory until a brand new factory for EMI Tape Ltd was completed in 1964 a short way up Dawley Road to the north.   This factory had only a short life, for tape production was transferred to the Uxbridge Road, Hayes, site of EMI in 1972. (5) The site of the EMI Tape factory and the area north of it up as far as the garden wall of Dawley House is today occupied by the Abenglen industrial estate served by a new road, Betam Road.   This was opened in 1983 and was intended for new and expanding firms, mostly small. (6)   Nearby was the Speedway industrial estate, opened earlier and, no doubt, taking its name from the former Speedway Cafe. Further north again, the site (formerly occupied by the UK Glass Co) Sir Robert McAlpine and Sons Ltd acquired in the early 1940's was called a 'Machinery Depot' about 1948 and 'Machinery Workshops' in 1951.   The latter was a new industrial building, with a distinctive roof composed of a series of barrel vaults.   After McAlpine's vacated this part of the site it was used by Acorn Anodising Co Ltd up until about 1987.   It was up for sale or letting in 1993.   McAlpine Helicopters was established on the canal-side site in 1979, and in 1988 Lord Brabazon of Tara, the Minister for Aviation and Shipping, opened the firm's new engineering centre for the servicing and sale of helicopters, the site having been doubled in size.   By 1991, the heliport was the night-time base for the Helicopter Emergency Medical Service, the Dauphine ambulance helicopter transferring to the helipad on top of the Princess Alexandra Wing of The London Hospital in Whitechapel in east London during the day to await calls to ferry seriously ill people for treatment. (7)   Osma Plastics Ltd, a firm making rainwater pipes etc, was established on the former Glaxo site by 1969. They had left by 1978. (8)   The site is now occupied by a new household rubbish dump and recycling centre.   Operated by Drinkwater Sabey Ltd, it was opened by the Mayor of Hillingdon   on   27 January 1993   to   replace   a   nearby   rubbish dump   closed   in   1990.   Some of the last of the brickmakers' cottages, Ship Row, were condemned as unfit for human habitation and demolished some years after the War.   In the early 1970's, it is believed, Rockfield Villa, by the canal near the 'Woolpack' bridge, was also demolished.   Divided into two dwellings and occupied by McAlpine's senior employees, it bore the inaccurate and misleading name plate 'Manor House' in its last years. (9)   Much more important was the demolition of the last Dawley House by EMI, its owners, in 1951.   This will be discussed later.   A new road, Swallowfield Way, was constructed about the late 1970's to connect Dawley Road with that part of Rigby Lane south of the canal, improving access for further factories and warehouses in the area between canal and railway, known as the Alder Industrial Estate.

It was in the north part of the former Dawley estate, north of the canal, that the most drastic and far-reaching changes in the post-war period were to take place. What industry and housing there was in this area was mainly contained in the south-east corner, near the canal and Dawley Road, apart from an enclave opposite Botwell Common Road, including the 'Cottage in the Wall' (a 20th century building); a builders yard (then Wilson & Wylie Ltd); the printing works of the 'Hayes News' (in the 1960's) and the Ram Recording Studios. (10)   Also, by 1962, a second gasholder joined the first one near the middle of Dawley. (11)   Rigby's Row of cottages was knocked down in 1954 (12) although the adjoining row, Bolingbroke Cottages, built later and in better condition, survived until 1990.   Horsley Smith & Co, owners of both the last-named terraced rows of cottages since 1946, outlasted one but not the other, disappearing from the local scene about 1964. (13)   Rapp Metals Ltd occupied a 7 acre site in the same area from about 1965. (14)   An aerial view of their 100,000 square foot warehouse, opened in 1967, showed that its frontage in Bolingbroke Way (part of the old Dawley Road by-passed by a new stretch of road) extended to where Rigby's Row used to be. (15)   The firm later became a division of Alcan Metal Centres Ltd and moved from Dawley some time after 1983. A sad loss was The Dawley Cottage (also known as The White House), demolished in 1990 to make way for a car park.   This building had served as a beer house for generations of brickfield and gravel workers and canal boatmen and, although it had become a private dwelling by the 1950's, it could easily have been converted back into a popular 'character' public house with the development of the area.   Aside from the parts just described, the rest of Dawley north of the canal could, by the 1960's, justly answer to the description of 'derelict' - 'a moonscape'.   Brick working had been followed by gravel working, as discussed, followed, in turn, by rubbish infill. The Hayes and Harlington Urban District Council bought from Edmund William Fane De Salis in November 1948 a 22 acre site by the west boundary of Dawley, with the canal on the south side, for use as a refuse disposal tip, although the site, or at least part of it, was occupied by the UDC by 1944. (16) Most of Dawley north of the canal consisted of very uneven and broken ground, partly also unstable and polluted by waste infill. Despite all these disadvantages, however, it had considerable attraction, in conjunction with a similarly ravaged area of Yiewsley adjoining to the west, as being one of the few large areas near Heathrow that was available for development. The plans for this area, and their eventual fruition, will be discussed in a later chapter.

CHAPTER 37

THE LAST 'DAWLEY HOUSE' -
OCCUPIERS, INTERNAL LAYOUT, DEMOLITION

The post-World War II decade saw the demolition of the last building to be called 'Dawley House', so this seems to be a suitable point in the story of Dawley to summarise the occupiers of this house for the 150 years or so of its existence; also to discuss what can be learnt of its internal layout from the recollections of people who knew it.

As has been explained earlier, when the mansion of Dawley was demolished about 1780, a small house was created from part of a wing: more precisely, from the laundry, pantry and dairy building on the north side of the courtyard. This house was probably intended for the use of tenant farmers rather than members of the De Salis family who owned it for about 130 years. Lord Bolingbroke had called his splendid mansion a 'farm', but this final successor house may well have also been called Dawley Farm when it was built, for the very good reason that it was indeed a farmhouse. There were farm buildings at the south-west corner of the courtyard in 1821 (1), although it is not known if these were created at the same time as the house. Latterly, at any rate, these buildings did include a farmhouse and two cottages, as well as barns etc, and by 1865 (on the OS map) they were called Dawley Farm, as opposed to Dawley House. The tenants of the house after about 1851 were not farmers, but it is not always clear before this date if the tenants of 'Dawley Farm' always occupied the house.

It seems that possibly the first tenant occupiers of Dawley House were members of the Tattersall family when they had a stud farm at Dawley. The last member of the family at Dawley was George Tattersall, who was there until 1838. (2) By 1839 until at least 1852, Warwick Bagley was farming at Dawley, and occupying the house for part of this time (3), although in the 1841 Census, Thomas Pool, bailiff (presumably in the employ of the De Salis family) was shown to be in residence there.

With the arrival of brickmaking at Dawley, Thomas Jolly, described in the Census as 'excavator', and probably a master brickmaker, was shown as in residence in 1851. In November 1853, as mentioned earlier, Messrs Thomas and William Rhodes leased from the De Salis' a 35 acre site adjoining Dawley Road and including Dawley House, although it is not recorded if either or both of them occupied the house. The map referring to this lease shows a smaller building joined to the east side of the house, as well as quite separate farm buildings to the south and south-east of the courtyard. A rectangular area, enclosed on three sides, immediately north of the house is described as 'kitchen garden'. By the time of the following Census, 1861, another brick manufacturer, Thomas Maynard, was at Dawley and certainly later, if not then, occupied the house. By 1865 the 25in OS map does not show the above-mentioned small building attached to the house, although it does show an ice house (an early form of refrigerator, using ice gathered in the winter) about 200 feet to the west, in an orchard. Its date of construction is not known, and no other record of its existence has been traced.

Thomas Maynard died in 1876 (4) and his widow Eliza Maynard was shown as head of the family at Dawley in the 1881 Census, where the house is described as 'Dawley Court'. Henry A Odell, another brick manufacturer, had taken over by 1882, when the name 'Dawley Court' was retained, although it later reverted to Dawley House. (The De Salis family may have taken exception to the house of one of their tenants bearing the same name as their seat at Hillingdon.) Odell appears to have remained at Dawley until 1896, one Gerald Harrison first being shown as occupier in the 1897 Electoral Register. He was there until at least 1900, although the tenant for 1901, if there was one, has not been traced in any records. In 1902-1904 Miss Maud Clayton Brown was at Dawley House. Her name suggests that she may have been related to Thomas Clayton, owner of brickfields and gravel pits in the area and developer of the industrial estate in nearby Hayes. A Mrs Fannie Agar moved from Wistowe House in Hayes Town into Dawley House in 1905 and stayed there until at least 1911, to be succeeded by Miss Louisa May Gray, who is said to have been a member of the legal department of the Gramophone Company.

No reference to tenants in 1913 has been traced, and it was at this time that Dawley House was converted into two dwellings - known as Dawley House west and Dawley House east. Dawley House west was the larger part and included the original front door. A new main entrance for Dawley House east was created at the east side of the building. The gardens, front and rear, were also divided and a hedge was planted in front of the house, immediately to the east of the front door, to run south. The relative importance of the two dwellings can be gathered from their rateable values which (in 1933) were west 51, east 34. The first occupiers (in 1914) of the divided house were Miss L M Gray (the earlier sole tenant), Dawley House west, and Francis E Bowater, Dawley House east. Bowater was a member of the paper-making family and was related to a Lord Mayor of London. He ran a small cork-making factory, located in a barn at Dawley Farm near the south-east part of the courtyard. Bowater stayed only for a year or so (5) and by 1917 Dawley House east was occupied by a Miss Gerrie; Dawley House west by Mrs Evelyn French (who remained there until at least 1923). The United Kingdom Glass Company, who had completed their factory on a site to the north, leased Dawley House east for 5 years from 1 December 1917 at £55 per annum, the lease renewed later. William Robert Johnson, the Glass Company's manager, was installed there at first, it is understood (6); and from about 1923 until 1928, I G Elias, also a manager or senior employee of the Company, took over. It is not known exactly when Mrs French left Dawley, but Owen Ernest Barnes leased Dawley House west for three years from 17 April 1926 at £65 per annum. Barnes was to be the last tenant of the De Salis family at Dawley House. (7)

The Gramophone Company Ltd, by an agreement dated 5 April 1928, leased from Cecil Fane De Salis the area of and including Dawley House, subject to existing tenancies. This was a preliminary step towards a conveyance of 19 July 1929 by which the Company purchased this land outright for the sum of £9650. (8) The tenancies would by then have expired and The Gramophone Company used Dawley House to accommodate various, mainly experimental, departmental sections. The earliest use of the house by the Gramophone Company before World War II seems to have been for the testing of both standard and experimental radio receivers under 'home' (as opposed to factory) conditions. In the courtyard a short way south of the house a tall aerial mast was erected for monitoring radio stations in the calibration of scales. There was another, much smaller, aerial mast on the roof, inside the front wall parapet. (9) By 1939 a small section that was the part of the Research Division concerned with cutting waxes in connection with tubes for television cameras had moved into a room at Dawley House. A vibration-free environment, away from the factories, was needed, and a pit was dug through the foundations of the house for the placement of a heavy concrete block on which to mount the wax-cutting machine. (10)

During the War, the house appears to have been allowed to fall into dereliction. An architect, R Theodore Beck, inspected the house in 1943 and reported that it was '..... in very bad condition. The interior contains nothing of interest and the principal staircase of no great merit has collapsed'. (11) Walter H Godfrey, Director of the National Buildings Record, however, commented, after seeing Beck's report together with exterior photographs of Dawley House, 'The house is a particularly interesting example of an early 18th century type, the detail has great distinction and it could be a great gain if the building could be preserved. As a manager's house, a rest house or for some similar purpose it would seem possible to convert it to usefulness and so maintain it on its old site'. (12) Walter Godfrey's comments evidently impressed The Gramophone Company, because Dawley House was not demolished (as had evidently been proposed) but repaired and by the late 1940's a variety of sections, most of them in support of the EMI

Abbey Road Studios, were using rooms in it. These included microphone testing, transformer assembly, a battery room, a laboratory, and radio design. (13) The TV camera wax-cutting section was still there, and a member of the staff recalls that their room contained the row of mechanical call-bells dating back to when the house was a private residence.

The need for the house declined, however, with the erection of a new Research Building near the main factory complex in Hayes, and the various sections moved out. (The heavy concrete block for mounting the wax-cutting machine was taken out and installed in the Research Building, mounted on springs that overcame any vibration problems.) (14) EMI having no further use for the building, and, apparently, with no voice raised in protest, Dawley House was demolished in the Spring of 1951. (15)

Neither Theodore Beck nor Walter Godfrey was aware that the house was the work of James Gibbs. Whether or not this knowledge would have made any difference at that time, not long after the War, during which much more important buildings had been destroyed by enemy action, is not known, but EMI cannot, accordingly, be blamed for knowingly destroying one of the few domestic works by such a distinguished architect.

Fortunately, several good exterior photographs of Dawley House were taken, although no interior views are known to exist. It must be borne in mind that this building was originally intended to carry out three distinct domestic functions - that of laundry, pantry and dairy. At the same time, in the fashion of the period, service buildings, like this one, were often grouped in 'wings' either side of a courtyard that formed the principal approach to the mansion, with which they had to be architecturally in keeping, externally. Inside, their functions were all-important and, although there seems to have been no standard layout for a building comprising laundry, pantry and dairy, obviously it would have been nothing like the interior of the smallish gentleman's house that the building was made to look outside. It may be assumed, however, that when the service building was converted into a farmhouse for a tenant, the minimum of structural changes would have been made. A fully symmetrical interior arrangement for Dawley House cannot be assumed. The alterations in c 1912-1913 to create two dwellings must certainly have resulted in further assymmetry, although some of the changes after 1929 when the house reverted to a single owner/occupier (The Gramophone Company) may have, to some extent, reversed the process.

The part of Dawley House the least likely to have been changed throughout its history was the attic storey or garretts, which contained the quarters for servants. The hipped roof of the house, pitched on all sides, surrounded a hollow rectangle, like a light well or small courtyard, (16) although the area was roofed, probably with lead, at first floor ceiling level. Two dormer windows lighted the garrets at the front and, possibly, there were more dormers at the back. A small cupola, located behind the central raised part of the front wall parapet, also gave light to the attic. The cupola, it will be recalled, housed the wind vane which actuated the wind direction dial on the front wall of the house and is shown in an early 19th century watercolour. (17) Both dial and cupola had disappeared by the time that the first known photographs were taken.

The two main floors of the building both had a transverse corridor running from one side of the house to the other. A hall lay behind the front door and the main staircase ('of no great merit', per Theodore Beck) was at its far end. A second staircase (possibly dating only from the c1912-1913 conversion) was also at the rear of the house, in its north-east corner. There were two main rooms at the front, either side of the hall, and about five smaller rooms along the north side of the ground floor corridor. The second and fourth rooms each had sinks, so may have served as the kitchens of the east and west dwellings, respectively, after c 1912-1913. The room in the west part had a row of mechanically operated servant call-bells over the door.

Upstairs, there appear to have been three main rooms at the front of the house and four smaller rooms at the rear. The room at the north-west corner was the largest and included what would have been part of the corridor, which terminated here short of the west wall of the house.

There was a two-storey square projection with a hipped roof at the rear of the house in the centre. This part of the building was added to on its west side, apparently later, with a structure having a single-sloped roof - this extension possibly dating, again, from the conversion to two dwellings.

The original brick garden wall enclosing three sides of the gardens to the rear of the house was maintained intact at least until about 1930, as were the wing walls linking the front of the house with the north part of the hexagonal court yard. (18)

Early in the 20th century, the last Dawley House acquired its own entrance lodge. Located by the Dawley Road approximately 220 yards north of where the Earl of Tankerville's lodge had been, it was a single-storey brick building with a slate roof. It was on the north side of an entrance in the former estate wall which had iron gates and brick gate posts with white ball finials. (19) In 1926, Dawley House west was described as having a 'coachhouse or garage outside and leaning against the wall of the garden'. (20)

CHAPTER 38

STOCKLEY PARK

Despite its unattractive appearance, the largely undeveloped area of Dawley north of the canal, together with the adjoining land in Yiewsley, similarly unprepossessing, was well appreciated for its potential for development by successive Councils of the London Borough of Hillingdon, which had become heir on its foundation in 1965 to these parts of two separate Urban Districts. Although the area was designated as Green Belt, it was clear that drastic and expensive changes would have to be made to justify the description and, at the same time, to make good economic and social use of this tract of land. Accordingly, with the blessing of both the Leader of the Council and the Leader of the Opposition, the Borough's Director of Planning produced in November 1979 a Planning Brief for what was designated the 'Stockley Special Project'. (1) The name was derived from the fact that the land at Dawley and Yiewsley lay either side of Stockley Road. The part of Dawley north of the canal that was included at the east side of the Stockley Special Project represented rather less than one third of the whole area of 315 acres then under consideration. Of Dawley, the south-east part either side of Rigby Lane, including Bolingbroke Cottages, the Alcan buildings and George Wimpey's depot, and a piece of land fronting Dawley Road and Bolingbroke Way owned by Costain's were outside the Special Project's boundary. Also, at this stage, the boundary did not include a small triangle of land at the north tip of Dawley and joining a larger site in Hillingdon that was owned by Bovis and intended for housing development. Inside the boundary of the Special Project another piece of land owned by Costain and the North Thames Gas Board (where two gasholders were located) was excluded from the plans. In the Special Project area as a whole, Drinkwater Sabey Ltd was the major landowner, with 242 acres. As part of their business activities, nearly all their land had been excavated for gravel and mostly backfilled with industrial and domestic rubbish. Two 'lakes' (both outside Dawley) had not been backfilled, and only one, comparatively small, area (also outside Dawley) had been restored with a top surface after backfilling. In Dawley, Drinkwater Sabey's owned only some 12 acres, 9.4 acres of which was unexcavated. This adjoined on the south side 15.47 acres of land belonging to the Council which, likewise, was untouched by gravel digging and had been used for cattle grazing. This unexcavated area of nearly 25 acres, fronting on to Dawley Road (most of it roughly north of the point of the Botwell Common Road junction) was proposed as the main site for 'enabling' development. In addition to the unexcavated site mentioned above, the Council owned a larger area of roughly 35 acres of excavated and backfilled land in that part of Dawley partly bounded by the canal in the south and partly by the old Harlington boundary in the west. The proposals, briefly, envisaged the greater part of the area, capped with topsoil and made safe, being restored to open space compatible with Green Belt standards, to be self-financing and carried out by a developer attracted by the 25 acre 'enabling' site. It was felt that, partly because existing public transport facilities were limited, warehousing would be the best option for the industrial development. This was to be in the Dawley part of the scheme, with a similar area earmarked for equestrian activities just to the south, based on existing livery stables in Bolingbroke Way. The remaining area of Dawley covered by the Special Project (omitting the excluded portion) was earmarked as part of the 'landscaped open space' that stretched as far as Stockley Road. Beyond, to the west, a 'district park' was envisaged. All these proposals were subject to public consultation, and the final planning brief that emerged would have to be considered by the Greater London Council and the Secretary of State for the Environment.

The Stockley Park Special Planning Brief issued at the end of 1979 was modified after discussion and, by 1981, Trust Securities Holdings Ltd, who had acquired Drinkwater Sabey, emerged as the developer of what had become known officially as Stockley Park. Although the essential philosophy remained, the details were changed drastically for what had become a 325 acre site, soon to be extended to 350 acres. The 'enabling development' was changed from warehousing to a 'science and commercial park' with buildings to be designed and built to a high standard. This was to be located roughly in the middle of the south part of the site, bordered by the canal and partly in the Dawley area. The equestrian site was transferred to the north at Goulds Green, outside Dawley, and the 'landscaped open space' was to be largely devoted to a golf course, partly in Dawley. A second golf course was proposed west of Stockley Road. The developers undertook to convert Stockley Road into a dual carriageway - the Yiewsley By-Pass - at their own expense. The breakdown, by area, for the whole 350 acres of Stockley Park was 250 acres for leisure pursuits - golf, playing fields etc, and 100 acres for the business park. It was anticipated that 40% of the latter would be offices, 40% light industry, and 20% warehousing.

In 1984 the development was taken over by Stockley plc, which in turn was financially strengthened in 1988 by a consortium known as Stockley Park Consortium Ltd, the present site owners. Work started in April 1985 and the first building was completed in November. Stockley Park was officially opened by HRH The Prince of Wales on 6 June 1986 and the first company, the Japanese firm of Fujitsu, moved in their new premises at the end of the year. (2) Stockley Park has proved to be a highly successful enterprise, and many international companies have established themselves there. These include (in 1996), to mention only some of those within the area of the former Dawley estate, such well-known names as American Express, Apple Computer, Dow Chemical Co, Panasonic Europe, Reebok International and Time Life UK. Glaxo - now Glaxo Wellcome UK Ltd - have premises west of the Stockley Road, although only about half a mile from the site of their original Glaxo pharmaceutical works at Dawley. The public park and recreational facilities were handed over to Hillingdon Borough Council in June 1993. The environmental advantage is undeniable, with the previous 'moonscape' converted into grassland and golf courses, with the buildings in landscaped surroundings, partly hidden by the 140,000 trees planted on the site.

Any traces of historical significance had largely been eliminated already by the previous uses of the site although, sadly, it was felt necessary to remove The Dawley Cottage, the former canalside pub. Far less of a loss was the two gasholders, thought in 1979 to be a permanent feature of the site. However, improved gas technology had made them redundant by 1987 and Stockley plc negotiated for the site and removed them. On the credit side, an archaeological 'dig' in the north of Dawley was sponsored by Stockley plc and revealed a previously unknown Iron Age site (see Chapter 1); also the Dawley estate wall, broken down and damaged in many places, has been restored sympathetically to its full height for much of its length by the developers.

Phase 2 of Stockley Park - the addition of the former Wimpey/Alcan site and its development, was granted planning permission by Hillingdon Borough Council in 1990. This involved the demolition of Bolingbroke Cottages, but carries with it an undertaking to restore a further stretch of the former estate wall in this area. (3) The Earl of Uxbridge's wall will then once again serve its original purpose, although enclosing a park of a kind entirely unknown in the 18th century. However, as a man reputed to be very interested in finance, the alliance of a successful business enterprise with visual amenity on part of his land might perhaps have met with Lord Uxbridge's approval.

CHAPTER 39

DAWLEY TODAY - SURVIVALS AND TRACES OF THE PAST

There can have been few country estates that have been so comprehensively eliminated by industrial and commercial development as Dawley.

The great house itself was, of course, demolished at will by its owner, as were its predecessors on the manor and estate. Then, within a decade or so, came the Grand Junction Canal which cut the estate in two. This was followed, within forty years, by the Great Western Railway which created a third division, the house site isolated between rails and water, leaving an estate, already in several ownerships, that would no longer hold any attraction as a gentleman's country seat. What disturbance to the site that these intrusions caused was relatively slight compared to the brickmaking which followed, lowering the ground surface for a large area between the railway and the canal and north of the latter. (1) Deep digging for gravel, mainly in the north part of the former estate and extensive housing development south of the railway completed the destruction of evidence regarding the site of the mansion house of c1672, and the formal gardens that existed both to the south and west of it. Something that is no more than a damp reminder of the grounds of the earlier Dawley manor house at Pinkwell does exist - from time to time - in the Bourne Farm Playing Field at the west end of Bourne Avenue. In the 19th century this area formed part of a field called 'The Aldergrove'. (2) The name implied a wet area suited to alder trees, and the field included, in fact, the remains of the 200 yard pond shown in Jenner's c1721 plan. The site of this pond shows up in aerial photographs and the field is liable to flooding after heavy rain. (3)

What then, survived of 17th-18th century Dawley into the 20th century? One remarkable survival was the dovecote shown in Kip's engraving of c1700. Converted into two cottages, it lasted until about 1932, to appear in at least one photograph (4) and remained in the memories of old people (some of whom had lived in it as children) well into the 1980's. (5) Of the mansion built c1672, also depicted by Kip, no traces have, as far as is known, ever been found - the canal, brick and gravel workings having completely removed any vestigal foundations that might have been left after the bulk of the materials had been removed in the 18th century - probably as hard core for later buildings. Of the house built by Lord Tankerville about 1720 and enlarged by Lord Bolingbroke within the next decade, what is presumed to be some of the brick foundations were seen by the present writer in 1983. This was during the time that foundations were being dug for the Abenglen industrial estate and, although photographs were taken, regrettably, it was not possible for an archaeological investigation to be carried out. (6) Although some of the brickwork was credibly footings for the mansion demolished c1780, two arched brick culverts, approximately 2ft 6ins wide, both running approximately south-west across the courtyard site, could not be related to any known facts regarding any buildings in this area. It will be recalled that brick footings and culverts were also noted in this part in 1939. The culverts were presumably for drainage, but may be the substance of the reputed 'subterraneous passage' leading to Drayton reported by H O Meyers in 1857. (7)

The building on the north side of the courtyard serving the mansion, also designed by James Gibbs for Bolingbroke, and converted from a laundry-cum-dairy into a dwelling house, was demolished as late as 1951. It was photographed externally on several occasions and inspected by an architect (although apparently not internally) but no contemporary record - photographs or measured drawings - of its internal layout appears to have been made.

The oldest still surviving remnant of the Dawley estate is, in fact, the length of unbuttressed garden wall that ran behind the laundry, pantry and dairy building and other service buildings on the north side of the courtyard and, when complete, turned south to join the north front of the east wing of the mansion house. This wall is shown on Rocque's map of 1754. Fortunately, the architects of the Abenglen estate took a sympathetic view when informed of its historic significance, and the wall has been preserved and now forms part of the north boundary of this industrial estate. (8)

Not shown on Rocque's map, because it is later, is the estate wall built by the Earl of Uxbridge about 1760 along the east side of his Dawley estate. Although broken for entry points in several places, and robbed in others for hard core, the wall has probably survived into the 20th century because it continued to form a useful boundary beside the Dawley Road. Rebuilt and refurbished to its original height in both materials and style by Stockley plc, the wall continues to serve as a boundary (although incursion by the plague is no longer feared) for much of its original length and is a very visible reminder of Dawley's past.

APPENDIX I   **THE BENNETS OF DAWLEY - OUTLINE FAMILY TREE**

Richard Bennet of Clapcote, Berkshire

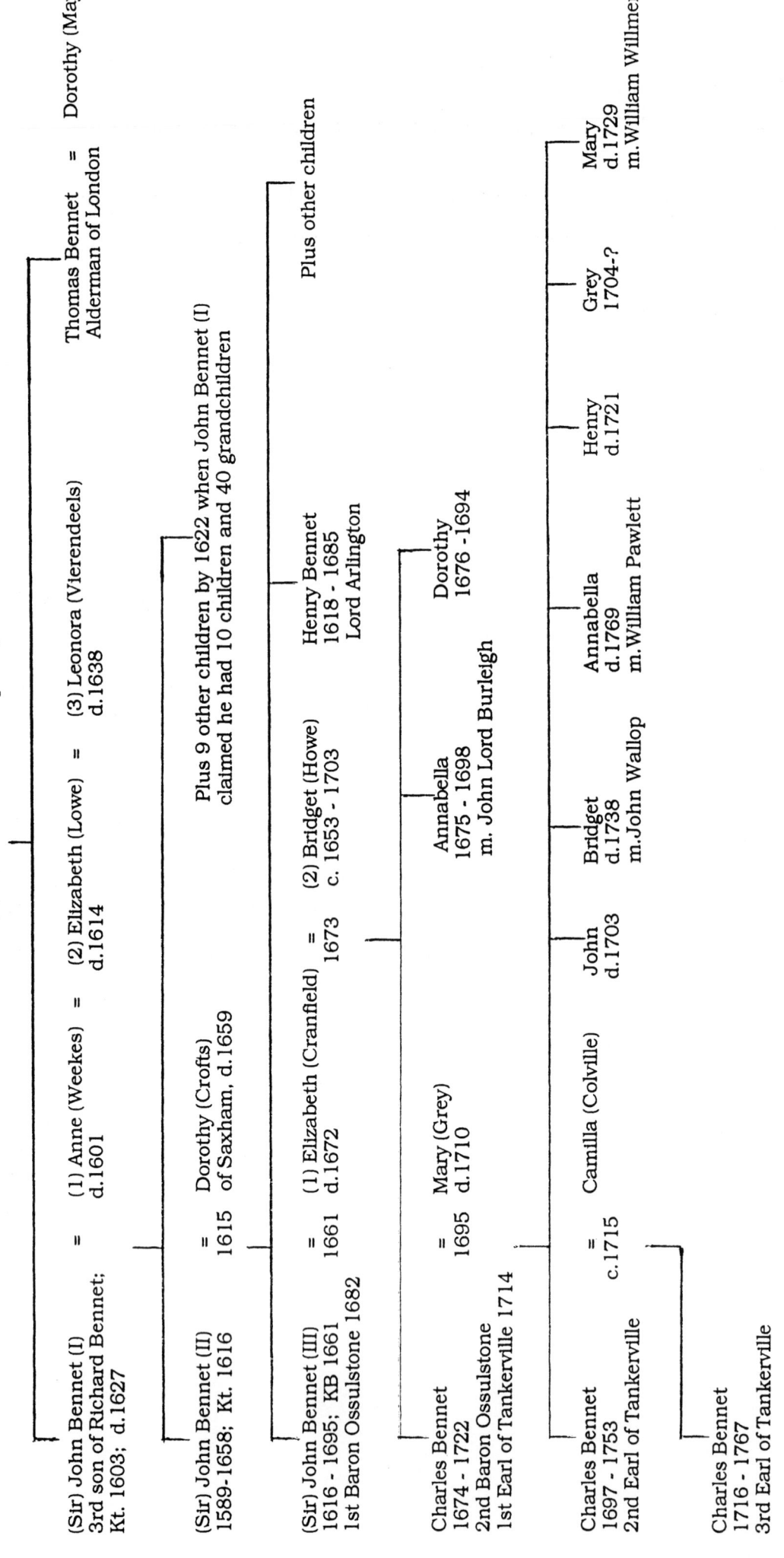

(Sir) John Bennet (I)
3rd son of Richard Bennet;
Kt. 1603; d.1627

= (1) Anne (Weekes) = (2) Elizabeth (Lowe) = (3) Leonora (Vierendeels)
d.1601   d.1614   d.1638

Thomas Bennet = Dorothy (May)
Alderman of London

Plus 9 other children by 1622 when John Bennet (I)
claimed he had 10 children and 40 grandchildren

(Sir) John Bennet (II) = Dorothy (Crofts)
1589-1658: Kt. 1616   1615   of Saxham, d.1659

Plus other children

Henry Bennet
1618 - 1685
Lord Arlington

(Sir) John Bennet (III) = (1) Elizabeth (Cranfield) = (2) Bridget (Howe)
1616 - 1695; KB 1661   1661   d.1672   1673   c. 1653 - 1703
1st Baron Ossulstone 1682

Dorothy
1676 -1694

Annabella
1675 - 1698
m. John Lord Burleigh

Charles Bennet = Mary (Grey)
1674 - 1722   1695   d.1710
2nd Baron Ossulstone
1st Earl of Tankerville 1714

Bridget
d.1738
m.John Wallop

Annabella
d.1769
m.William Pawlett

Mary
d.1729
m.William Willmer

Henry
d.1721

Grey
1704-?

John
d.1703

Charles Bennet = Camilla (Colville)
1697 - 1753   c.1715
2nd Earl of Tankerville

Charles Bennet
1716 - 1767
3rd Earl of Tankerville

Sources: "The Complete Peerage ... " by G.E.C., revised (London 1945); Burke's Peerage and Baronetage; Alumni Oxoniensis; Harlington Parish Registers; "Henry Bennet, Earl of Arlington" by V Barbour (Oxford 1914); "Little Saxham Parish Registers, 1559-1850", ed. by S.H.A.H. (Woodbridge 1901); Bridget Bennet's notebook, contained in P.R.O. C104/82. ("The Uxbridge Record", Autumn 1994 {Journal of the Uxbridge Local History and Archives Society), article on The Place, Uxbridge by Dr Richard T Spence, contains interesting information on the Bennets, with reference sources, although some of this does not appear to accord with details given elsewhere.)

APPENDIX 2

Dawley Manor Farm, Dawley Court, Little Dawley and Dawley Lodge

These buildings, none of which were in Dawley and all are now demolished, are at times the cause of some confusion with the manor house of Dawley or its outbuildings, so it is felt desirable to include brief notes on them here.

Dawley Manor Farm, High Street, Harlington

This farmhouse, destroyed in 1963 when the M4 motorway was built, was often confused with what Lord Bolingbroke called 'Dawley Farm' - the mansion house of Dawley.   In Harlington proper, with no known connection with Dawley, this timber-framed building of 17th century date, or earlier, may have succeeded the nearby moated site as the manor house of Harlington, it is suggested in the Victoria County History. (1)

Dawley Court, Hillingdon

Originally known as Gould's Green House, this Tudor (or earlier) building was probably renamed by the De Salis family (who owned property in Harlington, including Dawley) when they acquired it. (2)   It was demolished in 1929, or soon after, and a housing estate built on the site.   The lodge house of Dawley Court in Harlington Road still exists, incidentally.   Dawley Court has sometimes been confused with the manor house of Dawley, possibly because the earliest known references to the latter are to 'Dawley Courte'.

Little Dawley, Church Road, Hayes

Elizabeth Hunt, the Hayes historian (3), wrote '... Little Dawley is said to have been built of materials from Dawley House ...'.   It bore a brick dated 1787, according to a former resident (4), and such a date would have been consistent with its late Georgian appearance and accord with the availability of materials following the probable time of demolition of Dawley house.   This cannot be proved, however, since Little Dawley was demolished in 1973.   Incidentally, the Hayes entries in Uxbridge directories between about 1853 and the 1890's often refer to what is certainly this building as 'Dawley House'.

Dawley Lodge, Gould's Green

This 19th (?) century house in Judge Heath Lane was known as 'The Rose-house' in the 1820's, probably after its then owner, William Rose.   In the 1841 Census it had become 'Dawley Cottage'; in 1851 'Vine Cottage', but Dawley Cottage again in 1881 (Census).   The name 'Dawley Lodge' was given by the De Salis family . (5)   The house, demolished in 1964, was not in Dawley or Harlington, although it may at one time have been an outlier to the Dawley estate.

APPENDIX 3 (See Chapter 35)

Pillboxes surrounding the Royal Ordnance Factory at Dawley (now Public Record Office, Hayes) numbered clockwise. (NGR = location by approximate National Grid Reference)

1. Concrete pillbox, hexagonal, facing S, with on N side (rear) a circular brick gun pit, internal diameter approximately 6¹/₂ft. This pillbox is just outside the NE perimeter of the ROF site, and is set into the south abutment of a bridge (removed early 20th century) that crossed the GWR line at Dawley. NGR 08237963

2. Brick pillbox with concrete roof, square, facing E with blast wall at rear. Walls c14ins thick (1 header, 1 stretcher), roof c8ins. This is just inside the E perimeter fence of the site, immediately N of a damp tree-covered area where was the north pond of the two at Pinkwell marked on the 1865 OS map, and later. NGR 08147953

3. Concrete pillbox, hexagonal, facing E, at LH side of main entrance to site, at end of Bourne Avenue. Removed 1992. NGR 08137935

4. Concrete pillbox, hexagonal, facing S, in middle of a long N-S tree-covered area, approximately in centre of S area of site. NGR 07867931

5. Brick pillbox with concrete roof, square. Similar to 2. Facing N with blast wall at rear. This is approximately 15-20 ft N of 4 and apparently put there to protect its rear. NGR 07867932

6. Brick pillbox with concrete roof, square, at SW entrance to site, at Stockley Road. Similar to 2. There is a gatekeeper's brick building nearby, which appears to be semi-fortified. Both of these buildings demolished by 1996 during construction of Heathrow Express rail link. NGR 07687931

7. Concrete pillbox, hexagonal, facing NW, near NW perimeter of site, just S of railway and N of the boiler house. NGR 07957968

8. Brick pillbox with concrete roof, square, located on top of a larger rectangular brick building. This is roughly near the centre of the N side of the site, near the railway. This pillbox removed by 1996. NGR 08057965

NOTES

It should be explained that no general bibliography is given here because, apart from the Victoria County History (Middlesex, volume III) no single work covers the history of Dawley in any depth. All published works referred to are listed below, together with all primary sources and, as far as possible, all the names of individual informants. A select list of works on Viscount Bolingbroke, however, is given in the Notes for Chapter 18 because so much has been written about him, without unfortunately including much detail about his Dawley estate.

The following abbreviations have been used: DNB - The Dictionary of National Biography; EMI - Electric and Musical Industries Ltd (formerly known as The Gramophone Company); GLRO/MRO - Greater London Record Office, which absorbed the Middlesex Record Office and in 1997 was renamed London Metropolitan Archives; OS - Ordnance Survey maps, in both 25 inch and 6 inch to the mile scale, in editions from 1865 to 1935 in the main; PRO - Public Record Office; VCH - Victoria County History.

References to 'Advertiser' and/or 'Gazette' all relate to the principal local newspaper for the area, established in 1840 and published in Buckinghamshire, Middlesex, Uxbridge and other editions at various times, under one or other of these titles.

'Local Directory' refers to King's Uxbridge Directory, which included a Harlington section from about 1887 to 1932, or Lucy and Birch's Uxbridge Directory which also covered Harlington from about 1887, but ceased about 1916. Kelly's (originally 'Post Office') Directory of Middlesex and Surrey, later Middlesex alone, is identified as 'Kelly's' when cited.

Chapter 1.

1. The A437 is named 'Harlington Road' for a short distance along the north part of the Dawley boundary, and thence to the Uxbridge Road. Also see Chapter 11.

2. See Chapter 10 for a discussion of Jenner's plan of Dawley. (PRO ref MPH246).

3. See Desmond Collins 'Early Man in West Middlesex' (HMSO, 1978) on which this account of the Palaeolithic era is based.

4. The Museum of London 'Iron Age settlement at Dawley, west London' [pamphlet - Jonathan Cotton, 1985].

5. See, inter alia, Keith Branigan (Ed) 'The Archaeology of the Chilterns' (Chess Valley Archaeological and Historical Society, 1994).

6. See article by C Morris 'Uxbridge Road' in the Journal of the Hayes and Harlington Local History Society, Spring 1983, reproduced with permission from the Uxbridge Local History and Archives Society's journal.

7. Domesday Book - there are various translations, of which a version in more modern English is in 'Domesday Book [volume] 11 Middlesex', Ed John Morris (Phillimore, 1975).

8. VCH Middlesex, Vol III, p267.

9. Ibid p264. The supposition regarding relationship to John Aubrey is mine.

Chapter 1 (cont'd)

10.   Ibid p264 and DNB.   The supposition that this Lord of the Manor was Sir Thomas More's son-in-law is mine.   Margaret appears in a sketch by Holbein of Sir Thomas More's family.

11.   Ibid p264.

Chapter 2.

1.   G E Bate 'And so make a City here'.   (Thomason's, Hounslow, 1948). The author does not quote his source for the date.

2.   'Shott' - also known as selion: a cultivated strip in an open field (pre-inclosure).

3.   Quoted by Rachel De Salis 'Hillingdon Through Eleven Centuries' (Lucy and Birch, Uxbridge, 1926), p18.

4.   GLRO Acc 530/ED8/14.

5.   J E B Gover 'The Place Names of Middlesex' (Longmans, Green, 1922).

6.   Elizabeth Hunt   'Hayes, "Past and Present" '   (Uxbridge, 1861) (Reprinted, together with her 'Reminiscences of Hayes' (1916) by the Hayes and Harlington Local History Society, 1982, under the title 'The Hayes of Elizabeth Hunt (1832-1916)'.

7.   DNB.   Hayes was only one of his many livings.   He was Bishop, successively, of Bristol, Lichfield, and Coventry.

8.   'Queen Elizabeth's Progresses', Vol IV part 3 (page 26).   Printed by and for John Nichols & Son.   (London, 1821).

9.   See, for example, A L Rowse 'The Elizabethan Renaissance' (Macmillan, 1971).

10.   For a good account of this house and its owners see R T Spence in 'The Uxbridge Record' (Uxbridge Local History and Archives Society, Autumn 1994).

11.   GLRO has copies of both the 1664 and 1674 assessments.   There is nothing in the latter to suggest that George Selby's house still existed.

12.   In Camden Society, 1st series, pp148-152, he is given as of Allhallows, Kent.

13.   This biographical information is based on Camden Society, op cit; P W Hasler 'The House of Commons' 1558-1603 (Vol I)(HMSO, 1981); and 'Alumni Cantabrigensis' Part 1, Vol I.   (Cambridge UP, 1922).

14.   Also spelled Laetitia, and given as Lettice in P W Hasler, 'The House of Commons' (op cit).   Daughter of Edward Fitzgerald Nicholas David, Earl of Kildare.

15.   VCH Essex, Vol IV, p161.

16.   VCH Middlesex, Vol III, p275.

Chapter 2 (cont'd)

17.   'Queen Elizabeth's Progresses', op cit (see note 8, above).

18.   VCH Middlesex, Vol III, pp262-264; GLRO (MRO) Acc 446/ED 196-198.

Chapter 3.

1.   A general account of the later members of the Bennet family is in Chapter 9.

2.   DNB (on which the greater part of this account is based), but 'Alumni Oxonsiensis' (see note 7 below) states that he was the second son.

3.   Walter C Metcalfe 'A Book of Knights Banneret, Knights of the Bath and Knights Bachelor' (Mitchell & Hughes, London, 1885) p145.

4.   Sir John claimed in 1622 to have 10 children and 40 grandchildren. (DNB).

5.   R T Spence, 'The Uxbridge Record', op cit (see note 10, Chapter 2).

6.   VCH Middlesex, Vol IV, p114.

7.   Joseph Foote 'Alumni Oxonsiensis' Vol I - early series. (Kraus Reprint Ltd, Liechenstein, 1968).

8.   Harlington Parish Registers.

9.   State Papers, Interregnum, A.22 p276, quoted in Violet Barbour 'Henry Bennet, Earl of Arlington' (OUP, 1914), p9.

10.   The Act of Oblivion was passed in 1660 as an attempt to wipe out the enmities of the Civil War period.

11.   Violet Barbour, op cit (see note 9 above).

12.   GLRO (MRO) Acc 446/ED258.

13.   GLRO Acc 1066 (Middx).

14.   Transactions of the London & Middlesex Archaeological Society (LAMAS), Vol II (1864) p120 (quoting from Dom Charles II, Vol 13, No 47).

15.   See letter from Elizabeth Legh, quoted below (note 17).

16.   PRO - included in C104/82. This book has a brown leather cover with a gold pattern; tie-up tapes. Inside - 'Scrope Howe gave this book 1669'.

17.   This letter, undated but written about 1673-75, is from Elizabeth, wife of Richard Legh of Lyme (Cheshire) to her brother-in-law, Thomas Legh. Sir John Bennet's 'Sister Carr', referred to, was Elizabeth, who had married Sir Robert Carr of Sleaford. See Lady Newton 'The House of Lyme' (Heinemann, 1917) pp270-271.

Chapter 3 (cont'd)

18.   G Redford & T H Riches 'The History of the Ancient Town of Uxbridge' (Uxbridge 1818, reprinted 1885) pp218-219.   Sir John Bennet (III) was created Baron Ossulston (although he usually signed himself 'Ossulstone') on 24 November 1682.

19.   This account is based on Violet Barbour, op cit (see note 9 above).

Chapter 4.

1.   LAMAS (see note 14, Chapter 3) Vol II, p120.

2.   R Latham & W Matthews (Eds) 'Diary of Samuel Pepys' Vol VI, 1665 (G Bell, 1972).

3.   See 'A genealogical & heraldic history of the extinct and dormant Baronetcies of England'.   J Burke and J B Burke (London 1838 and reprint).   Strangely, George Selby is described as 'knight' by his widow in BM Add Ch 19008 (see below).

4.   Dame Arabella Bryors' original mortgage was for £3400-, of which £1600- had been paid by 29 May 1657 - see above (Chapter 3).

5.   LAMAS Vol II, p120, op cit.

6.   See note 3 above.

7.   BM Add Ch 19008.

8.   BM Add Ch 19003 and 19004.   GLRO (MRO) Acc 446/ED259 also refers to this transaction.

9.   Robert Cecil's Hatfield House was built partly using bricks from the old Hatfield Palace.   (Guide book).

Chapter 5.

1.   VCH Middlesex. Vol III pp261-263.

2.   Ibid.

3.   Herbert Wilson 'Eight Hundred Years of Harlington Parish Church' (Lucy and Birch, Uxbridge, 1909) p30.   The chalice and flagon bear the Bennet coat of arms and date mark for 1672.

4.   Lady Newton 'The House of Lyme' op cit p250.

5.   GEC 'The Complete Peerage, or a history of the House of Lords and all its Members from the earliest times'.   (St Catherine's Press, London, 1945, revised edition).

6.   For Hugh May, see, inter alia, H M Colvin 'A Biographical Dictionary of English Architects, 1660-1840.   (John Murray, 1954).

7.   Survey of London, (The Athlone Press, University of London. Published for the Greater London Council), Vol XXIX, p77.

8.   See note 16, Chapter 3.

Chapter 5 (cont'd)

9.   The south-east wing of Dingley Hall, Northants, was built by Sir Edward Griffin in 1670-1680, using, it has been convincingly suggested, as his architect Hugh May, who was related to his wife.   See N Pevsner, 'Northamptonshire' (Penguin, 1961).

Chapter 6.

1.   See John Harris 'The Artist and the Country House' (Sotheby Parke Bernet, 1979) pp 91-95.

2.   PRO MPH 246.   Jenner's Plan of Dawley is further discussed in Chapter 10.

3.   Ibid.   The tiny sketch of it is coloured as brick.

4.   Kip's engraving of c1700 compared to features in Jenner's scale plan of c1721, and size measured from the latter.

5.   At Botwell Common, just the other side of Dawley Road to the east, the natural water level is typically 1.7m and 4.2m below the ground surface.   See Planning Application by Redland Aggregates dated 23/11/90.

6.   H Inigo Triggs, in 'Formal Gardens in England and Scotland' (Batsford, 1902), evidently didn't believe that Kip's engraving was accurate, because he re-drew the windows as 3 panes wide and 6 high.

7.   See John Harris 'William Talman Maverick Architect' (Allen & Unwin, 1982).

8.   Ibid.

Chapter 7.

1.   PRO - included in C104/82.   This book has a plain dark brown leather cover.   Inside - 'B. Ossulstone 1688'.

2.   Ibid.

3.   PRO - included in C104/82.   Paper, sewn, c 6" wide, 14$^{1}/_{2}$" high.

4.   Camblet - a light-weight material of wool and silk or wool and cotton. The name derives from the belief that camel hair was originally used.

5.   PRO - that for 1716 is included in C104/82.   Papers, sewn, c 6" wide, 14$^{1}/_{2}$" high.   That for 1722 - discussed more fully in later chapters - is in C104/147 part 1, in a book with a yellow hard cover inscribed 'No 7 Meres & Nott'.   There is also a second copy in a parchment cover.

Chapter 8.

1.   Kip's engraving of c1700 compared to features in Jenner's scale plan of c1721 and size measured from the latter.

Chapter 8 (cont'd)

2.   Plan measured from 25in OS map.

3.   Builders estimates contained in PRO C104/82. This is a loose sheet, folded, inside cover of 'Receipt Book 11 Feb 1700'.

4.   John Harris 'Talman' op cit. See note 7, Chapter 6.

5.   do.

6.   do.

7.   See note 3, Chapter 7.

8.   See 'A Country House Portrayed - Hampton Court, Herefordshire, 1699-1840' (Sabin Galleries Ltd, 1973) (Exhibition catalogue).

9.   See J Starkie Gardner ' English Ironwork of the XVIIth and XVIIIth Centuries' (Batsford, 1911) page 117.

10.   These have been designated 'the parterre gardens' for convenience of reference by the present writer. See Chapter 13.

11.   PRO C104/147 Part 1.

12.   GLRO Acc 446/EM 45 Middx. (Survey of Harlington, 1692).

13.   VCH Middlesex, Vol III (quoting PRO C66/3339 no 16).

14.   Ibid (quoting GLRO (MRO) Acc 446/EM 47).

15.   There is no natural high spot nearby, and Harlington church tower is too far away, so the artist must have relied on his imagination for some details, although he would have had access to the roof of the house itself.

Chapter 9.

1.   See note 16, Chapter 3.

2.   GEC 'The Complete Peerage' op cit. (See note 5, Chapter 5).

3.   See Brian Williams 'Stand and Deliver' (Hillingdon Borough Libraries, 1986) p46.

4.   The five volumes of the diaries, contained in two separate lots, are as follows:

In PRO C104/116 Pt2
Diary volume 'A'. Brown, leather-bound cover, c4$^{1}/_{2}$" x 7"
12 November 1703 - 10 March 1705/06

Diary volume 'B'. Brown, leather-bound cover, c5" x 8"
11 March 1705/06 - 23 June 1708

In PRO C104/113 Pt2
Diary volume 'C'. Brown, leather-bound cover c6" x 7$^{1}/_{2}$"
14 July 1708 - 21 May 1710

Chapter 9 (cont'd)

> Diary volume 'D'. Reddish wavy pattern cover c6¹/₂" x 9"
> 25 May 1710 - 13 May 1711
>
> Diary volume 'E'. Similar to 'D'
> 26 May 1711 - 19 December 1712

5.　See Survey of London (op cit. See note 7, Chapter 5) Vol XXIX, p78.

6.　George Cooke bought the estate of Rythes, Harefield, in 1705 and Belhammonds in 1713; the combined estate later became Harefield Park. Lord Ossulstone contributed to the election expenses of Cooke (by then knighted) in January 1722 (Thomas Robertson's 2nd Book, 1721, included in PRO C104/82). (Sir George purchased the Manor of Hayes from James Jennings in 1729, incidentally).

7.　GLRO Acc 446/EM 45 Middx.

8.　Robert Cooper was Rector of Harlington 1732-1747 and Archdeacon of Dorset. He died in 1752 aged 83. (See H Wilson '800 years of Harlington church' op cit).

9.　PRO - included in C104/82 - a book with a 'shot silk' pattern soft cover.

10.　GEC 'The Complete Peerage' op cit.

11.　Redford & Riches 'Uxbridge' op cit (see note 18, Chapter 3) pp125-126.

12.　PRO - included in C104/82 'Thomas Robertson's 1st Book 1716' page 112.

13.　Dr William Thorold occupied Place House, Uxbridge, from at least 1709 until 1728 or later. He married (as a widower) Mary Charlton at Boxley, Kent, in 1720 (Boxley Parish Church Registers). In the Uxbridge Burgage Roll for 1728, Thorold is shown as paying the highest rent to the Lord of the Manor and owning the greatest number of animals. Incidentally, an earlier occupier of Place House (after Dame Leonora Bennet) was Sir Christopher Abdy, who was related by marriage to Sir John Bennet (II). Their wives, Mary and Dorothy (Crofts) were sisters. It is tempting to believe that Thorold was also connected with the Bennets. (See notes on the Crown and Treaty House by John Mills, held in the Local Heritage collection, Uxbridge Library).

14.　Lord Ossulstone's diary (volume 'A'). John Bush, AM, was Vicar of Harmondsworth 1698-1713.

15.　GEC 'The Complete Peerage' op cit.

16.　Those interested should read 'Mary Cole, Countess of Berkeley' by Hope Costley-White (1961, reprint Havant, 1973).

17.　GEC 'The Complete Peerage' op cit.

Chapter 10.

1.　A payment to Jenner on 23 December 1719 was for, inter alia, 'the new measuring work' since 20 November 1719. (PRO C104/82 p6).

Chapter 10 (cont'd)

This payment might well have been to cover surveying work for the Plan of Dawley.

2.   PRO ref MPH246.

Chapter 11.

1.   GLRO (MRO) MSP AP/62, Sessions Book [SB] 645 page 53; SB 648 page 60.

2.   Botwell Heath lay east of the Dawley estate and north of the road to Norwood (the present North Hyde Road).

3.   GLRO (MRO) MSP AP/62, SB655 page 45; Lord Ossulstone's diary entries between 6 January 1706/07 and 27 April 1708.

4.   See note 1 above (SB645 page 53).

Chapter 12.

1.   PRO C104/116 - Lord Ossulstone's diary entries for 18/7/1706, 7/4/1708 and 25/6/1712.

2.   PRO - included in C104/82 - a loose sheet of paper inside cover of Receipt Book (commenced) 11 February 1700.

3.   PRO C104/116 Part 2 - Lord Ossulstone's diary entry 26/11/1703.

4.   Ibid. Diary entries 25-26/1/1704/05 and 26/3/1705/06.

5.   PRO - included in C104/82 - another loose sheet of paper, as in note 2 above.

6.   PRO C104/150. This refers to 12 acres leased by William & Anne Pannett on 29/11/1708. A separate tree map is included. A later abstract of title is in GLRO (MRO) Acc 446/Ed 236.

7.   Hubbards Farm, Colham Green, Hillingdon. A copy of this plan (the property of Mr J Shepherd) is included in the Local Heritage collection, Uxbridge Library.

Chapter 13.

1.   Lantern or lanthorn - as well as describing a form of artificial lighting, the term applies to an architectural feature, discussed below.

2.   See note 5, Chapter 12.

3.   PRO - included in C104/82, Receipt Book 1701/1722. On 30/5/1719 £6- was paid for a beehouse and beehive.

4.   See GLRO (MRO) Acc 446/EM 45 Middx.

5.   See VCH Buckinghamshire, Vol III, p258.

Chapter 13 (cont'd)

6. However, hundreds of Protestant families were forced to flee from the Palatinate province of the Rhine around 1709. These included some of the name of Switzer. Stephen Switzer (1682?-1745), the celebrated gardener, was born in England (see DNB) but concentrated research might reveal a Dawley connection with his German namesakes.

7. PRO - included in C104/82, Receipt Book 1701-1722.

8. See David Green 'The Gardens and Parks at Hampton Court and Bushey' (HMSO, 1974).

9. David Green - Ibid; also see J Starkie Gardner, op cit (see note 9, Chapter 8).

10. Dawley canal - measured from Jenner's plan of c1721; Hampton Court canal - measured from Bridgeman's map reproduced in David Green op cit (see note 8 above).

11. PRO - included in C104/82. The list was compiled on 21/5/1722 following the Earl's death.

12. See, inter alia, Derek Clifford 'A History of Garden Design' (Faber, 1962).

13. See note 2, Chapter 12.

14. PRO - included in C104/82, Receipt Book 1701-1722, entry 11/9/1716; Thomas Robertson's 1st Book, entry 6/10/1716.

15. PRO - included in C104/82, Gardener's account book, 1713-1722.

16. The Harlington Inclosure Award, 1821, names the field covering the area as 'The Lime Walk'.

17. PRO - included in C104/82 - 'An account of wages paid for work done in the wood in Dawley Park 25 November 1718 - 26 October 1719' (Book with yellow cover and gold pattern; tie-up tapes).

18. Ibid; also Gardener's account book 1713-1722 (e.g. digging and growing the maze in the wood).

19. Ibid (Gardener's Account Book)

20. PRO - included in C104/82 'Thomas Robertson's 1st Book, 1716'.

Chapter 14.

1. PRO - included in C104/82. Receipt Book 1701-1722, entry for 9/4/1715.

2. Ibid - entries for dates quoted in text.

3. Ibid. 'Thomas Robertson's 1st Book, 1716'.

4. Ibid. Receipt Book 1701-1722.

Chapter 14 (cont'd)

5. This was almost certainly Jeremy Delavell, carpenter, who was working on alterations to Lord Ossulstone's town house in St James's Square in 1705. See Survey of London (op cit) Vol XXIX, p78.

6. Lord Ossulstone's diary, volume 'E' (see note 4, Chapter 9).

7. H M Colvin 'Biographical Dictionary' op cit (see note 6, Chapter 5).

8. Ibid.

9. A 'Bagnio Room' is included in the 1722 Inventory of Dawley, although in sequence it still follows the rooms of the old mansion. Strangely, there is no reference to a bagnio in the 1715/16 Inventory.

10. 'Follies' were usually positioned to provide a distant eye-catching feature, viewed from the house. This Dawley structure is close to both the houses of c1670 and 1720, but not obviously lined up with either. The so-called 'Tattingstone Wonder' near Ipswich, Suffolk, has a superficial similarity to the Dawley building, but was built to disguise estate cottages as a church in the late 18th century. See J W Whitelaw 'Follies' (Shire Publications, 1982).

11. Thomas Newcomen's first engine was built in 1712.

12. Most likely Thomas Holland (1646?-1730) who took out patents in 1691 and 1716 for raising water from mines, or supplying towns etc. See Bennet Woodcraft 'Alphabetical Index of Patentees of Inventions 1617-1852' (London, 1854. Reprint 1969); also R B Prosser's MS List in BM Add MS 54500B. I am indebted to Dr R T Smith for this information.

13. PRO - included in C104/82. Receipt Book 1701-1722.

14. Ibid.

15. Ibid.

16. Hand-in-Hand Fire Office, London. The policy was dated June 19th 1753 and numbered 74224, 25 and 26 for the three parts of the mansion and 74227 for the service buildings. The Register ledger is in the Guildhall Library collection (ref. I 3, p75) and owners' copies of the policy are GLRO (MRO) Acc 446/H9-10.

17. PRO - as note 13, above.

18. Ibid.

19. But see Chapter 14 for discussion of a new stable built at Pinkwell.

20. See Kerry Downes 'English Baroque Architecture' (A Zwemmer, 1966).

21. The National Trust 'Uppark, Sussex', 1983 (guide book).

Chapter 15.

1. See above (Chapter 14).

2. See Kerry Downes op cit (note 20, Chapter 14).

Chapter 15 (cont'd)

3. Kerry Downes (op cit) considers John Price as the possible architect of Barnsley Park (built 1720-21) because of the owner's connection with the Duke of Chandos, but believes Hawksmoor, or even Gibbs or Archer, as more likely candidates. David Verey (Pevsner's 'The Buildings of England - Gloucestershire: The Cotswolds', Penguin, 1989) favours John James. The present writer merely offers the choice ! The plan of Barnsley Park, however, foreshadows to some extent what Gibbs did later in enlarging the building presently being discussed. Another possible example of John Price's work is Bradmore House, Hammersmith, built between 1720 and 1723, of which the rebuilt garden front remains. See Michel Burrell (ed) 'Bradmore House, Hammersmith' (London, 1996) page 21.

4. John Jenner's Plan of Dawley c1721 bears the Board of Ordnance mark, incidentally.

5. See Christopher Hussey 'English Country Houses Early Georgian 1715-1760' (Country Life, 1955).

6. Dubois' biographical details are based on H M Colvin (op cit). For 41 Brewer Street see Survey of London (op cit) Vol XXXI, p121.

7. PRO - included in C104/82 'Thomas Robertson's 1st Book 1716'.

8. See James Lees-Milne 'English Country Houses Baroque 1685-1715' (Country Life, 1970); also plans in National Monuments Record File 61859.

9. See William Collier 'Historic Buildings, Thames Valley' (Spurbooks, 1973).

10. See Royal Commission on the Historical Monuments of England (RCHM) 'Salisbury: The Houses of the Close' (HMSO, 1993).

11. See H Montgomery-Massingberd ' "The Field" book of Country Houses and their Owners' (M Joseph, 1981).

12. PRO - included in C104/82: Receipt Book 1701-1722. A list of costs of the various items is followed by accounts of payments made. The estimates are on three sides of a loose sheet, c7$^{1}/_{2}$" x 12".

13. Few details are known of the Jenners. John appears to have died between 1726 and 1729. He undertook alterations to Lord Tankerville's London house with his son, James, who carried on the work after his death. See Survey of London (op cit) Vol XXIX, pp78-79.

14. See Chapter 16. Anthony Adams' payment (including painting) was dated 14/8/1721, recorded in Receipt Book 1701/1722 included in PRO C104/82.

Chapter 16.

1. See Chapter 17.

2. Henry Bennet had died in 1721 and was buried at Harlington on 24 August. Grey did not survive him for very long: he died in 1724 and was buried, also at Harlington, on 21 November.

Chapter 16 (cont'd)

3. This is discussed fully in Chapter 10.

4. I am indebted to Miss Wendy Hefford, Deputy Curator, Textiles and Dress, Victoria and Albert Museum, for the information on and likely identification of the Dawley tapestries: personal communication of 8/1/1992 refers. They are illustrated in W G Thompson 'Tapestry-Weaving in England' (1914).

5. Harlington Parish Registers.

Chapter 17.

1. PRO - included in C104/147 Part 1: a large book with a yellow cover inscribed 'No 7 Meres & Nott'. The first four pages cover the Earl's Will and Codicil; the remaining 55 pages list his possessions at Dawley, London and Uppark; also servants and their wages.

2. A new Sash Maree, presumably the same vehicle or one of its type, was purchased in 1716 - see below; also Chapter 28, item 74 in sale.

3. For details of horse-drawn vehicles I have consulted 'Discovering Horse Drawn Carriages' (1976) and 'A Dictionary of Horse Drawn Vehicles' (1988), both by D J Smith. Mr H S Middleton, Curator, Maidstone Museums, has also provided helpful information.

4. PRO - included in C104/82 - Thomas Robertson's 1st Book, 1716; Receipt Book 1701-1722; Receipt Book 1713-1719.

5. The (8th) Earl of Tankerville, in a personal communication of 14/8/1958, said 'I myself doubt this very much, for I think it highly unlikely that in those days any calves removed from the herd at Chillingham (older animals cannot be caught) would have survived the weeks of transport necessary to get them from Chillingham to Harlington'.

6. PRO C104/147 Pt 1; Stephen Dowell 'A History of Taxation and Taxes in England' (1884, 3rd ed. 1965). The variations in Land Tax, 1693-1724, are recorded in a book, yellow cover, tuck-in flap, endorsed 'An account of the farms rents 1724' included in PRO C104/82.

7. See note 1 above.

8. PRO - included in C104/82 - 'Thomas Robertson's 1st Book, 1716'.

9. Harlington Parish Registers.

10. Source - as in note 1 above. An earlier list, with servants' dates of entry from November 1716 onwards was compiled by Thomas Robertson in his '1st Book, 1716' - see note 8 above. This is discussed further below.

11. Individual entries in Thomas Robertson's 1st Book - see note 10.

12. 'The Ipswich Journal', 1725 - report dated 'London Sept 21'. I am indebted to Miss Julia Zouch for this item.

Chapter 18.

1.   For the Earl of Tankerville's Will see note 1, Chapter 17.

2.   GLRO (MRO) Acc 278 (the lease); GLRO (MRO) Acc 446/ED 205 (the sale).

3.   See the 'Proceedings of The Huguenot Society of London', Vols 13 & 15, in University College, London.   Mr G L Read has been of great help here.

4.   This is a select list of works on Bolingbroke, with emphasis on those throwing light on his life at Dawley.

      Cooke, George Wingrove 'Memoirs of Lord Bolingbroke' (2 vols)
            (Richard Bentley, London, 1835)

      Dickinson, H T   'Bolingbroke'   (Constable, 1970)

      Goldsmith, Oliver 'The Life of Lord Bolingbroke' (1770) included in
            'The Miscellaneous Works of Oliver Goldsmith'
            (Macmillan, London, 1899)

      Hassall, Arthur 'Life of Viscount Bolingbroke'
            (W H Allen, London, 1889)

      Hopkinson, M R 'Married to Mercury - a sketch of Lord Bolingbroke
            and his wives' (Constable, London, 1936)

      Macknight, Thomas 'The Life of Henry St John Viscount Bolingbroke'
            (Chapman & Hall, London, 1863)

      Petrie, Sir Charles 'Bolingbroke' (Collins, London, 1937)

      Sichel, Walter 'Bolingbroke and his Times - The Sequel'
            (1901, reprinted Greenwood Press, New York, 1968)
      (Sichel includes a valuable Appendix of letters from, to and about
      Bolingbroke)

5.   Dickinson - see details in note 4 above.

6.   Sichel p212 - see details in note 4 above.

Chapter 19.

1.   Allen Bathurst, Baron Bathurst of Battlesden (1684-1775) who had an estate at Richings (or Riskins) Park, Iver, nearby.

2.   Burke's Peerage and Baronetage; GEC The Complete Peerage (op cit).

3.   'A Book of Architecture containing Designs of Buildings and Ornaments by James Gibbs' (London, 1728).

4.   'The Gentleman's Magazine', August 1802, page 725 (plate facing).

5.   Hand-in-Hand Fire Office - see note 16, Chapter 14.

6.   James Gibbs 'Architecture' - op cit - see note 3 above.

Chapter 19 (cont'd)

7.   See discussion below (Chapter 23) of the remote possibility of the introduction of Indian architectural features by Edward Stephenson.

8.   GLRO (MRO) Acc 446/H22/2.

9.   Ibid.

10.   George Sherburn (ed) 'The Correspondence of Alexander Pope' (Oxford, 1956), Vol II, p503; Goldsmith (see note 4, Chapter 18) p464.

11.   Goldsmith   Ibid.

12.   'The Gentleman's Magazine', June 1731, p262.

13.   'Letters written by the late Right Honourable Lady Luxborough to William Shenstone Esq,' (London, 1775) pp139-140.

14.   Sherburn   op cit   Vol II, p525.

15.   Geoffrey Beard 'Craftsmen and Interior Decoration in England 1660-1820' (Bloomsbury Books, 1981).

16.   Hopkinson (see note 4, Chapter 18) p169.

17.   GLRO (MRO) Acc 446/H22/4.

18.   'The Gentleman's Magazine' op cit - see note 12 above.

19.   The present writer has seen only views of the garden front.

20.   Sherburn op cit Vol II p400, note in Index. James, 3rd Earl of Berkeley had his main seat at Berkeley Castle, Gloucestershire. He was a distinguished Naval officer who became Vice-Admiral of Great Britain, Lord Lieutenant of Gloucestershire 1710, and Lincolnshire 1727. He died in 1736 (Burke's Peerage). Cranford House was largely rebuilt in 1722. (See also note 17, Chapter 21).

21.   Sichel (see note 4, Chapter 18) p517.

22.   Sherburn op cit Vol II, p525.

Chapter 20.

1.   John Rocque 'A Topographical map of the County of Middlesex' ('Carte topographique de la Comte de Middlesex') (1754). Scale 2" : 1 mile.

2.   The 'turrett clock' and the wind dial at Dawley were cleaned and repaired in April-May 1770. (See GLRO (MRO) Acc 446/H22/16).

3.   See 'Hayes and Harlington Official Guide' [1952 edition] page 11.

4.   This watercolour, artist unknown, captioned 'Dawley House Middx', is in the Guildhall Library collection. It dates probably to the early 19th century, between say, 1800 and 1820. Another watercolour, in a similar style and with an identical border, in the Local Heritage collection, Uxbridge Library, captioned 'Colham Mills' is dated 'c1805'.

Chapter 20 (cont'd)

5.   H O Meyers 'A Lecture on the Village of Harlington' (J Gotelee, Hounslow, 1857) page 8.

6.   In a report for EMI by Walter H Godfrey, FSA, Director & Secretary, The National Buildings Record, in response to a letter dated 9 March 1943 from R Theodore Beck, FRIBA. (EMI archives).

7.   Terry Friedman 'James Gibbs' (Yale University Press, 1984) includes a plan and elevation on p126.

8.   BM Add MS 27732, f166.

9.   There is also a local belief that circus animals were once kept there.

10.   Hassall (see note 4, Chapter 18) p178.

11.   Sherburn op cit Vol II, p332 (Pope's letter to Swift dated 15 October 1725).

Chapter 21.

1.   Quoted by Edward Walford 'Greater London A narrative of its History its people and its Places' (Cassell, 1883, 1898 etc. Reprint Alderman Press, 1985).

2.   See Chapter 19.

3.   'The Gentleman's Magazine', June 1731, page 262. (Fogg's Weekly Journal, No 128, 26 June 1731 is given as (another) source by M R Brownell 'Alexander Pope and the Arts of Georgian England' (Oxford, 1978) p227. The poem was published anonymously but attributed to Pope.

4.   'A Further Account of Rural or Extensive Gardening', probably written c1730 but published 1742 as an appendix to 'Ichnographica Rustica'. See D Jacques in 'Garden History' (journal), 1976.

5.   Sherburn op cit Vol II, p327.

6.   See Macknight (note 4, Chapter 18) p587. Swift in a letter enquired of Bolingbroke about the yew hedges and the mount. Quoted by M R Brownell op cit (see note 3 above).

7.   Ashmolean Museum, Oxford - James Gibbs Collection, iii 90a.

8.   See, inter alia, Macknight (note 4, Chapter 18) pp568-569.

9.   In 'Imitations of Horace' (1733).

10.   Sherburn op cit Vol II, p403 (footnote 2).

11.   Ibid p401.

12.   Ibid p399. (Gay also wrote about this incident to Swift).

13.   Gordon S Maxwell 'Highwayman's Heath' (Thomasons, Hounslow, 1935) p366. Macknight (note 4, Chapter 18) p565, says 'Gulliver's Travels' was 'discussed' at Dawley.

Chapter 21 (cont'd)

14.   'The Oxford Companion to English Literature' (Oxford, 1993).

15.   VCH Middlesex, Vol III, p272.

16.   H Wilson '800 years...' (op cit - see note 3, Chapter 5) includes biographical details and a portrait.

17.   See, for example, Gay's letter to Swift, September 1726 (Sherburn op cit Vol II, p400).   The 17th century house at Cranford was largely added to and rebuilt about 1722, per dates on rainwater heads.   It was further extended about 70 years later, and demolished in 1944. (Royal Commission on Historical Monuments England.   Inventory Middlesex (1937); VCH Middlesex Vol III, and local information).

18.   Harlington Parish Registers.

Chapter 22.

1.   M R Hopkinson (see note 4, Chapter 18) p188.

2.   Sichel (op cit) quotes Bolingbroke, writing from France on 25 June 'It will be 3 weeks tomorrow since we sailed from Greenwich' (p537).

3.   M R Hopkinson (note 4, Chapter 18) p249 (quoting from HMC Part V, Denbigh Papers).

4.   Sichel op cit p544.

5.   Macknight op cit p622.

6.   Ibid p622.   The letter to Lady Denbigh is quoted in Hopkinson p248.

7.   Sherburn op cit Vol IV p106.

8.   Ibid pp113-124.

9.   Ibid p113.

10.   Ibid p136.

11.   See note 1, Chapter 19.

12.   Sherburn op cit Vol IV p148.

13.   Burward was Bolingbroke's farm agent.

14.   House and land were, in fact, sold separately, much later, by Lord Paget (see below).

15.   Sherburn op cit Vol IV p153.

16.   Ibid Vol IV p173.

17.   Ibid Vol IV p177.

Chapter 22 (cont'd)

18. The monument, by Roubiliac, is in the north side of the gallery. It consists of a shrouded urn, surmounted by Bolingbroke's coat of arms below which are low relief profiles of Bolingbroke and his second wife. (Battersea Church History and Guide Book, 1975).

Chapter 23.

1. Chief sources are: (a) India Office Library and Records. 'Bengal General Proceedings', period August-September 1728. (b) J F Crosthwaite 'Researches and Reminiscences' (Keswick, 1902). Short biography of Governor Stephenson, pp19-22. (c) Brigadier J W Kaye 'Governor's House, Keswick' in Transactions of the Cumberland & Westmorland Antiquarian & Archaeological Society, Vol 66 (New Series) (Kendal, 1966) pp339-341. (d) Romney Sedgwick 'The History of Parliament: The House of Commons 1715-1754 [Vol] II Members E - Y, 1715-1754 (HMSO, 1970) p445.

2. Robert Clive took 15 months to reach Madras in 1743-44, after running aground in Brazil en route. The voyage was considered uneventful ! (C Lestock Reid 'Commerce and Conquest' (C and J Temple Ltd, 1947)).

3. Printed obituaries; memorial in Crosthwaite Church (see note 28).

4. A house at Tranquebar on the Coromandel coast was once the property of one Edward Stevenson, but this was in the Danish enclave of India. See Sten Nilsson 'European Architecture in India, 1750-1850' (Faber 1968) p54.

5. J F Crosthwaite - see note 1 above.

6. P Morant 'The History and Antiquities of Essex (1768) Vol 2, p520. Information kindly supplied by the Essex Record Office and Mrs Edith Freeman of Sudbury.

7. J W Kaye - see note 1 above.

8. See G H Hamilton 'Queen Square, its neighbourhood and its Institutions' (Leonard Parsons, 1926); H Phillips 'Mid Georgian London' (Collins, 1964).

9. J W Kaye op cit - see note 1 above.

10. Ibid.

11. Romney Sedgwick - see note 1 above.

12. Harlington Parish Registers.

13. Romney Sedgwick op cit - see note 1 above.

14. 'An Act ...... for repairing the Highways between Tyburn and Uxbridge', 12 George I, and additional Trustees in 15 George II (1742). Copies of these Acts, together with the Minute Books, are held in Kensington Library.

15. Harlington Parish Registers.

Chapter 23 (cont'd)

16. VCH Middlesex, Vol III, p270.

17. GLRO (MRO) Acc 446/ED 269.

18. GLRO (MRO) Acc 446/ED 270.

19. Harlington Parish Registers.

20. GLRO (MRO) Acc 446/ED 236.

21. See note 16, Chapter 14.

22. GLRO (MRO) Acc 446/ED 237.

23. Ibid. The sale Indenture is GLRO (MRO) Acc 446/ED 378.

24. Endorsed on ledger entry for Hand-in-Hand insurance policy 74224-74227 (see note 16, Chapter 14).

25. For example, GLRO (MRO) Acc 446/H22/37 and H22/47.

26. DNB; VCH Hertfordshire, Vol III pp487-488. (Could the John Deane who purchased the Manor of Wormley Bury from the Humes have been Edward Stephenson's successor as Governor of Bengal ? See above).

27. See Romney Sedgwick etc, op cit - see note 1 above.

28. The memorial reads 'Edward Stephenson Esqr. Late Governor of Bengal, Obt Septr 7th 1768 aetat 77'.

29. 'The Gentleman's Magazine', January 1783 - obituary.

30. Ibid. August 1802 - figure 1, page 725.

31. See Chapter 19.

32. See G H R Tillotson 'Architectural Guides for Travellers ; Mughal India' (Penguin, 1991).

33. See D Verey 'The Buildings of England - Gloucestershire: The Cotswolds' (Penguin, 2nd ed 1979); C Hussey 'English Country Houses Late Georgian, 1800-1840 (Country Life 1955). Even earlier than Daylesford and Sezincote was Castle Hall, Milford Haven, originally built between 1770 and 1775 for a retired Governor of Bengal. Thought to have had some details in the 'Hindoo style', it was remodelled in the Italian style in 1855 and demolished before World War II. See 'Property Services Agency Historic Buildings Register', Volume I (1982).

Chapter 24.

1. Evidence that this was still a recognised local feature in 1744 is the reference to the 'Corner of the Pales near the visto upon Goulds Green' in the Perambulation of Hayes in that year. See Journal of the Hayes and Harlington Local History Society, Autumn 1977.

2. GLRO (MRO) Acc 46/EF 22.

Chapter 24 (cont'd)

3. See note 16, Chapter 13.

Chapter 25.

1. 'The old mansion ... ... was pulled down by the late Earl of Uxbridge, about the year 1750' per the Rev Daniel Lysons, 1800. See note 14, Chapter 27, below.

2. DNB. One Peter Walters (the same ?) was described as the land jobber in a transaction in which Bolingbroke helped the Earl of Essex - see Sichel op cit p221.

3. GLRO (MRO) Acc 446/ED/237.

4. GLRO (MRO) Acc 446/ED/378.

5. Irken - location not established.

6. See note 16, Chapter 14.

7. Ibid.

8. GLRO (MRO) Acc 446/EM50.

9. Ibid (EM50/11).

10. See note 2, Chapter 24.

11. Hubbards Farm - see note 7, Chapter 12.

12. GLRO (MRO) Acc 530/ED/8/1. (Lease of land: Farringeton to Rayner, dated 16 April 1586. It has to be said, however, that 'Gate' may still have had the Old English meaning of 'a way').

13. GLRO (Middx) Acc No 1066.

14. Ibid.

15. Harlington Parish Registers.

16. See also note 1, Chapter 24.

17. Officers of the Greater London Council Historic Buildings Division; Arup Associates 'Stockley Park Dawley Wall Proposed Renovation'. Report No 2.171 28th July 1987.

18. See note 5, Chapter 20.

19. See note 6, Chapter 2.

20. Mrs J Wadsworth (nee De Salis) - personal communication 13.5.1956.

21. The Hayes Parish Register records that 6 out of the total 22 deaths in 1752 were due to smallpox. The totals for the next 5 years (1753-1757) were 16, 18, 12, 18, 22. For Harlington in 1752-1757, the totals were 8, 5, 13, 10, 7, 5, causes of death not being recorded in this register.

Chapter 25 (cont'd)

22.   See Charles F Mullett 'The Cattle Distemper in Mid-Eighteenth Century England' in 'Agricultural History', Vol 20 (1946), pp144-165.

23.   See O & N Hamilton 'Royal Greenwich' (Greenwich, 1969) p101.

24.   James Boswell 'The Life of Johnson' (1791, Penguin edition 1979) p296.

25.   Mystic significance has sometimes been attributed to certain forms of wall decoration, but no evidence has come to light that this was so at Dawley.

26.   See note 16, Chapter 14.   The renewal document is GLRO (MRO) Acc 446/H9-10.

Chapter 26.

1.   GLRO (MRO) Acc 446/EF 21 - William Eldridge's Account Book, 31 August 1760 - August 1761.

2.   See note 6, Chapter 2.

3.   See Chapter 4.

4.   The materials are itemised in GLRO (MRO) Acc 446/EF21 (see note 1 above).

5.   GLRO MR/HT/55.   Even Sir Robert Vyner at Ickenham (Swakeleys) was only assessed at 39 hearths.

6.   GLRO (MRO) Acc 446/EF 21.

7.   See Gordon S Maxwell op cit (See note 13, Chapter 21).

8.   In the collection of the Hayes and Harlington Local History Society.

9.   Ex info Mrs F M Symmons, daughter of the one-time owner of Church Farm; photographs in the collection of the Hayes and Harlington Local History Society.

Chapter 27.

1.   June Sampson 'All change - Kingston, Surbiton and New Malden in the 19th Century' (News Origin, 1985, revised 1991) pp16-17.   (I am obliged to Mrs C Cotton for this source).

2.   GLRO (MRO) Acc 46/H22.

3.   Ibid (H22/2).

4.   June Sampson op cit (see note 1 above); Burke's Peerage.

5.   GLRO (MRO) Acc 446/H22/23.   'Coal' then meant charcoal; Scotch coal (or 'sea coal' etc) meant mined coal.

6.   Ibid (H22/16).   Gatford was an Uxbridge man.

Chapter 27 (cont'd)

7.   See note 4, Chapter 20.

8.   GLRO (MRO) Acc 446/H22/60.

9.   Ibid   (H22/14).

10.   Ibid   (H22/60).

11.   Ibid   (H22/1, 41, 42, 59).

12.   Ibid   H22/19, 31).   For sale in 1772 see Chapter 28.

13.   Ibid   (H22/47, 56).

14.   Rev Daniel Lysons 'An Historical Account of those Parishes in the County of Middlesex which are not described in the Environs of London'. (London, 1800).

15.   DNB.

Chapter 28.

1.   Dr O C White drew my attention to this item. Grateful thanks are due to Messrs Christie's of London, whose archivist Mr J Rex-Parkes kindly allowed me to see their file copy of the catalogue, which is annotated with the amounts raised.

2.   Chaise marine - see note 2, Chapter 17.

Chapter 29.

1.   See D Lysons op cit (note 14, Chapter 27).

2.   Hassall op cit p187.

3.   Personal communication (1963) from Mrs M E Gibbs, who occupied Little Dawley 1933 - c1947.

4.   See Journal of the Hayes and Harlington Local History Society, Spring 1988.

5.   See Rachel De Salis (op cit). (See note 3, Chapter 2).

6.   H O Meyers op cit, etc.

7.   Edward Walford op cit (see note 1, Chapter 21);   personal communication Mrs J Wadsworth, 1956 (see note 20, Chapter 25).

8.   See note 4, Chapter 20.

9.   Ibid.

10.   The earliest photograph traced is that reproduced in Gordon S Maxwell 'Highwayman's Heath' op cit (1935).

11.   GLRO Acc 969/63. There is a discussion of this site in Chapter 32.

Chapter 30.

1.   The canal route through Dawley was not as intended; the line should have run due west from Southall, just north of Cranford Park and Harlington village. As, probably, the land required could not be obtained, the Dawley route was adopted,   saving about ³/₄ mile of canal, but at the expense of the deep cutting. (A H Faulkner 'The Grand Junction Canal' (David & Charles 1972)).

2.   J G James 'Ralph Dodd, The Very Ingenious Schemer'.   Paper presented to The Newcomen Society, 14 January, 1976.

3.   C Hadfield 'The Canals of the East Midlands' (David & Charles, 1970).

4.   See 'Report of the Committee of Magistrates ..... respecting the Public Bridges in the County of Middlesex' (London, 1826).

5.   See Vincent Orchard 'Tattersalls' (Hutchinson, London, 1953).

6.   Ibid.

7.   Pigot & Co's London & Provincial Commercial Directory, 1827-1828.

8.   GLRO (MRO) DP 141.

9.   'The Register of Electors ...... County of Middlesex, 1838' - Parish of Harlington.   (Copy in Local Heritage collection, Uxbridge Library).

10.   Mrs V Hammond kindly drew this to my attention.

Chapter 31.

1.   GLRO (MRO) DP 141. See Chapter 30.

2.   Archibald Williams 'Brunel and After'. (Great Western Railway, 1925; reprint 1972).

3.   This bridge was still shown on the 1914 OS map.

Chapter 32.

1.   VCH Middlesex, Vol IV p30.

2.   Ex info P T Sherwood. Sometimes the agricultural loam would be shaved off and put aside, the clay used, and the loam put back. (See Miss A M Pollard, Middlesex Local History Council Bulletin No 6, January, 1958).

3.   See Kip engraving of Dawley c1700 where a smoking brick kiln is shown.

4.   A Thomas Jolly was described as 'beer retailer' at Yeading in an 1882 directory. He may well have also been carrying out brickmaking there.

5.   GLRO (MRO) 969/63.

6.   GLRO (MRO) 969/64a & b. The cottages, Rigby's Row, were claimed to be 80 years old when demolished in 1954. See 'Gazette', 29/10/1954.

Chapter 32 (cont'd)

7.   Buckinghamshire Advertiser 8 April 1871.

8.   Ibid.   7 October 1871.

9.   Ibid.   2 August 1873.

10.   Ibid.   20 May 1876.

11.   Ibid.   2 September 1876.

12.   Harlington Census, 1881.

13.   Balance Sheet of T Maynard, deceased, 31 October 1878. (Hayes and Harlington Museum collection HHM636/5).

14.   EMI archives - Indenture dated 30/12/1899 - schedule of hereditaments.

15.   Stockley Park Consortium Ltd - Conveyance E W F De Salis to Hayes and Harlington UDC dated 15/11/48.

16.   See VCH Middlesex Vol IV pp199-200 (West Drayton); also Desmond Collins 'Early Man in West Middlesex' op cit.

17.   OS Map, 1865.

18.   EMI archives - see map enclosed with Indenture dated 30/12/1899.

19.   Per Mrs K E Norman, then owner/occupier The Dawley Cottage.

20.   Ibid.

21.   Local Directories.

22.   Mrs K E Norman (see note 19 above). There was a skittle alley on the south side of the yard; also, at one time, stabling for six canal-boat horses. A well was in use until 1963, when mains water was laid on.

23.   Uxbridge Gazette, 15 February 1973, p13.

Chapter 33.

1.   See Journal of the Hayes and Harlington Local History Society, Spring 1987, which includes an account by a Member of the Society (Mr E Hammond) who lived there as a child.

2.   Electoral Register, 1890.

3.   Ex info Mrs E M Howard.

4.   Hayes and Harlington UDC Rate Book, 1933.

5.   Per date plaque on front wall of terrace.

6.   According to local informants (Mrs M Grace (nee Hammond) and her sister Miss G Hammond), a Mr Lowe, foreman to the Clayton brickworks, lived at 'Manor Lodge' (sic). This has not been confirmed (see below).

Chapter 33 (cont'd)

7.   Electoral Register, 1905; local directory.

8.   Ex info Mrs Reed, granddaughter of Alfred Maynard; local directories.

9.   Ex info Mrs E M Howard.

10.   Dawley Infants School log books, 2 volumes. Local Heritage Collection, Uxbridge Library, Acc Nos 2300A and B.

11.   Ex info Mrs Grace and Miss Hammond (see note 6 above) who lived there as children.

12.   Ex info J Hearne; local directories.

13.   EMI archives - Indenture dated 30/12/1899.

14.   Ex info C Gadbury, who lived there as a child.

15.   Local directories.

16.   Harlington Census, 1881.

17.   EMI archives - internal correspondence referring to a conveyance C F De Salis to D Colville Stewart dated 20/5/1921.

18.   OS maps.

19.   Journal of the Hayes and Harlington Local History Society, Autumn 1971.

20.   Ex info C F Rose (son of Mr G Rose); local directories.

21.   Journal of the Hayes and Harlington Local History Society, Autumn 1980 - article by P T Sherwood and B T White. Subsequent research has modified some of the conclusions reached then. (See also Chapter 26).

22.   Bournes Bridge Cottages and Bourne Farm Cottages were demolished in the 1960's.

23.   Journal of the Hayes and Harlington Local History Society op cit (note 19 above).

Chapter 34.

1.   Ex info Mrs Grace and Miss Hammond.

2.   Post Office Directory of Middlesex.

3.   EMI archives - Indenture dated 30/12/1899 op cit.

4.   Ex info Mrs Grace and Miss Hammond.

5.   Local directories; Maynards trade card (copy in Local Heritage collection, Uxbridge Library).

6.   D Collins 'Early Man in W Middlesex' op cit (see note 3, Chapter 1).

Chapter 34 (cont'd)

7.   F P Larkin 'The Industrial Development of Western London' in Great Western Railway Magazine, February 1908.

8.   Local directories; Kelly's Middlesex Directories.

9.   Despite the varying descriptions, the factory site at Dawley was probably unchanged.

10.   Bottles in the collection of the Hayes and Harlington Museum, Acc Nos HHM 443/1, 455, 315, 426.

11.   Kelly's Middlesex Directory, 1899.

12.   EMI archives.

13.   E A Alexander was still shown as the site owner on a conveyance map as late as 1941 (EMI archives).

14.   Ex info Mrs Grace and Miss Hammond.

15.   'Order of Service' (printed pamphlet) Hayes and Harlington Museum Acc No HHM 17/1.

16.   Neville Manning 'The First 50 Years. The Story of St Jerome's Church, Dawley' (1983).

17.   Advertiser and Gazette, 12 November 1915, p8.

18.   Ibid. 30 November 1917, p6, and 7 December 1917, p6.

19.   The front doorsteps are well below road level - a reminder that the cottages were built where brick earth had been extracted.

20.   Ex info J V Hammond.

21.   EMI archives - Indenture dated 30/12/1899.

22.   Ex info Mrs E M Howard; picture postcard of Hayes Station.

23.   Ex info Mrs Grace and Miss Hammond.

24.   See map in A Rawlinson 'The Defence of London 1915-1918' (Andrew Melrose, 3rd ed 1924).

25.   The local newspaper carried many reports of distant gunfire and explosions etc but none of bombs having been dropped in the area.

26.   Advertiser and Gazette, 21 September 1917, p3.

Chapter 35.

1.   See Chapter 33.

2.   Ex info J Hearne. This would appear to be George Bromley Jones trading as 'Bee and Jay'. (Kelly's Middlesex Directory, 1937).

3.   Per photocopies of conveyances kindly provided by Stockley Park Consortium Ltd (Hayes and Harlington Museum Collection Acc HHM 802/1-3).

4.   VCH Middlesex, Vol III, p260.

5.   EMI archives - map dated 19 July 1929.

6.   Ex info kindly provided by Mr J A Hunt, Glaxo historian, and Mr A Wood, Librarian.

7.   Hayes and Harlington UDC Rate Books, 1933 and 1940.

8.   Ex info Mr J A Hunt op cit - see note 6 above.

9.   Ex info J V Hammond.

10.   EMI archives - map dated 10/1/1945. Messrs R H Green and Silley Weir re-rigged the sailing ship 'Cutty Sark' about 1955 after she had been placed in the special dock at Greenwich constructed by Sir Robert McAlpine and Sons - their former neighbours at Dawley.   See F G Carr 'Maritime Greenwich' (Pitkin, 1974).

11.   EMI archives - map dated 10/1/1945.

12.   Hayes and Harlington UDC Rate Book, 1933.

13.   Ex info J V Hammond; Hayes and Harlington UDC Rate Book, 1940.

14.   OS Maps.

15.   See Journal of the Hayes and Harlington Local History Society, Spring 1994.

16.   The boundaries were: land of the UK Glass Co in the north; Chappell & Co's sports field in the west; and (with minor exclusions) the GWR line and Dawley road in the south and east, respectively.

17.   EMI archives.

18.   VCH Warwickshire, Vol VIII, pp175 and 177;   Rudge-Whitworth catalogue, 1939, where, in an artist's impression of the factory, the wording 'Bicycles Motor Cycles Service Repairs' is shown on the front of the buildings; 'Don't trudge it Rudge it' Bryan Reynolds (Haynes, 1977).

19.   The directory is in alphabetical order of residents, but the principal roads appear to be represented, all or in part.

20.   VCH Middlesex, Vol III, p272.

21.   Information kindly supplied by the School.

22.   Even so, the proposals might have aroused opposition.

23.   Mr J Marshall has pointed this out to me.

24.   Officially 'Hayes Cemetry, Shepiston Lane' (Cherry Lane renamed).

25.   'Public Air Raid Shelters in the Hayes and Harlington UDC' - 1st interim report of Engineer and Surveyor. (A copy is in the Local Heritage collection, Uxbridge Library).

Chapter 35 (cont'd)

26. This shelter belonged to EMI - see amended Map of Public Shelters [6" OS map, annotated]. (A copy is in the Local Heritage collection, Uxbridge Library).

27. EMI archives - correspondence between Alfred Clayton and Mr Boden, 19/3/1940.

28. Hayes and Harlington UDC Rate Book, June 1939.

29. Log book of Air Attack incidents (Local Heritage collection, Uxbridge Library).

30. Ex info J Marshall.

31. Ex info K Surman. The searchlight site, and also the location of the Bofors gun, is confirmed by Mrs K E Norman (nee George) who lived at 'The Dawley Cottage' throughout the War.

32. See Appendix 3.

33. See L B Whittaker 'Stand Down - Orders of Battle ...... Home Guard, November 1944'. (Ray Westlake, Newport, 1990).

34. Derek Martin 'Thorn EMI 50 years of Radar' (Thorn EMI Electronics, 1986) pp13 and 16.

35. Ex info J Marshall and personal observation by the present writer.

Chapter 36.

1. The precise date does not seem to be available, even from the PRO itself !

2. See Gazette 11/8/1967 and 13/12/1979; Hillingdon Mirror 23/2/1971; and PRO file ref PRO 55.

3. P Hall and C Brown (editors) 'Hayes on Record' (Hermes Plates, Reading, 1993); D Martin '50 years of Radar' op cit. (See note 34, Chapter 35).

4. See Gazette 26/8/1992, p9.

5. P Hall and C Brown 'Hayes on Record' op cit; Gazette 26/9/1963.

6. See 'The Leader', 20/10/1983.

7. See Gazette, 21/8/1991.

8. Osma Plastics - see Gazette 21/8/1991 and 'The Informer', 3/6/1988; also Hayes and Harlington Local History Society photograph HHLHS 443, taken 12/7/1969.

9. Ex info J V Hammond; personal observation by the present writer.

10. Kemp's Hayes and Harlington Directories 1963/64 and 1965/66 etc.

11. VCH Middlesex, Vol III, p260.

Chapter 36 (cont'd)

12. See Gazette, 29/10/54 p4.

13. Kemp's Hayes and Harlington Directories - as note 10 above.

14. Ibid   ; also Hillingdon Mirror 19/9/1967 p11.

15. 'The London Borough of Hillingdon' [Official Guide Book], 1971 - p148 (advt).

16. Conveyance document held by Stockley Park Consortium Ltd.

Chapter 37.

1. Harlington Inclosure Award map.

2. Register of Electors, Middlesex - see note 9, Chapter 30.

3. Kelly's Directory of Middlesex and Surrey, 1852, states that a 'still remaining wing of Dawley or Doyley House ...... now inhabited by Mr Warwick Bagley, a market gardener.

4. See Gazette 2/9/1876 where he was described as of 'Dawley House, Hayes'.

5. Local Directories. These are the principal source of information on Dawley House tenants, together with some local informants. No directory entry for Dawley House in 1916 has been discovered.

6. Local information. Johnson was there in 1922 (Kelly's Directory); no definite information for earlier period.

7. EMI archives - 'Agreement' document C De Salis/O E Barnes.

8. Ibid. 'Agreement' and Conveyance documents.

9. Per photographs taken not later than April 1937 (one reproduced in 'The Voice', Vol XXI, No 4, April 1937).

10. Ex info Mr A G Seeley and Mr R F Crowther, both of whom worked for EMI in Dawley House.

11. Letter dated 9/3/1943 written by R Theodore Beck (see note 6, Chapter 20).

12. Report by Walter H Godfrey to EMI (see note 6, Chapter 20).

13. Ex info as note 10 above.

14. Ibid   (A G Seeley).

15. Hayes and Harlington Official Guide [1952 edition] p11.

16. Per aerial photograph of c1932.

17. See note 4, Chapter 20.

18. Photographs; OS map.

Chapter 37 (cont'd)

19.   Verbal description by Mrs Grace and Miss Hammond op cit; EMI archives - map with Conveyance dated 19/7/1929 etc.

20.   EMI archives - Agreement 17/4/1926, C De Salis and O E Barnes.

Chapter 38.

1.   'Stockley Special Project Planning Brief' (J D Wardell, Director of Planning) (London Borough of Hillingdon, November 1979).

2.   'London Borough of Hillingdon Reporter' [news sheet] January 1982; Stockley Park Newsletters; Millbrook Facilities Management - Tenant Information (list and plan of Stockley Park tenants); Local newspapers.

3.   A car-breaking business vacated part of the site behind the wall in Bolingbroke Way in 1994. This included the important section of the wall with the diamond-shaped decoration, which had started to sustain damage. Also in 1994, a section of the estate wall south of the entrance to Hendricks Lovells builders yard was demolished and replaced with a new replica wall at an angle to the road. This was for road safety reasons. (Per local newspaper; local informants).

Chapter 39.

1.   See note 19, Chapter 34.

2.   See Harlington Tithe Award map.

3.   Mr P T Sherwood has drawn attention to this fact.

4.   See aerial photograph of c1932.

5.   See note 1, Chapter 33.

6.   The photographs, taken by P T Sherwood and B T White, are in the collection of the Hayes and Harlington Local History Society.

7.   H O Meyers op cit. Similar brick culverts were discovered during an archaeological excavation of the site of Drayton Manor House, West Drayton, in 1979-1980. (See J Cotton in 'The London Archaeologist', Winter 1981).

8.   The garden wall can be viewed from roads inside the Abenglen Industrial Estate.

Appendix 2 - Notes

1.   VCH Middlesex, Vol IV, p263.

2.   See Rachel De Salis op cit (note 3, Chapter 2).

3.   Elizabeth Hunt op cit Reminiscences, p12 (see note 6, Chapter 2).

Appendix 2 (cont'd)

4.   Mrs M E Gibbs op cit (see note 3, Chapter 29).

5.   House names from Hillingdon Censuses and local directories; also Rachel De Salis op cit (see note 3, Chapter 2).